Integrating the Forty Acres

Integrating the
40 ACRES

The Fifty-Year Struggle for Racial Equality at the University of Texas

Dwonna Goldstone

The University of Georgia Press   *Athens & London*

© 2006 by the University of Georgia Press
Athens, Georgia 30602
All rights reserved
Designed by Erin Kirk New
Set in Bulmer by BookComp, Inc.
Printed and bound by Maple-Vail
The paper in this book meets the guidelines
for permanence and durability of the
Committee on Production Guidelines for
Book Longevity of the Council on Library
Resources.

Printed in the United States of America
10 09 08 07 06 C 5 4 3 2 1

British Library Cataloging-in-Publication
Data available

Library of Congress
Cataloging-in-Publication Data

Goldstone, Dwonna Naomi, 1968–
Integrating the 40 acres : the fifty-year
struggle for racial equality at the
University of Texas / Dwonna Goldstone.
p. cm.
Includes bibliographical references
and index.
ISBN-13: 978-0-8203-2828-7
(cloth : alk. paper)
ISBN-10: 0-8203-2828-6
(cloth : alk. paper)
1. College integration—Texas—History.
2. African Americans—Education
(Higher)—Texas—History.   3. University
of Texas at Austin—Students—History.
I. Title: Integrating the forty acres.
II. Title.
LC214.22.T48 G65 2006
378.1'9829960764—dc22   2006005469

Contents

The past isn't dead; it isn't even past. —William Faulkner

Preface

In October 1956, a faculty committee chose African American
Barbara Smith to play the female lead in a University of Texas production of
the opera *Dido and Aeneas*. Because the committee had chosen two white men
to play the male lead, the opera would have an interracial cast. After Texas
legislator Jerry Sadler learned of the casting, he demanded Smith's removal
from the cast. Sadler and another Texas representative threatened to vote against
appropriations for the university because the people of Texas did not "want
mixing of Negroes and whites publicly." Perhaps afraid that the university would
lose funding, UT president Logan Wilson removed Smith from the opera. As this
episode demonstrates, although racial integration occurred in the classrooms at
the University of Texas at Austin, white administrators and legislators worked
to preserve other aspects of segregation and the white supremacy it bolstered.
No one doubted Smith's talents as a singer, but her appearance was enough
to threaten what whites had come to expect under segregation. And like other
white southerners, white university administrators and Texas legislators seemed
obsessed with miscegenation.

The nation's celebration of the fiftieth anniversary of the U.S. Supreme Court's decision in *Brown v. Board of Education* has led to strong interest in that decision's meaning and effects. Sheryll Casin's *The Failures of Integration: How Race and Class Are Undermining the American Dream*; Derrick Bell's *Silent Covenants: "Brown v. Board of Education" and the Unfulfilled Hopes for Racial Reform*; Charles Clotfelter's *After "Brown": The Rise and Retreat of School Desegregation*; and Charles Ogletree's *All Deliberate Speed: Reflections on the First Half-Century of "Brown v. Board of Education"* all attempt to explore why, despite a Supreme Court decision that many believed would become the "Holy Grail of racial justice," America's public schools remain racially separate and in some cases "educationally ineffective."[1]

The experience of racial integration at the University of Texas does not generally inform the contemporary conversation about race in America, but the history is both relevant and instructive. Theorists of race in the United States have recently expressed skepticism about the original imperatives of racial desegregation since the civil rights movement. Despite the demise of Jim Crow segregation and formal exclusion, racial inequalities and disparities continue to exist. Many commentators have wondered whether "racism in America is . . . a curable aberration—as we all believed it was at some earlier point" or instead constitutes "a key component in this country's stability." Other commentators have wondered whether racism has never been eradicated from this country in part because the primary motives behind de jure segregation never centered on formal racial equality, especially for African Americans. Perhaps embarrassed by Soviet propaganda that called attention to America's hypocrisy with regard to its treatment of African Americans, the federal government sought to eliminate the most obvious and most vulgar signs of racial segregation after World War II. Instead of eliminating all forms of racial inequality, however, the United States may have addressed only the surface expressions.[2]

This book explores the ways in which the University of Texas at Austin desegregated in theory if not in practice in response to federal mandates, most notably from *Sweatt v. Painter* and *Brown v. Board of Education*. In the face of federally mandated desegregation, UT administrators had the difficult challenge of maintaining white supremacy while undoing the most visible signs of formal racial segregation. As this volume shows, racial integration remained unpopular with major segments of the Texas population. Sensitive to those sentiments, administrators permitted black students to attend the university yet worked to allay white Texans' concerns regarding the diminution of the social, cultural, and political distance between blacks and whites. Despite formal desegregation, UT administrators ensured that the campus's blacks and whites remained separated in other meaningful ways.

Why did Texas seem to straddle this line between segregation and desegregation? UT administrators and members of the Board of Regents conceived of the Austin campus as neither South nor West but in between. While some Texans acknowledged that the state had a history of white supremacy resembling that of other southern states, other state residents wanted to distance themselves from the more blatant forms of racial segregation.[3] During the 1950s and 1960s, the regents did not want their university to acquire a reputation for lawlessness and Negro hating that was becoming common among "southern" places and institutions because of their intransigence. Board members knew all too well how costly a bad reputation could be and consequently acquiesced to the Supreme Court's decision in *Sweatt* but did as little as possible to help black students. Moreover, administrators worked to limit integration as much as they legally could—for example, by refusing to allow black women to live in university dormitories and forbidding black men from playing on the school's intercollegiate athletic teams. They acted out of the long-standing fear that too much integration would endanger what most white supremacists valued most—the virginity and purity of white women.

The policy of limited integration had its costs, most of which were borne by the African American students at UT, who although formally admitted were made to feel unwelcome. In addition to housing and intercollegiate sports, other on- and off-campus activities and eating facilities remained closed to black students, and the experience of contesting these forms of exclusion profoundly shaped black students' views of the university. Limited integration failed to secure meaningful racial equality and left deep scars on African Americans.

In today's "color-blind" society, racism and white supremacy have become more subtle, eschewing overt discrimination while embracing less dramatic, quiet racial bias that sometimes goes by the name of "race neutrality." Perhaps as a result, white students continue to bring legal challenges against the "unfair advantage" provided by affirmative action policies at the nation's colleges and universities. Contrary to popular beliefs, Americans have never wholeheartedly embraced racial equality, as is evidenced by the fact that racial integration was and remains limited and belies several arguments about the end of racism in the United States.[4]

Chapter 1 of this volume describes the events leading to Heman Sweatt's 1946 attempt to enroll in the University of Texas School of Law and the subsequent admission of the first African Americans to the university. Chapters 2 and 3 explore the ways in which white administrators and the campus community worked to limit integration in the 1950s and early 1960s as well as the efforts by black and white students to expand integration on campus and in surrounding businesses. Chapter 4 discusses UT housing and the efforts both to close and to open it to black students, while chapter 5 examines the lengthy process of integrating intercollegiate athletics at UT. Chapter 6 reports on desegregation at UT since 1964. The epilogue discusses *Hopwood v. Texas*, the court case that ended affirmative action in Texas public colleges and universities, and the lingering effects of limited integration at UT.

In her preface to *The First Black Actors on the Great White Way*, Susan Curtis challenges us to "reconsider how we historians and American studies scholars imagine America." Today, fifty-five years after Sweatt and sixteen other black students first enrolled in Austin, less than 4 percent of the UT student body is black. In many ways, the desegregation of the University of Texas summarizes the difficult journey of the Old and New South and of our nation as a whole. For many black alumni, this journey might serve as a sort of reconciliation—and reclamation—of their unknown (and often ignored) trek through history.[5] Moreover, knowing what their predecessors endured might provide current African American students with a measure of comfort in a sometimes isolating and uncomfortable environment. Theirs is a compelling story. I hope I have done it justice.

This volume does not address the experiences of other racial and ethnic minorities, including Mexican Americans, Native Americans, or Asian Americans. The book focuses specifically on the experiences of African Americans, who for historical and other reasons faced some of the most humiliating forms of segregation in Texas and elsewhere. Although almost all minority groups have faced discrimination in the United States, white supremacists have reserved most of their ire for African Americans. Moreover, UT administrators worried very little about the admission of other groups.[6] Their preoccupation with racial integration centered primarily on African Americans, and this book tells their story.

Integrating the Forty Acres

The Texas way of life, indeed, represents an extension into the twentieth century of certain ideas that animated all Americans up to the First World War. Here is the land of opportunity, where anybody can rise to the "top," where tomorrow is unpredictable and yesterday unnecessary. Here the intrepid individual, the risk, the adventure, the fabulous reward, have somehow come to fruition in a world largely occupied with the less romantic problems of social "security" and social "science." It is possible for the modern American to feel somewhat nostalgic about Texas, however he may smile—or cringe—at its excesses. —*Fortune, U.S.A.: The Permanent Revolution* (1952), quoted in Kirven, "Century of Warfare"

Introduction

For many of Texas's African American (and Mexican American) citizens, the opportunity for life, liberty, and the pursuit of happiness has constituted merely a fleeting dream. The history of African Americans in what is now Texas dates back to 1528, when two men, Estevan, a black Moor of Azamor in Morocco, and an unnamed slave of Captain Andrés Dorantes landed. Both men had survived a Spanish expedition to Florida under the leadership of Pánfilo de Narváez. Other blacks explored Texas and settled its territory over the next three hundred years, a period of Spanish and Mexican rule that was generally better for blacks than the subsequent years under U.S. rule. Most free blacks worked and lived in East Texas as farmers and agricultural laborers, although other African Americans lived in San Antonio, Brownsville, and Austin and worked as artisans, servants, barbers, tailors, masons, and dance instructors, among other professions.

However, reality for most Texas blacks, especially after 1821, involved slavery. Although slavery existed in Spanish Texas, it never developed into a basic societal institution, as had been the case in other parts of the South. Mexico allowed

Anglos to settle in Texas beginning in 1821 but at the same time forbade the sale or purchase of slaves and required that children of slaves be freed at age fourteen. Despite these laws, slavery greatly expanded in Texas as Anglo settlers brought along their slaves, either claiming that they were simply indentured servants for life or just outright breaking the law. When Texas became a part of the United States in 1845, white settlers were free to bring slaves. Life was hard for Texas slaves, most of whom worked in plantation cotton fields from sunup to sundown, enduring oppressive summer heat as well as cruel treatment by masters and overseers. Slavery eventually became important to Texas, and by 1860, one out of four white families owned slaves, and the state's total slave population had reached 182,566. On the eve of the Civil War, Texas ranked tenth in the nation in total slave population, and nearly a third of the state's residents were enslaved.[1]

Word of President Abraham Lincoln's January 1, 1863, Emancipation Proclamation did not reach Texas's slaves until more than five months later. Nonetheless, the news brought with it joy and hope for a new future. With the help of the Freedmen's Bureau, former slaves eagerly sought education, and in the first year after the bureau's creation, Texas boasted roughly a hundred black schools (including Sunday schools), with sixty-five instructors teaching 4,769 students, some of them adults. One teacher said that black students "love their school as white children do not." The curriculum of these new public schools included reading, geography, arithmetic, writing, rhetoric, singing, and the Bible. Because black Texans saw education as their avenue to a better life, they often used their meager funds to pay teachers or to construct school buildings. In Austin, for example, African Americans raised money to build a school on a lot furnished by the city council. Black and white teachers continued their efforts despite the threat of violent repercussions from whites who did not believe in educating African Americans.[2]

With the creation of schools for African Americans came a debate as to what the state's black children should learn. This debate lingered into the early 1900s, when scholars and "race men" Booker T. Washington and W. E. B. Du Bois argued about whether African Americans should be schooled in the classics (Du Bois's view) or should learn an industrial trade (as Washington argued). Du Bois placed a greater emphasis on liberal education and adamantly opposed the movement to create a special vocational curriculum—the black studies of an earlier generation—that taught African Americans how to cook, sew, and make bricks at a time when white college-bound youth were learning to read, write, and do mathematics. Conversely, Washington disparaged what he called "mere book learning" and argued that black schools and colleges should stress manual training. He even suggested that the classical curriculum represented a major cause of African Americans' failure more rapidly to improve their economic position.[3]

Following Washington's death, Du Bois and later Carter G. Woodson continued the discussions about African Americans in higher education. In one of his early essays on education, Du Bois wrote, "The Negro race, like all others, is going to be saved by its exceptional men." He believed that "the problem of education" focused on training a "Talented Tenth" to become "leaders of thought and missionaries of culture among their people." Du Bois thought it rank heresy to suggest that liberal education was the privilege of whites and a dangerous delusion for blacks and contended that the school system for African American children should differ "in no essential particular" from other educational systems. African American students, Du Bois believed, should pursue a "long and rigorous course of study similar to those which the world over have been designed to strengthen the intellectual powers [and] fortify character." Woodson was also concerned about contemporary educational conditions for African Americans, and in 1933, he published a series of essays later collected into a book, *The Mis-Education of the Negro*, that critiqued the contemporary status of Negro education in America. Woodson believed that black education should serve two purposes: preparation and training for movement into the mainstream of American political and economic life, and the inculcation of "race pride" in the younger generation of black Americans. In this way, Woodson wrote, African Americans would be in a position to compete with others for society's limited resources and would do so as black men and women proud of their heritage in this country and throughout the world. At the time of his writing, Woodson ironically believed that the greatest threat to African American education and general advancement was "the educated class of Negroes," who failed to use their education for the betterment of the entire race. Woodson asked "whether these 'educated' persons are actually equipped to face the ordeal before them or unconsciously contribute to their own undoing by perpetuating the regime of the oppressor?" Like Du Bois, Woodson believed that men of scholarship "must show us the right way and lead us into the light which shines brighter and brighter."[4]

In 1865, members of the Texas legislature amended the state constitution to "encourage" separate schools for white and black children. A year later, members of the Texas Constitutional Convention recommended that income derived from a tax for "educational purposes" be collected yearly and that sums collected "from Africans, or persons of African descent, shall be exclusively appropriated for the

maintenance of a system of public schools for the Africans and their children."
The desired result of funding "colored" schools only with taxes collected from
African Americans was quite obvious: black schools would almost certainly lag far
behind white schools because African Americans had only limited opportunities
to earn money. In 1876, legislators adjusted the law to state that "in no case shall
any school, consisting partly of white and partly of colored children, receive
any aid from the available school fund, but the two races shall always be taught
in separate public free schools."[5] Even though legislators had never passed a
law specifically requiring the separation of black and white children in public
schools, laws on the books made integration in the public schools difficult if not
impossible.

Even with the rise of Jim Crow education, the Freedmen's Bureau, black religious denominations, and northern philanthropists and missionaries stepped
in to help African Americans build and establish institutions of higher learning.[6]
By the late 1800s, most private black colleges were organized into elementary,
intermediate or grammar, secondary, and college departments. What many white
students learned in elementary and secondary schools, African American students learned in college. The curriculum for black children usually emphasized
vocational skills. To this end, the Texas legislature passed an 1874 act that
established an "Agricultural and Mechanical College of Texas for the benefit of
the colored youth." Now known as Prairie View A & M, the school followed
the Tuskegee and Hampton philosophy of black industrial education, which not
only sought "to develop habits of industry, build character, and instill a feeling
for the dignity of labor," as Washington would argue, but had as its "primary
mission [training] a cadre of conservative black teachers who were expected to
help adjust the African-American minority to a subordinate social role in the
southern political economy."[7] The school's construction served as a politically
expedient device to reconcile racist white Texans to the idea of universal common
schooling for African American children and to pacify Reconstructionists who
supported new forms of external control over blacks.

With conversations about what African Americans should learn came discussions about educational opportunities (or lack thereof) for white Texans.
According to historian Joe B. Frantz, Anglo settlers had envisioned a Texas
state university beginning in the 1830s: "Almost every constitution since the
beginning of the republic had called for a university of some sort to be organized
'at an early date.' " Participants to the 1876 Constitutional Convention were
the first to make this university a reality, agreeing that "the Legislature shall . . .
establish . . . a university of the first class." However, they left the decision about

the location of this university to a future legislature. Governor Oran M. Roberts began to encourage the legislature to decide where to build this state university in 1879, but the legislators did not act until 1881, when they managed only to agree on the idea of "one university and one only," without settling on a site. The Texas teachers' association then proposed that the state create a medical school separate from the main university. In March 1881, the legislature agreed to hold an election on the second Tuesday in September to decide on sites for both the main campus and the medical branch. Legislators nominated six potential sites for the University of Texas: Austin, Waco, Albany, Graham, Williams' Ranch, and Matagorda.

The most likely spot for the university was in Austin, the centrally located state capital, a site that would enable the legislature to avoid sectional antagonisms. Governor Roberts and Lieutenant Governor L. J. Storey heavily lobbied for Austin. Legislator F. D. Wilkes did not want the university in Austin because he believed that the city was a "dead town, with no vim, no push, no enterprise, and morals of the worse kind . . . from the heads of government on down." Legislator M. D. Herring, who wanted the university built in Waco, said that Austin "had never supported an institution of higher education, whereas Waco was successfully maintaining Waco University." He also warned that a state university in Austin "would fall prey to the whims of political parties." Still others wondered whether Austin's "vices of gambling and prostitution prevailed to [such] an alarming extent" that they would render the city "an unfit place for the location."[8]

Ironically, an African American man lobbied black Texans, who constituted an important voting bloc in 1881, to cast their ballots in favor of placing the university in Austin. Rev. Jacob Fontaine, a minister, educator, and newspaper owner, traveled throughout the state to encourage black groups to vote for Austin. According to the *Austin Democratic Statesman*, Fontaine "is doing good service for the university down about San Antonio, Seguin and other places. He held a big meeting at Seguin the other night and delivered a stirring address favoring Austin for the location of the university." Several days later, Fontaine's church held "a big convention" in San Antonio. He took a vote on the university question, and 118 of the 120 ministers present said that they would vote for Austin. Each minister then "pledged himself to work for Austin." In September, three days before the election, Fontaine spoke with African American voters in Marlin, Tyler, Waco, and elsewhere, taking straw polls in areas where "Austin's competition was the greatest." When the election was held, Austin won in a landslide, garnering more than 30,000 votes—far more than second-place Tyler, which received just under 19,000. The decision to separate the medical branch and the main university won by a two-to-one margin, with 29,741 voters selecting Galveston to host the medical school, more than doubling Houston's 12,586 votes.[9]

Now that the citizens had selected a site for the state's flagship institution of higher education, construction could begin on the "university of the first class." Governor Roberts nominated eight men to serve as the new university's Board of Regents. While Abner Cook, an experienced builder, began working on the west wing of what would later be known as Old Main, board members began organizing the academic departments at the University of Texas. Using the University of Virginia as a model, the regents organized the new institution into nine academic departments: English and history; chemistry; natural philosophy, astronomy, mechanics, and meteorology; natural history and botany; mathematics and practical engineering; mines, geology, and mineralogy; moral philosophy and ethics and political economy; ancient languages (Greek and Latin); and modern languages (Spanish, French, and German). Each department would have only one professor. Five of the first University of Texas faculty members had served in the Confederate Army or had otherwise participated in the Civil War; in addition, at least three members of the inaugural Board of Regents had served as officers in the Confederate Army.[10]

Schooled in the southern traditions of slavery, segregation, and Jim Crow, the regents created a university for the white citizens of Texas (though a small number of Mexican Americans enrolled and graduated from the University of Texas in its early days). The university would teach the white children of the state's most prominent citizens a (distorted) history of the South, providing (both consciously and unconsciously) lessons about the white hegemonic structure of southern—and American—society.[11]

In its early days, the university garnered very little respect in the academic world. Few professors, especially those from the North, left the school once they arrived because, according to Alvin Johnson, a professor of economics from 1908 to 1909, they had "adapted [their] teaching, research, and style of speaking and writing to 'the independent state of Texas, with its Lone Star floating from the capitol tower.'" University leaders were pessimistic about the future of the school, with one departing president telling his successor, "Texas is governed by hookworm and malaria; there's no hope for the university." Politicians paid little attention to the activities on the Austin campus and seemed unaware of the fact that professors taught controversial subjects such as evolution and socialism. In 1914, however, Governor Jim Ferguson, "the poor people's friend," demanded that the UT President R. E. Vinson fire six professors. When asked why he wanted the professors fired, Ferguson said, "I am the Governor of Texas; I don't have to give reasons." However, he also stated that there was a "political ring in the university" and that "a professor at this school went down and presided at a county convention with a crowd that refused to endorse this administration." Vinson refused to discharge the men without conducting an investigation, and the conflict between the president and the governor lingered on for three years and ended only after Ferguson was disgraced: the state Senate eventually convicted him on ten charges of "misapplication, embezzlement, and diversion of public funds." Vinson remained the school's president until 1923.[12]

Despite Vinson's seeming victory in the fight, it had the long-term effect of shifting control of the campus—from the activities of the administration to those of the professors and the students—from the president's office to the Board of Regents, who were appointed by the governor. Perhaps worried that the university was becoming too "autocratic or aristocratic in its ways or customs" and beginning to "arrogate to itself an unwarranted superiority over the great masses of the people who make higher education possible," as Ferguson had asserted, regents were now charged with making sure that the campus represented the people of the state. To this end, the regents declared that "no infidel, atheist, or agnostic [could] be employed in any capacity in the University of Texas." After receiving word from a state senator that an economics professor might be a socialist, the Board of Regents asked the faculty to be more careful in its "presentation of economic, political, and social theory" so that it would be "practically impossible for students of reasonable ability and for the citizens of Texas to misunderstand the attitude of this institution toward such radical theories." As the 1920s progressed, the University of Texas campus was quickly becoming an "ordinary Southern-Southwestern place where cultural and moral conservatisms were the weapons that were used to enforce a profound prejudice." And the members of the Board of Regents held tightly to the handles of these weapons.[13]

During the 1940s, Texans became obsessed with the possibility that communists were infiltrating the university campus. In 1940, U.S. Congressman Martin Dies "declared that there was a communist cell at the university and subpoenaed a dozen students and one professor." Though he had no proof, Dies announced that there were "two revolutionary groups on campus, Stalinists and Trotskyites." University of Texas President Homer Rainey called for Dies to produce evidence to support his charges, and Dies subsequently admitted that "no subversion existed at the University of Texas." Despite the fact that Dies and other Texas legislators claimed that they simply wanted to obliterate any and all communist influences from the University of Texas, their ultimate goal was to stamp out any and all liberal elements on campus and in the state at large.[14]

The Board of Regents, however, was not finished. Wondering who in the English department had placed John Dos Passos's *USA* on the supplementary reading list for a sophomore English class, the regents questioned the textbook committee. And even though the English department agreed to drop the book from its reading list, the regents continued their investigation, wanting to fire the person responsible. "No teacher who would put that book in for a sophomore to read is fit to teach in a penitentiary or reform school—let alone a university," Regent Orville Bullington said. "As long as I'm a regent I'm going to repress that book and put out any teacher who teaches it."[15]

Though the regents had had some success in limiting the kinds of discussions that occurred on UT's campus, a few Texas politicians still believed that the university constituted a bastion of liberal activities that needed to be quashed, alleging that certain professors violated the rules against teaching subversion (communism, socialism, Marxism, or any derivative thereof). Thus, with the support and encouragement of the governors who appointed them, the men of the Board of Regents set out to limit academic freedom by attempting to restrict what professors taught (and thought). The regents were prepared to fire any professor who refused to adhere to these new rules. In addition, the regents stopped approving grants for "radical" research projects and revised tenure rules so that faculty could be fired without a hearing. Southern Baptists were elated that the University of Texas was to be purged of socialists, communists, infidels, homosexuals, and all those who did not fit the "Texas" mold. In the spring of 1942, Rainey and the regents clashed over the board's attempt to dismiss three young economics professors who had attended a Dallas meeting at which they had tried to argue in favor of the forty-hour workweek and overtime pay. As board member D. F. Strickland wrote to Rainey, the board's actions were intended to remind the president that he "had no business 'urging or suggesting' anything at all to" them. The incident ended with Rainey's firing, demonstrating the extent to which the Board of Regents would go to curtail what it saw as liberal elements on campus.[16]

In 1946, an African American man, Heman Marion Sweatt, presented his transcript to the registrar in an attempt to gain entry into the University of Texas School of Law. After being rejected, he took his case to the courts; in 1950, the U.S. Supreme Court handed down its decision in *Sweatt v. Painter*, forcing the desegregation of the University of Texas's graduate and professional programs.

Fourteen years later, the Board of Regents desegregated the entire university community.

For many reasons, few people know the story of integration at the University of Texas at Austin. This story, like others of the civil rights movement, often gets lost in the way that many people, including historians, view Texas—that is, as an anomaly. For scholars of the West, Texas's slave legacy makes it too southern for inclusion in discussions of that region. Similarly, the presence and influence of numerous Mexican Americans makes the state too western to fit into examinations of the South. Moreover, civil rights campaigns in Texas were mostly local in nature and did not provoke the kind of national exposure received by efforts in Birmingham, Alabama; Philadelphia, Mississippi; or Nashville, Tennessee. Thus, even though important U.S. Supreme Court civil rights decisions occurred in Texas cases—including *Smith v. Allwright* and *Sweatt v. Painter*—the state has for the most part remained out of the national spotlight in discussions of the civil rights movement.

Many people today think of Texas as a western state. For example, George W. Bush's 2000 and 2004 presidential campaigns promoted the state not as part of the South but as part of the West, with the candidate frequently sporting cowboy boots and a cowboy hat, speaking of the Mexican influences on Texas, and showing his ability (or lack thereof) to speak Spanish. At his first inauguration, Bush even wore cowboy boots with his black tuxedo. Because of this perception of Texas as part of the West, when current historians write about the history of the South and of southern race relations, events in Texas often get lost in the storytelling. Yet many characteristics qualify Texas as a southern state. Like twelve other southern states, Texas seceded from the Union and joined the Confederacy in the Civil War. Texas's significant slave population made the state much like such southern stalwarts as Mississippi, South Carolina, and Alabama. During Reconstruction, Texas, like other southern states, enacted a set of Black Codes: the delegates to the 1866 Constitutional Convention prohibited African Americans from testifying in court cases except against other blacks, disenfranchised even literate blacks, and required blacks to ride in separate railroad cars. The first Texas legislature further restricted black freedoms in the state by passing measures that prohibited African Americans from holding public office, serving on juries, and marrying outside of their race.[17]

As was the case elsewhere in the South, white Texans also perpetuated random acts of violence against the state's black citizenry. Lynchings became particularly common in eastern and central Texas, home to the majority of the state's blacks. In the last two decades of the nineteenth century, between three and five hundred black Texans were lynched, though the rate of lynchings declined from eighteen per year during the 1890s to ten per year from 1899 to 1903. Most black victims had been accused of murder or rape of white women, but some had been accused of such petty crimes as theft and being "sassy" to white persons. Though some whites and most blacks opposed lynching, white newspapers and white leaders condoned these acts as necessary to "control the Negro." In the late 1950s and early 1960s, African Americans continued to face violent intimidation in many parts of the state.[18] While many white Texans would not have supported violence against African Americans, most would probably have agreed with the words of one white Brooklyn, Texas, woman: "I approve of [blacks]. They should have the same rights. But I wouldn't want to live with them." A 1948 poll conducted indicated that 66 percent of white Texans opposed equal rights for African Americans.[19]

Although Texas differed little from Mississippi, which seemed the most resistant to dismantling segregation, or Alabama, which provided images of the civil rights struggle that have become embedded in American memory, the leaders of the civil rights movement perceived Texas's whites as less hard-nosed than other southern whites about granting African Americans their civil rights. The National Association for the Advancement of Colored People (NAACP) had a stronger presence in Texas than in other southern states, where local governments frequently prohibited the chapters from forming.[20] The NAACP consequently decided to challenge segregated colleges and universities in Texas, where the group's lawyers believed that the relatively moderate racial climate would permit them to win their cases. Such was the logic behind *Sweatt v. Painter*.

Books on blacks in higher education are replete with stories about governors and other elected officials "standing at the schoolhouse door" to prevent African Americans from taking a seat in the classroom.[21] These texts often omit the story of integration at the University of Texas, however. Although a U.S. Supreme Court decision led to the admission of the first black students, the rest of the story of integration at UT includes little fanfare, a stark contrast with events elsewhere in the South. In 1961 for example, Charlayne Hunter and Hamilton Holmes, the first two black students admitted to the University of Georgia, were greeted by a "boisterous, if not hostile, crowd of white humanity." Five years earlier, African American Autherine Lucy had been driven from the University of Alabama campus after three days of tumultuous demonstrations, and in 1963, Alabama Governor George Wallace stood in defiance of the Kennedy administration as he vowed to keep the institution's doors forever closed to black students. When James Meredith became the first African American to enroll at Ole Miss in 1962, federal marshals had to protect him from white mobs that included Governor Ross Barnett and members of the Mississippi Board of Regents. At the University of Texas, no such dramatic confrontations occurred; in fact, some white students openly welcomed the first black enrollees, though most whites ignored the blacks. Despite their commitment to traditional southern principles, the regents vowed to fight any lawsuit only until all legal remedies were exhausted: "I do not propose that we should arm ourselves, bodily prevent marshalls from escorting negroes into dormitories, and instigate another Mississippi," wrote Regent A. G. McNeese in November 1962. "If we lose, we lose—but we have shown to the people to whom we are responsible and, more important politically, to the Legislature, that we defended our cause and theirs through every legal channel available to us." The regents knew that progress was coming, and they realized, in the words of historian E. C. Barksdale, that it would be "far better . . . for the image of the South in the eyes of the world [to be] taken in hand by its own leaders and led into reality rather than be hooked and gaffed by federal bayonets until it comes flopping, floundering in like a helpless trout."[22] The board members wanted no lives lost, no bloodshed, and no embarrassment to the school. They knew when to stop fighting the inevitable, even if Texas's governors and other white citizens did not.

Regents and university administrators struggled to both appease popular opinion and follow the new law of the land. As board member W. W. Heath, formerly an opponent of integration, told a reporter in 1965, "The thing I'm proudest of—and I'm proud in a way of integration—is that we did what we had to do and should have done in the matter of human rights and that sort of thing. We did it under pressure from both sides—one side saying we were dragging our feet, and those on the other side who, when we moved an inch, were calling us nigger-loving s.o.b.'s and that sort of thing. . . . It was like being on a tight rope."[23]

The regents generally emphasized total integration in the academic process while disavowing any major responsibility for African American students' social and extracurricular integration, which the board claimed did not constitute part of the academic process. This policy of social segregation systematically denied black students equal educational opportunities, and when UT students of both races pressed the regents for full integration, the board replied that it reviewed African American student problems at least once a year and was gauging the process. In essence, board members wanted black students to wait just a little longer for equality. The regents believed that a general policy of gradualism would constitute a suitable compromise among Texans' varying viewpoints on integration.[24] Board members knew that many white Texans would require time to accept the fact that African Americans—especially African American men— would be attending school with their "virginal" white daughters. In looking out for the university's total welfare, the regents could not ignore good public relations, both in the state as a whole and in particular in the legislature (which set the university's funding). This approach resulted in a policy that served to maintain the racial status quo at the state's flagship university. Consequently, UT's struggle to integrate constituted both a southern and western experience— southern in the sense that the state resisted integration, western in the sense that it did not resist too hard.

At Ole Miss and the University of Alabama, after black students enrolled, the furor over their admission generally died down and they joined in most facets of university life. These two schools seem generally to have confronted, negotiated, and moved beyond their racist pasts, and African Americans today make up an important proportion of the student bodies. In contrast, at the University of Texas, where change happened incrementally, much racial progress still has not arrived. White Texans seem to have engaged in a collective denial of the school's racist past, with many whites explaining the dearth of minorities at the school with such statements as, "Well, they're just not qualified to get in." Although African Americans comprise some 15 percent of the state's population, less than 4 percent of UT's students are black. Mexican Americans, who comprise some 30 percent of the state's population, make up only 7 percent of the UT student body.[25]

The Board of Regents' policy of gradualism with regard to desegregation stood in direct conflict with black students' desires to become full members of the university community. As in other civil rights campaigns of the 1950s and 1960s, black (and white) UT students debated, marched, protested, and partook in other forms of civil disobedience as a way of demanding equal treatment and equal opportunity on the campus that they supported with their (or their parents') tax dollars. The student newspaper, the *Daily Texan*, stood at the forefront of efforts to ensure equal treatment for African American students.

The story of those southern colleges and universities that integrated "peacefully" has been lost in the retelling—and reconstruction—of the history of the South. Thus, those chronicles by which we measure how far the United States has come in terms of race relations are distorted. "If we look closely at Ole Miss," Nadine Cohodas wrote in her history of integration at that school, "we continue to see a reflection of our contemporary society—determined and even idealistic at times in pursuit of racial parity, but unsure of how well we have shed the past, how we might properly measure our progress, and perhaps, how clearly we envision our future."[26] However, to understand the entire story of the South, historians must also look to those schools where the road to integration was not paved with violence.

Few people have written about the experiences of African American students at the University of Texas.[27] *Integrating the Forty Acres* goes beyond this previous scholarship, first by looking into the University of Texas's role in shaping ideas of race on campus and then by exploring how African American students, with the help of their white peers, negotiated the challenge of making a place for themselves in such an unpropitious and difficult environment. Examining this process provides a better understanding of why black students felt uncomfortable and unwelcome at UT in the 1950s and 1960s and why many of them still feel this way today. In addition, looking at desegregation at one southern university provides insight into the larger issues of the civil rights movement and African American progress in higher education.

A negro, Heman Sweatt, of Houston, Texas, has applied for admission as a student in the law school of the University of Texas, claiming that the University is the only state institution of higher learning in this State furnishing facilities and instruction for the proper training in the profession of law. The applicant, who is a citizen of Texas, is scholastically qualified for admission. . . . It is also noted that it has not been the policy of the University to admit negroes as students and this is probably the first instance in which a negro has presented himself for registration as a student. —Texas Attorney General Grover Sellers to UT President Theophilus Painter, February 28, 1946

1 African Americans at the School of Law

When the University of Texas School of Law opened in 1881, there was little need for a discussion about whether African Americans would be allowed to attend the school: southerners' insistence on strict racial segregation made it a moot point. The University of Texas would remain a school for white Texans and white professors such as W. S. Simkins, who had served as a first sergeant in the Confederate Army and gone on to become a judge, founder of the *Peregrinus* (the School of Law yearbook), a member of the Ku Klux Klan, and professor of law at the University of Texas from 1899 until his death in 1929. Colonel Simkins (as he was known around the law school) was quite popular with law students. Each year on the first day of class, he addressed the first-year law students on the ideals of the profession, telling them "of the great importance of aspiration and inspiration." After his wife died, Simkins became known around the university as "quite a lady's man," paying "formal calls several times a month" to the sororities, "for no other apparent reason than to get to kiss the young ladies goodbye when he [left]."[1]

Although no evidence indicates that Colonel Simkins sought the continued exclusion of African American students from the law school, in either 1914 or 1916 he delivered a speech, "Why the Ku Klux Klan," to students at a campus Dixie Day celebration. In his speech, later published in the 1916 Commencement edition of the *Alcalde* (the University of Texas alumni magazine), Simkins explained why he had helped found a Florida branch of the KKK during Reconstruction: the Klan and other secret organizations "sprang out of a great necessity for readjusting social conditions . . . at a time when Southern men were face to face with negro domination thrust upon them by federal law harshly executed by hated emissaries from other states." Not wanting to sit idly by while the Florida legislature passed bills that insisted on equal rights—and therefore social equality, these whites reasoned—Simkins and his cohorts did the only thing they could: they formed a chapter of the Klan.[2] That Simkins delivered this speech on the grounds of the University of Texas and that the speech was reprinted in the alumni magazine clearly suggest that the time—as well as the University of Texas—belonged to people like Simkins. Thus, it is no surprise that it took a lawsuit to force the admittance of African Americans to his law school.

On February 26, 1946, Heman Marion Sweatt, an African American postal worker with, as he said, "a yen to become a lawyer," applied for admission to the University of Texas Law School. Because the state constitution required segregated educational facilities for its black and white students, University of Texas President Theophilus Painter explained to Sweatt that the state would establish a "separate but equal" law school for African Americans. The team of lawyers from the National Association for the Advancement of Colored People (NAACP) who represented Sweatt filed a suit to force the University of Texas to admit him. When the Supreme Court decided in 1950 that Sweatt had a "personal and present" right to a "legal education equivalent to that offered by the State to students of other races," desegregation had come to the University of Texas.[3] This chapter will discuss Sweatt's lawsuit, explore the experiences of the first African Americans at the University of Texas's law and graduate schools, and examine the ways in which the Board of Regents worked with university administrators to keep African Americans from fully participating in campus life.

The Stage Is Set

The first attempt to integrate the University of Texas began not in 1946 with Heman Sweatt but in 1885, when an African American student applied for admission. The school denied him admission based solely on his skin color.

The second attempt came in October 1938, when George L. Allen, the Austin district manager for the Excelsior Life Insurance Company, arrived at Geology Building 14 for a seminar on business psychology and salesmanship. His appearance stunned the class, since the university did not admit African Americans. According to historian Joe B. Frantz, before "a confused UT registrar type could figure what to do," Allen had registered for several classes, "paid his fees," and begun the seminar. The professor, unsure about what to do, allowed Allen to sit in.[4]

Allen had no desire to attend the University of Texas. In conjunction with the Dallas branch of the NAACP, he had attempted to register so that the school would deny him admission. The NAACP would then threaten to sue the state of Texas, hoping to force the legislature to provide black Texans with scholarships to out-of-state institutions. "The only wrench in the whole machine," Allen recalled, "was that they admitted me." Ten days after he enrolled, Professor C. P. Brewer called Allen to a conference at the Driskill Hotel in downtown Austin and informed him that he would have to withdraw from the course. Allen refused. In response, the registrar's office canceled his admission and prevented his return to class. He and the NAACP then threatened to sue, and within nine months, the legislature had voted to establish an out-of-state scholarship program. Texas would now pay tuition at out-of-state institutions for African Americans who wanted to pursue an education beyond a bachelor of arts degree. Most went to schools in the North and West. Marion Curry, for example, went to Columbia University in New York. "It was a great deal," he said, "because I got to go to a better school anyway and the state of Texas paid for it."[5]

Other black Texans, believing that the out-of-state scholarship program did not sufficiently address the poor quality and quantity of public schools for the state's African American children, moved their families out of the state. Charles Bolivar's parents took him and his eight brothers and sisters to California so that they could receive a quality education and have a greater choice in colleges. "I don't mean this in a negative way," he said, "but Huston-Tillotson was just not an adequate substitute for the University of Texas. My parents wanted us to have the opportunity to attend the school for which we were best qualified, so they moved us to California."[6]

Although some African American Texans seemed happy with the out-of-state scholarship program, many of them saw it as an intermediate goal in the "fight to get Negroes admitted to the University of Texas," as the founders of the Texas State Conference of NAACP Branches stated in 1937. The members of the UT Board of Regents, however, made it quite clear that the university would strongly resist admitting African Americans. In a 1944 letter to John A. Lomax, a folklorist and former director of the university's Ex-Students' Association, Regent Orville Bullington wrote, "There is not the slightest danger of any negro attending the University of Texas, regardless of what Franklin D, Eleanor, or the Supreme Court says, so long as you have a Board of Regents with as much intestinal fortitude as the present one has."[7]

The chair of the Board of Regents, Dudley K. Woodward, who some observers believed had ambitions to be the university's first chancellor, wrote regularly to Gibb Gilchrist, the president of Texas A & M, that UT had a "moral responsibility" to educate African Americans with professional and graduate ambitions. To Woodward, however, "moral responsibility" simply meant establishing a separate institution for African Americans. On November 1, 1944, the regents fired UT President Homer P. Rainey in part because of his "liberal" views on race. Rainey's opponents argued that because he had addressed interracial audiences and encouraged the development of black educational facilities, he believed in social equality and a desegregated university. Rainey denied that he believed such things, instead arguing that he believed in separate educational facilities. The regents appointed Theophilus S. Painter, an internationally respected geneticist, to succeed Rainey. Painter had accepted the job after promising the faculty that he would not take it, apparently because the faculty wanted an outside candidate who would not be so attached to the wishes of the regents, and many UT professors saw him as "a narrow-minded and vindictive soul who pursued vendettas against the student newspaper and encouraged the presence of the FBI on campus to eliminate 'subversion.' " Although Painter was a staunch segregationist, he did not think that the state was doing enough to provide a quality education for its African American citizens. He said, "Like many others, I feel the people of this state have not faced up to their obligations in the matter of Negro education, and I think all of us should join together and meet those needs."[8]

By this time, many African American Texans had become dissatisfied with the out-of-state scholarship program. Although the Supreme Court had outlawed this practice in *Missouri ex rel. Gaines v. Canada* (1938), many southern states, including Texas, continued providing out-of-state scholarships for African American students to avoid building separate educational institutions. In the early 1940s the Texas legislature had appropriated only the inadequate sum of $25,000 annually for out-of-state aid to all African American students. In 1945 the scholarship aid committee denied aid to some sixty African Americans because of a lack of funds. In addition, the out-of-state scholarship program placed an unfair burden on black students, who had to leave behind family and friends. Furthermore, many of the African American students who left the state to study law and in other graduate and professional programs did not return after completing their education. As a result, Texas's black community did not receive the full benefits of this program. Some whites also disliked the program, seeing the costs as prohibitive and believing that there was no guarantee that an individual African American would not sue for admittance to the University of Texas.[9]

The Texas State Conference of NAACP Branches carefully planned for a lawsuit against the University of Texas. In 1945, almost a year before Sweatt attempted to enroll, the Texas NAACP had asked its lawyer, William J. Durham, to prepare an opinion on whether the group could file a suit against the University of Texas. On April 9, 1945, A. Maceo Smith, the state's NAACP leader and executive secretary, sent a copy of Durham's review to Thurgood Marshall, the head attorney in the NAACP Legal Defense and Education Fund. The review stated that the Texas State Conference of NAACP Branches was ready to file suit and was requesting that Marshall come to Texas. When the Texas NAACP met in Dallas on June 2, 1945, its members announced that they would file a lawsuit against the University of Texas to ensure equalization of educational opportunities at the graduate and professional levels. A few weeks later, the organization retained Durham for the proposed action and set about securing money and a plaintiff for the pending lawsuit.[10]

Getting funds for a lawsuit against UT was easier than getting a plaintiff. Carter W. Wesley, publisher of the *Houston Informer*, a black weekly, encouraged people to donate money by publishing tallies of the amount raised, and by October the NAACP had four thousand dollars for the suit. But few people wanted to have their lives disrupted—and possibly placed in jeopardy—by serving as a plaintiff in a lawsuit. In addition, the plaintiff needed to have a bachelor's degree from an accredited college and be willing to attend the University of Texas after the suit was won. With this in mind, Smith, Wesley, and Kenneth Lampkin, an Austin attorney, interviewed five candidates, but none met the qualifications. Another candidate, Grover Washington, met all of the qualifications; however, "the disapproval of his family caused him to withdraw." Smith then asked Durham's legal assistant, Crawford B. Bunkley Jr., who held a law degree from the University of Michigan, to apply to enter the UT master's in law program. Although Bunkley had little desire to attend UT, he agreed to apply "so that the case would not be held up for want of a plaintiff." The NAACP decided not to go forward with Bunkley as the plaintiff after learning that "universities sometimes reserve the right to select the students for [master's] programs," thus making clear-cut racial discrimination difficult to prove. On October 12, 1945, Marshall finally received some good news. Lulu White, the NAACP's state director of branches, had found a plaintiff. [11]

Many people saw Heman Sweatt as an unlikely candidate for admission to law school. At age thirty-three, he was older than most students. Moreover, according to historian Michael Gillette, in size and appearance "Sweatt was an unlikely challenger to face the state of Texas." He stood five feet, six inches tall, weighed only 135 pounds, was slightly balding, wore glasses, and had a "narrow, neatly-clipped moustache." But Sweatt's father, who had graduated from Prairie View College, had instilled in his children a desire for education and social activism. Before Heman was born, the elder Sweatt had helped to organize black railway clerks who were denied insurance by the Mutual Benefit Association. [12]

After graduating from a segregated high school in Houston in 1930, Heman Sweatt attended Wiley College in Marshall, Texas, where he studied biology under James H. Morton, a civil rights activist who later became president of the Austin NAACP branch. Sweatt received an undergraduate degree in 1934 and returned to Houston, where he worked at a variety of jobs. In 1936 Sweatt became a teacher and acting principal in Cleburne, Texas, at what he described as "the most unsupervised school system for blacks that heaven ever conceived." After a year at Cleburne, Sweatt decided to attend graduate school at the University of Michigan. He originally planned to attend medical school, but after his uncle's Standard Life Insurance Company failed, thereby scuttling his plans for financing his education, Sweatt enrolled in Michigan's public health program. While there, Sweatt became friendly with Lloyd Gaines, the man whose lawsuit had forced the state of Missouri to establish a law school for its African American residents. [13]

Sweatt returned to Houston in the spring of 1938 after two semesters in Ann Arbor because Michigan's long, cold winters made him constantly ill. He took a job as a substitute mail carrier and married his high school sweetheart, Constantine Mitchell, in April 1940. Sweatt continued to work as a postal carrier and became involved in trying to eliminate racial discrimination at the post office, activities that sparked his interest in studying law. In a 1946 interview with the *Daily Texan*, Sweatt said, "I decided that I wanted to be a lawyer. I didn't want to go a thousand miles away from my home and my people to do it, so I applied for admission to the University of Texas." Sweatt further explained his reasons in "Why I Want to Attend the University of Texas," an article he wrote for the *Texas Ranger*, a liberal Texas monthly, after filing his lawsuit: "My answer simply and conclusively is: For the same reason that there are other Texans studying there. It is the best law school in Texas, and the only one that can offer me equal training to that available for other students."[14]

Sweatt's father "heartily approved" of his son's participation in the lawsuit and expressed pride at being associated with it. Constantine Sweatt was at first less enthusiastic, fearing that a lawsuit would ruin the family financially or that the family would become victims of racial violence. Sweatt's mother and one of his sisters, Erma, who had graduated from Columbia University, offered their "unqualified support." A brother, Jack, who attended the University of Michigan, opposed the plan because he believed that Heman was too old to succeed in law school. Another brother, John, also opposed the suit, believing that it would do little to end segregation in Texas. "The only way this white man is going to be whipped," John Sweatt said, "is for Uncle Joe Stalin to come over here and just blow the hell out of him." Eventually, however, the entire family pledged its support.[15]

Sweatt v. Painter

The state of Texas knew that a lawsuit was coming. In 1941, School of Law Dean Charles T. McCormick had received a letter from his friend, attorney Alexander B. Andrews of Raleigh, North Carolina, that spoke of the U.S. Supreme Court's decision in *Gaines v. Canada* and the NAACP's promise to continue the fight to integrate the nation's colleges and universities. In accordance with the provisions of the *Gaines* decision, on June 1, 1945, the Texas legislature enacted a measure that changed the name of Prairie View State Normal and Industrial College for Negroes to Prairie View University. Section 2 of the act provided for the establishment at Prairie View of courses in law, medicine, engineering, pharmacy, journalism, and any other "generally recognized college course" taught at the University of Texas "whenever there is demand for same." These courses were to be "substantially equivalent" to those offered in Austin. Nevertheless, on February 26, 1946, when Heman Sweatt attempted to register at the University of Texas, neither Prairie View nor any other institution of higher education in Texas offered a law school for African Americans.[16]

Before registering at UT, Sweatt went to Samuel Huston College in Austin (now Huston-Tillotson College), where he joined a group of NAACP representatives, including Lulu White; R. A. Hester, president of the Texas chapter of the NAACP; and Dr. B. E. Howell, president of Huston College, who accompanied Sweatt to the university registrar's office. There, the group met with President

Painter; E. J. Matthews, the university registrar, who had once boasted that he had "no more than the normal amount of prejudice against Negroes"; and other university officials. Speaking on behalf of Sweatt's group, Hester asked what the university had done to provide educational opportunities for the state's black citizens. Painter explained that the only avenue available to African American students was the out-of-state scholarship program.[17]

A dialogue between the two men ensued. Painter eventually suggested that "a small beginning ought to be made and then courses added as demand indicated, believing that a limited graduated program could be set up by September" at Prairie View. Hester and the others refused to accept this plan because the legislature had not appropriated funds for this initiative. Sweatt then asked for an opportunity to speak. He said that the state had the money "and the law and the constitution provide for me to have the training." He said that he needed the education and that he could not "go out of state to school, and I cannot wait indefinitely until some provision is made." Sweatt then presented his transcript and requested admission to the university's law school. Matthews responded that funds would be made available for Sweatt's education elsewhere and warned him that African Americans stood to lose everything if he filed a lawsuit. University Vice President J. C. Dolley advised Sweatt to "think twice and to choose the course that offered him the most promise of success." Sweatt declined both options, after which Painter held Sweatt's application until he could get a ruling from the attorney general's office. Painter's letter to the attorney general asked in part "whether or not a person of Negro ancestry, otherwise qualified for admission into the University of Texas, may be legally admitted as a student in this institution." Texas Attorney General Grover Sellers replied that even though Sweatt, an African American, was "scholastically qualified for admission . . . the wise and long-continued policy of segregation of races in educational institutions" should continue.[18]

Sweatt then filed suit against the university in the 126th District Court of Travis County. His petition asked Judge Roy C. Archer to order the university to admit him, arguing that his exclusion on the basis of his race denied him equal protection under the Fourteenth Amendment. Archer ruled that if the state established "a course of legal instruction substantially equivalent to that offered at The University of Texas" by December 17, the "writ of mandamus sought herein will be denied." The University of Texas and Texas A & M University worked quickly to establish a separate law school. The new institution would be located in Houston in conjunction with Prairie View University, have a faculty of two black divorce attorneys, and open the following February. After six months, however, no black law school existed: creating the facility was taking longer than the state had anticipated. Sweatt petitioned again but was again denied by Judge Archer, and Sweatt appealed the ruling to the Court of Civil Appeals, which remanded the case to the district court for a full hearing in May 1947.[19]

While Sweatt's case was winding its way through legal channels, the state legislature hastily appropriated $2.75 million to create a new institution, the Texas State University for Negroes (TSUN). The legislature may have moved so swiftly out of a fear that, as one senator warned, "If we don't do something quickly, the United States Supreme Court will rule that your child and my child will have to attend school with Negroes." Because state officials knew that they had to create an interim law school before the May hearing, the legislature authorized the establishment of a temporary facility in Austin. The university leased the basement of a building from a petroleum firm located behind the State Capitol and set up the law school of the Texas State University for Negroes. Nicknamed the Basement College, the TSUN Law School had only one furnished classroom with six arm-desk chairs and a blackboard; a second classroom was empty except for an old water heater. In addition to his duties as dean of the UT Law School, McCormick would serve as the part-time dean of the black law school; similarly, Matthews would add to his portfolio the position of part-time TSUN Law School registrar, and UT law librarian Helen Hargrave would also serve as the new school's part-time librarian. In addition, three UT Law School faculty members—Leo W. Leary, Starling T. Morris, and Chalmers M. Hudspeth—received dual appointments.[20]

With an emergency appropriation of $100,000, Hargrave, McCormick, university administrators, and the Texas Attorney General's Office set out to assemble a law library for the black law school, with the "ultimate goal" of at least equaling the UT Law School library. (Employees of the Attorney General's Office believed that a good library was needed to win the *Sweatt* lawsuit.) Hargrave compiled a list of the books necessary to fulfill the "recommendations of the Association of American Law Schools and the Association of American Law Libraries" and asked alumni to donate any volumes they owned. The effort resulted in roughly nine hundred books for the TSUN library.[21]

According to Governor Beauford Jester, blacks responded in a "very wholesome and very satisfying" manner to the new TSUN. Craig Cullinan, chair of the TSUN Board of Directors, told Jester that registrations would "total between 2,500 and 3,000 students." When no black students registered for the spring term at the black law school, however, Jester became "perplexed." Joseph J. Rhoads, president of Bishop College in Marshall, Texas, and of the Texas Council of Negro Organizations, stated that his group would "have no part" of the new university and that admittance to the University of Texas at Austin was the only solution to the problem of equal educational opportunities. This statement supported Attorney General Price Daniel's assertion that the "primary purpose of some Negroes is to break down the segregation laws, not primarily to obtain an education." Some whites believed that so few African Americans had applied for admission to the law school because of possible damage to Sweatt's case. Kenneth Lampkin, an attorney for Sweatt, dismissed this point, remarking that he believed that other Negroes enrolling would "not hurt the cause" because Sweatt was "seeking an 'individual right' guaranteed him under the fourteenth amendment."[22]

Although the state was desperate for people to enroll in the TSUN Law School, McCormick turned down Earnest Jones's application because he was "not qualified to enter the School of Law at the Texas State University for Negroes because of [his] lack of college training." TSUN required three years of college work for nonveterans, two years of college work for veterans. (In comparison, applicants to UT's law school needed a bachelor's degree from an accredited college or university.) Finally, six months after the TSUN Law School opened its doors, its first student enrolled. He was Henry E. Doyle, a thirty-seven-year-old Austin schoolteacher and grocer who was to also serve as the school's janitor. Doyle had graduated from Austin's Anderson High School and Sam Huston College and had taken courses at Columbia University. Doyle explained that he would prefer to learn in a small class since "you become just a number in larger classes" and that the black law school lacked students because "Negroes are already employed." Two other African Americans, Heullan (Virgil) Lott and Fornie Ussery Brown, soon registered. Professor Corwin Johnson, a UT law professor who also taught at TSUN, said that Lott and Doyle "turned out to be very good students" who never had an attendance problem even though his class met at 7:45 a.m.: "They were both very dedicated." Although Johnson did not believe in segregated education, he also supported the black law school because "segregated education is better than nothing." Sweatt refused to enroll in the black law school despite a personal letter from the school assuring him that it would offer black students "equal training and educational opportunities." Sweatt simply told the court, "I don't believe in segregation."[23]

When the time came for Sweatt's May 1947 hearing in Austin, some University of Texas law professors dismissed their students early so that they could watch the proceedings, in which Daniel and his assistant, Joe Greenhill, faced off against Marshall. McCormick testified that "facilities of the Law School for

Negro citizens furnished to Negro citizens an equal opportunity for study in law and procedure; that considering the respective use by the respective number of students, the physical facilities offered by the Negro Law School were substantially equal to those offered at the University of Texas Law School." TSUN was, McCormick said, "equal, if not superior, in every respect to the University law school to which Heman Marion Sweatt, Houston Negro, has been asking admission since February 1946." When asked whether tradition and history constituted important elements of a good law school, McCormick replied that they merely provided "a source of pride." D. A. Simmons, a Houston attorney and former president of several bar associations, testified that the TSUN Law School met the necessary standards "if University professors taught the courses." The state had argued that although the basement law school was not "monetarily" equivalent to the University of Texas Law School, it did afford African American law students the opportunity for an equal or "substantially equivalent" legal education. Few observers were surprised that Judge Archer again ruled in the state's favor. The NAACP again appealed, and the case eventually worked its way up to the U.S. Supreme Court.[24]

By the spring of 1948, UT President Painter was becoming "a little disturbed" that the TSUN Board of Trustees was not "acting vigorously enough in preparing to meet the demands for medical and dental education the coming fall." Fearing that such foot-dragging would open the way for blacks to demand admission to the university, Painter devised another plan to keep out Sweatt and other African Americans. Writing to Board of Regents Chair Woodward regarding "the general problem of Negro education," Painter stated his belief that "the Negroes" were determined "to make it as embarrassing as possible and as expensive as possible" for the state to maintain separate institutions for blacks and whites. "In the end," he wrote, "the financial burden will be extremely heavy to the State, and, as you have often said, it is the price we pay for segregation." Painter suggested changing the out-of-state scholarship program to make "all races . . . eligible." The state could then avoid having to establish separate schools for African Americans "when the demand for a certain subject" falls below a certain level in "White or Negro schools." Painter reasoned that if Texas sent blacks and whites out of the state for school, African Americans could not legally demand access to white educational facilities in the state.[25]

Many UT students supported Sweatt's lawsuit. Student representatives from seventeen campus organizations voted unanimously to support the drive to raise funds for Sweatt's legal battle and adopted a petition that stated, "We, the undersigned, hereby endorse and intend to support the National Association for the

Advancement of Colored People's efforts for equal educational opportunities." The Lutheran Students Association of the University of Texas adopted a resolution that "fully endorse[d] the principle of equal educational opportunities for all Texans, irrespective of race or color." Rev. Edward Brown, the associate secretary of the university Young Men's Christian Association, declared that Christians "must do away with racial segregation" because "before God we are all the same." Students on UT's campus also organized a chapter of the NAACP, "the first officially chartered in a white Southern university, and the only chapter in a white Texas school." On April 11, 1949, thirty-five African American students from Dallas's Bishop College attempted to register for graduate school at UT. When the registrar would not give them the necessary forms, the students left quietly and were joined by eleven white university students for a protest march to the Capitol, during which the students carried signs that read "Civil Rights Are Everybody's Rights" and "Separate and Equal Education Is a Mockery."[26]

Some university faculty and alumni also backed Sweatt's effort. UT English professor and Texas folklorist J. Frank Dobie spoke out publicly in support of Sweatt's lawsuit and of integration in general: "If the state establishes a law school in every way equal to the University of Texas Law School, then I shall say no more about the Sweatt case, but if the state sets up only a farce, then I am for admitting Sweatt and other qualified Negroes to the University of Texas." Sweatt would send a letter to Dobie thanking him for his "great assistance given the cause of liberalism in this state" and asking Dobie to read a few of his chapters from his unfinished novel. Sweatt said that his novel "aimed at interpreting 'legal discrimination' " as he witnessed it "in the treatment of the Negro employee of the United States Post Office." UT graduate Gwendolyn Tubb wrote to Painter of her experiences at Columbia University and the University of Chicago, where she sat next to African American students, "most of whom were far superior in intelligence to the 'average' Texas University student."[27]

Other members of the University of Texas community stood on the other side of the fence. In a letter to the editor of the *Texas Ranger*, someone identified only as "J.B." declared that "UT was built by enterprising and visioned white leaders for white men and women." Law student Edwin H. White believed that the "imposition of the Negro race on the white (by virtue of Northern influence) will lead to the inevitable destruction of one race!" Mrs. J. R. Rice of Wichita Falls wrote to President Painter to offer her "congratulations on your stand against admittance of Negro students to our great Southern Institution. If we of the South do not guard against Negro equality we are hopelessly lost." And George W. Willey sent a telegram to Painter announcing that "if that Nigger is allowed to enter the University of Texas just consider me no longer an ex student of the University of Texas."[28]

The segregation question, of course, occupied everyone's thoughts. In a poll by members of Alpha Phi Omega, a national service fraternity, and Orange Jackets, an honorary service organization for women, nearly 56 percent of students at the University of Texas generally favored the admission of African American students to graduate programs, though not necessarily undergraduate study. More than 65 percent of law students favored desegregation, while fewer than 18 percent strongly opposed the admission of African Americans to undergraduate programs. On the whole, men and veterans favored complete admission, while women and nonveterans favored admission of African Americans only to graduate programs. The broader white public had somewhat different opinions, however: a poll of Texas residents found that 69 percent of whites would object if "one or two Negro law students were allowed to study in the University of Texas at Austin." When asked whether African Americans who had finished college and wanted to study advanced courses should be allowed to enter the university if those courses were not offered elsewhere in the state, only 34 percent of whites responded in the affirmative.[29]

Another challenge to the university's segregation policy arose in December 1947, when W. Astor Kirk applied to graduate school in political science. Kirk, a twenty-eight-year-old professor at Austin's Tillotson College, had earned bachelor's and master's degrees at Howard University in Washington, D.C. He had inquired about studying at TSUN, but the school lacked adequate library and faculty for him to get a Ph.D. The university informed Kirk that he could get an out-of-state scholarship for his studies, even though the Supreme Court had ruled this practice illegal in its *Gaines* decision handed down nine years earlier. In 1949 Kirk was admitted to TSUN with the understanding that courses not taught there "would be offered to him separately and apart from the campus in Austin." In 1950 the university allowed Kirk to enroll but insisted that he take his classes alone at the Young Men's Christian Association since no other black students had registered. Kirk dropped out and threatened to file suit. The university then permitted Kirk to take his classes on campus but seated him at the back of the classroom with a metal ring around his desk so that "his blackness wouldn't rub off on the white students." Kirk again threatened to sue, but the university changed its policy after the Supreme Court's June 5, 1950, ruling in *McLaurin v. Oklahoma*.[30]

The lawyers for the state of Texas and for Heman Sweatt argued their case before the Supreme Court on April 4, 1950, and the Court rendered its unanimous decision two months later, on June 5. By this time, the TSUN Law School had moved to Houston, had five full-time professors, 23 students, a library of 16,500 volumes, a practice court, a legal aid association, and one alumnus who had been admitted to the Texas bar. In comparison, the University of Texas Law School had sixteen full-time professors, 850 students, a library of 65,000 volumes, a law review, moot court facilities, scholarship funds, an Order of the Coif affiliation, many distinguished alumni (including the state attorney general), and much tradition and prestige.

Aside from these obvious differences in the two law schools, the Court held that the fact that the black law school excluded from its student body the white population of Texas—85 percent of the population—meant that the "legal education offered petitioner [was] not substantially equal to that which he would receive if admitted to the University of Texas Law School." Although the state had gone to great lengths to prove that the two law schools were physically equal, the Court decided that "the University of Texas Law School possesses to a far greater degree those qualities which are incapable of objective measurement but which make for greatness in a law school," including faculty reputation, administrators' experience, alumni position and influence, community standing, traditions, and prestige. Thus, the Court decided, "the Equal Protection Clause of the Fourteenth Amendment requires that [Sweatt] be admitted to the University of Texas Law School."

1950–1960

The Supreme Court's decision in *Sweatt v. Painter* opened the door for African Americans to enter the University of Texas School of Law and other formerly all-white graduate programs. Some whites could not handle the new challenge of attending school with black students. In anticipation of the fall enrollment of Sweatt and five other African American men, crosses were burned on the law school's lawn in the summer of 1950. Law school dean W. Page Keeton received a letter from an acquaintance who wanted his son to complete his last year of law school at Baylor University to avoid going to school "with a nigger." Although no African American women enrolled at the law school in 1950, some "pure, lily-white, white women" became concerned about sharing bathrooms with black women whose mothers and grandmothers had been slaves and concubines. Many of those who objected to integration believed that outsiders and communists were shaping UT's dialogue on race: as sociology student E. H. Powell summed up that perspective, "Yankee Jews brought the virus of racial equality to our innocent boys and girls on fraternity-sorority row." Another group of white students told Keeton, "We don't want to go to the same restroom as these blacks are going to. We object to them. We want you to have a separate 'black only' restroom." Keeton refused to allow formal segregation within the law school but told the black students, "Look, I've got a group of rednecks here that object to using the same restroom you use. Now, they wanted me to set up a 'For Blacks Only' restroom. . . . But, will you voluntarily use just one of those men's rooms, instead of both of them? We won't put up any signs or anything." The black students agreed.[31]

Some white students did not object to the presence of African American law students. Powell, for example, privately "argued for racial integration," although he never acted publicly to support his beliefs. He recalled being "immersed in continual talk about race and social justice. . . . But the thought of organizing to compel the power structure to change its policy never occurred to me." White law students including Oscar Mauzy gathered at the nearby Hillsberg's Café to formulate ways to help the incoming black law students. Believing that the black students had attended inferior schools, the white group at first considered asking the faculty to automatically pass all black students and to spend as much time as possible with them; however, Mauzy and his peers subsequently decided that such an approach would amount to telling the black students that they indeed were not intelligent enough to be students at the UT School of Law. Moreover, because these future black lawyers would likely be serving black clients, the white students worried that if the black law students automatically passed their classes, they would not be able to adequately represent their future clients.[32]

Sweatt registered for classes on September 19, 1950, as cameras flashed. A total of seventeen African American students enrolled for graduate study that fall semester. Sweatt received a "mixed reception" at the law school. On his first Friday evening at UT, he found a Ku Klux Klan group waiting for him as he left school, and he headed home immediately after class each day to avoid harm. Although faculty members such as Jerre Williams and Charles McCormick tried to befriend and help Sweatt, others were openly hostile. Keeton warned Sweatt against making any "NAACP showmanship." Another faculty member turned his back and doodled on the chalkboard when Sweatt tried to ask a question after class. Judge Stanton taught a seminar in which he repeatedly used the word *nigger*. Remembered Sweatt, "I never heard of a case with so many niggers in it in all my life." One white classmate recalled that before Sweatt attended the law school, the judge had referred to all law students by their last names; however, he dropped this practice to avoid having to refer to Sweatt with the courtesy title "Mr."[33]

George Washington Jr. joined Sweatt as a member of the first class of African American students to enter the University of Texas Law School. A high school student during most of the Sweatt litigation, Washington had always known that he wanted to go to law school. According to his wife, Emma, Washington was more concerned with doing well in school than with "breaking any new ground." "He just didn't have time to worry about it," she said. "He was just there to get a law degree." Nevertheless, Washington knew that his days at the university were historic. Recalled Emma Washington, "He knew he was opening doors, and he knew it would be difficult."[34]

Although Sweatt remembered a majority of both law students and faculty members as opposing integration, law professor Corwin Johnson stated that only the senior faculty openly supported segregation: "I think it was generally understood that [segregation] was bad and that eventually the Supreme Court was going to get around to making it unconstitutional. I think that was the general feeling." Some members of the faculty told white students that if they did not like the Supreme Court's ruling, they should file their own lawsuits. Stanton told his students that if they wanted to work to prevent desegregation, they should do it within the system: "You didn't go around burning crosses. You didn't go around bombing people's houses. . . . You got yourself up a lawsuit, and you went through the traditional channels to get it changed."[35]

In his first year at the law school, Sweatt joined a student social committee and attended a few UT football games but turned in a lackluster academic performance. He failed several classes during his first year and audited them the following fall. The stress of law school took a toll on his health and marriage, and he eventually withdrew from UT, saying that he just was not prepared to do the work. Although he persistently declined to "point a finger at the University of Texas," he cited "four-and-a-half years of that case, two years in that school, 6½ years of that pressure" as perhaps having caused him long-term health problems, including a "weakness in my heart." Sweatt later received a scholarship to study social work at historically black Atlanta University and earned a master's degree in community organizing in 1954. He then moved to Cleveland, where he worked for the Urban League. He died of a heart attack in 1982.[36]

Only two of the six men admitted to the UT law school's first class of African Americans graduated, and by 1960, fewer than ten African Americans had received law degrees from the school. There is no question that law school posed a challenge for both black and white students: at the time, the graduation rate for white students hovered around 50 percent as a consequence of the law school's low admission standards. In 1951, Dean Keeton wrote to President Painter that three of the five first-year black law students (one had dropped out before school began) had "a lower average than that required for remaining in school, and the other two have an average which would result in their being placed on probation." Although Keeton found these results "unfortunate," he assured Painter that "the papers of these men [were] being graded on the basis of precisely the same standards that are employed in the grading of the papers of other students."[37]

In fact, few students or administrators took note of the experiences of African American law students at the University of Texas until 1960, when an article on "Integration at U.T." appeared in the *Texas Observer*. The piece quoted Betty McAdams, an African American second-year law student who had first enrolled at the University of Texas as an undergraduate in 1956, as saying that some of her most unpleasant experiences had been at the law school. She was surprised because she had thought the law school "would be a liberal place." Instead, "Many times I would be sitting in the lounge when a number of other girls were there," she said, "and some girl would come in and invite the others by name to come have coffee. They never asked me." When asked about her exclusion from these events, she was told that "some boys objected to girls having coffee breaks with negro girls." Another woman stated that African American women had previously been invited to attend the morning coffees but that some faculty wives were "surprised and reportedly disturbed," and in 1959 black women were not invited. In 1960, black women were invited but did not attend.[38]

After this article appeared, Keeton sent a memorandum to law professors Charles Alan Wright, Millard Ruud, Ernest Goldstein, and Peter Loiseaux that said that the *Observer* article indicated that "some of the Negro students were unhappy with the situation here at the Law School." He asked the professors "to serve as a committee to make such investigation as you care to make and then to make suggestions to me as to what, if anything, should be done." The committee learned that "Professor X" automatically gave a score of 63 to each "colored" student enrolled in his course, while black students taking the same course from other professors averaged above a 71. The committee believed that the point differential was too high to be explained on "the theory that the students were of different caliber." Black students told the committee that the same professor had talked about African Americans' supposed immorality while discussing a court case in class; not surprisingly, African American students avoided courses taught by that professor.[39]

However, most African American law students spoke well of their professors and of the school's administrative staff. McAdams believed that administrators had been very fair and that Assistant Dean T. J. Gibson III had handled matters "very fairly." A second African American student described Gibson and his staff as "polite and fair," while a third said that the administrative staff was "strictly on the up and up." Some African American students told the committee that faculty members sometimes made "ambiguous" remarks in class that might be incorrectly interpreted as racist. One such remark came from Dean T. H. Green, who said that African Americans participating in a sit-in at the law school were "compensating for being over-sexed." Green was apparently mimicking an editorial in the June 1960 issue of the law school magazine *Obiter Dicta* in which the editor, an ardent segregationist, poked fun at students who held pickets and sit-ins to protest discrimination. [40]

White students had different perceptions of how African Americans experienced the University of Texas Law School. A white law student named Matthews said that he had "never seen negro students shunned in the library" or witnessed any "ungentlemanly conduct toward negro students in the classroom." "Negro students," Matthews said, "tend to keep to themselves and be pretty quiet. [They] have acted well." Matthews also said that he had seen no official discrimination by anyone at the law school. Unofficially, however, incidents of discrimination occurred. An upper-division law student who was teaching first-years reported to the committee that a white female student had requested a seat away from an African American male student but that the situation was "handled so discreetly" as to cause "no incident." [41]

Matthews also noted that little interaction occurred between "white and negro students in the building" because integration "is a new experience for whites." Another white student, Mike Brimble, told the committee that he had told McAdams that "this integration is a new experience" and that he had "counseled patience to her." This was not an uncommon admonition. In *The Southern Case for School Segregation* (1962), James J. Kilpatrick argued that if any significant degree of desegregation were ever to take place in the South, "let alone any significant degree of integration in society as a whole," it could come only one way: "slowly, cautiously, voluntarily, some time in the near future." [42]

The committee found that as many as a third of the white students made a point of being friendly with the black students, studying with them, talking with them, and treating them as equals. One African American student told the committee that the "overfriendliness of some white students" at times made him "uneasy." Another African American said that although a few students went out of their way to be friendly, a much greater number were "positively rude." Another black student said that although some white students "are friendly and we study together," others "give you 'the eye.'" He said he had not experienced any discrimination in class or any "off color" remarks by teachers. Another African American student stated that he had personally experienced no "deliberate rudeness," although others had. McAdams believed that whites discriminated against her during her first year of law school. In contrast, African American law student Mary Simpson did not believe that discrimination against black law students had occurred and had experienced no classroom incidents. [43]

Although both black and white students overwhelmingly felt that the classrooms were integrated, they felt that extracurricular activities were not, largely as a result of student and faculty racism. Moreover, blacks believed that their exclusion from fraternities, sororities, and clubs associated with the law school kept them from the total law school experience and exacerbated distrust between black and white law students. Two law school events highlight this point. Male law school students traditionally elected "Miss Portia, the School of Law Sweetheart," which many law students perceived as "the greatest honor that can be bestowed upon a woman in a law class," reflecting "brains as well as beauty." The title was apparently so important that candidates were not announced until the last minute to prevent campaigning. In the spring of 1957, the male law students elected Albertine Bowie, an African American, as Portia. Few observers, including Dean Keeton, thought that the students had elected Bowie in good faith, instead believing that she had been selected as some sort of practical joke. To avoid controversy (and risk losing alumni money), Keeton persuaded a reluctant Bowie to turn down the crown. One black newspaper praised Bowie for being willing to stand for the honor of Miss Portia, thus "making it necessary for the demagogues to repudiate their own rules, to maintain their theory that the white race is better, per se, than the Negro race." [44]

Another incident involved a skit that Kappa Beta Pi, the female legal sorority, had planned for Assault and Flattery, an annual law student revue parodying different classes, professors, and the law school experience, on Law Day in 1959. Because the sorority lacked enough members to put on a skit, the group invited all female law students to participate. After two African American female law students "took a full place" in the skit, some white students questioned just how extensively the black women could and would participate in the final skit. The sorority then worked out a compromise—the black women would work behind the stage and otherwise help but would not appear on stage. The sorority then held a meeting of all female law students at which the issue was debated; the participants subsequently voted to boycott the skit if "restrictions were to be put on the activity of the Negro girls." In the end, no skit was performed. According to the committee's official findings, the controversy that developed about this incident "caused a marked deterioration in relations between white and Negro girls, which has continued to the present."[45]

The committee made several recommendations to Dean Keeton about ways to make the law school more comfortable for minority students. One suggestion was for administrators to pass out copies of a no-discrimination policy to staffers, student assistants, the officers of the Student Bar Association, and the editors of the *Texas Law Review*, *Obiter Dicta*, and the *Peregrinus*. The committee also recommended that the Placement Office be directed not to disclose to prospective employers law students' religious or racial background. Although these suggestions unquestionably had value, the committee failed to do something more important: it never recommended increasing the number of minority law students.[46]

Council on Legal Education Opportunity (CLEO)

By 1970, many whites had come to understand the need for more black and brown lawyers to help hold American society together. The assassination of Dr. Martin Luther King Jr. and the riots after his death provided just two examples that underscored the need for creative and prompt responses to these signs of social dislocation. While the Kerner Commission report stated that America was moving toward two distinct societies—one black and one white, separate and unequal—many people believed that such a disjunction already existed.[47] Society noted this phenomenon not out of a general benevolence but rather because African Americans and other minority groups had been more overtly expressing their profound sense of alienation and discontent with the workings of American society through such behaviors as rioting.

To address these issues, law schools began to examine ways to increase the number of minority lawyers. In 1967, African Americans constituted only 1 percent of all U.S. lawyers, compared with 12 percent of the U.S. population; Mexican Americans constituted less than 2 percent of lawyers versus about 10 percent of the U.S. population; and neither Arizona nor New Mexico, collectively home to more than 350,000 American Indians, had a single American Indian practicing law, and officials could remember no Indian ever graduating from those states' law schools. The entire state of Mississippi had only eight black lawyers in 1968, despite the fact that blacks comprised some 50 percent of the state's population. Texas had fewer than 90 African American lawyers despite a total black population of about 200,000; fewer than 350 black lawyers practiced in the entire South and Southwest. Of the 3,000 black lawyers in the United States, more than 70 percent worked in the six metropolitan areas of New York; Detroit; Cleveland; Washington, D.C.; Chicago; and Los Angeles. Although many blacks believed that white lawyers would not provide adequate service, entire African American communities had no African American lawyer to serve them. Moreover, few African Americans served as federal district court judges, state court judges, government administrators, or political functionaries.[48]

Some private organizations responded to the lack of minority lawyers by awarding scholarships to members of particular ethnic or racial groups. For example, the United Negro College Fund, the National Urban League, and the NAACP assisted African American students in pursuing undergraduate degrees, although most African Americans relied on university financial support for postgraduate work. Law schools throughout the country responded to the dearth of African American lawyers by sending representatives to historically black schools to encourage African American students to attend law school. Marc Franklin, a faculty member at Stanford University, visited Tuskegee Institute, where he met with several students who expressed interest in attending law school. Franklin helped to dispel some myths, most notably the notion that going to law school required students to major in political science; instead, he told aspiring law students to take courses in political science, history, economics, logic, and philosophy and to do as much writing as possible. Franklin found that finances posed the major barrier to attending law school for many students, who did not want to go further into debt after borrowing to finance their undergraduate education. This problem, Franklin wrote, was "aggravated by the relatively small scholarships available for law schools compared to other forms of graduate study."[49]

In January 1968, representatives of the American Bar Association, the Association of American Law Schools, the National Bar Association, and the Law School Admission Test Council formed the Council on Legal Education Opportunity (CLEO). The preceding year, U.S. law schools had graduated more than ten thousand whites and only two hundred African Americans. CLEO sought to increase the number of minority law students. American Bar Association President Lewis Powell appointed Texas's Keeton as CLEO's first chair. CLEO ran summer programs at select colleges and universities to help minority students get into law school. Although records describing the specific nature of UT's CLEO program have not survived, the program at Atlanta's Emory University was fairly typical. At Emory, CLEO sought primarily to help minority students prepare for the Law School Admission Test and sent letters to the deans or prelaw advisers at fifty-nine historically black colleges and universities, informing them of the nature of the program and requesting their assistance in publicizing it and in evaluating applicants. At the end of the eight-week summer CLEO program, the director helped successful participants gain admission to law school. The director of the Emory program made no attempt to contact any law school outside of the South, believing that if black students went to school in the South, they would be more likely to practice there. Nevertheless, the program garnered national publicity that brought placement inquiries from law schools throughout the United States. Iowa, Temple, Tulane, and Yale sent representatives to the Emory program to recruit, and Iowa, Emory, and Temple agreed to accept any student recommended by the CLEO faculty.[50]

In 1971, the University of Texas officially withdrew from the CLEO program. Professor Ruud believed that the university did so in part because of pressure from the regents, particularly Chair Frank Erwin, who had warned all university administrators to refrain from participating in any program that benefited a particular group. Two years earlier, the Board of Regents had passed a rule that no funds could be used "for the direct recruitment of students who otherwise would not have had an opportunity for higher education." Many people believed that Erwin ordered the elimination of CLEO not because the program constituted "reverse racism" but because he was a racist, although such charges are difficult to evaluate given his often contentious tenure on the board. African American and Mexican American students led unsuccessful protests demanding Erwin's ouster.[51]

Three years after the University of Texas ceased participating in CLEO, the number of African Americans admitted to the law school fell to zero. "This will have a bad effect on our reputation nationally and locally when people see that the University doesn't live up to its representations to the community," said law professor Edward Cohen. "It undoes all the work that people with good intentions at this University have done since *Sweatt v. Painter*."[52] More than two decades after Heman Sweatt and sixteen other African Americans had broken the color line at the University of Texas, the campus clearly was not yet open to all students.

I feel, as do hundreds of thousands of other Texans . . . that the Negro just don't have a place in the same schools and colleges that were intended to be strictly white. . . . I intend to do my part, as father of two little girls and one boy, to fight integration to the end. Failure of any white college or school to keep the Negroes out of it or them, means to me, that I just won't educate them in an integrated school or college. Every *Southern White* man and woman knows what the N.A.A.C.P.'s ultimate goal is[:] Intermarriage! —White Texan R. G. Hicks to the UT Board of Regents, March 10, 1956

The A.P. sent out a dispatch from Austin last week, to the effect that the Student Body of The University of Texas had voted to accept the Constitution of the United States and the Supreme Court's decision of May 1954, accepting qualified Negro students to the University. If this is true, accept the congratulations of a son of a Confederate veteran. —White Texan J. C. Osborne to UT President Logan Wilson, March 16, 1956

2 Desegregation of Educational Facilities

In February 1951, Oliver Brown, an employee of the Santa Fe Railroad and an assistant pastor from Topeka, Kansas, filed suit against the Topeka Board of Education on behalf of his nine-year-old daughter, Linda. Brown's suit focused on the fact that Topeka segregated its schoolchildren on the basis of their race and that African American children, who had to cross railroad tracks and a main industrial street to catch the school bus, faced danger every day. In addition, Brown's suit focused on "the humiliating fact of segregation." Although a three-judge federal panel originally rejected Brown's suit on the basis that Topeka's black schools were equal to those for white students, the suit eventually reached the Supreme Court, and on May 17, 1954, the Court held unanimously that separate educational facilities were inherently unequal. "To keep black children segregated solely on the basis of race," Chief Justice Earl Warren wrote in the *Brown v. Topeka Board of Education* opinion, "generates a feeling of inferiority as to their status in the community that may affect their hearts and minds in a way unlikely ever to be undone."[1]

At the time of the *Brown* decision, twenty-one states and the District of Columbia operated segregated school systems. Each state now had the task of deciding how to desegregate its public schools. Although some border states reluctantly agreed to comply with the Court's decision, in Texas and other Deep South states, many white citizens called for diehard defiance because they believed that *Brown*, which in essence overturned *Plessy v. Ferguson*, opened the door for race mixing between blacks and whites. At North Texas State College (today the University of North Texas) in Denton, administrators "hesitatingly" accepted the first African American graduate student, Tennyson Miller, in the summer of 1954. Privately conceding that they would lose a court challenge, college administrators nevertheless decided that it would be better to explain to white parents that "the federal courts, not the college, were responsible for the intermingling on campus of Negroes with their sons and daughters." Consequently, the first African American undergraduate there, Joe Louis Atkins, had to sue for admission with the help of Thurgood Marshall and the Legal Defense and Education Fund of the National Association for the Advancement of Colored People (NAACP).[2]

Even with the knowledge that most white Texans did not want black students to attend the state's flagship school, administrators at the University of Texas decided to admit qualified black undergraduates before any lawsuit went to court. No extant documents explain why university administrators or members of the Board of Regents chose not to maintain the policy of segregation until the courts explicitly ordered otherwise. Perhaps these university officials had already accepted that maintaining segregation was a lost cause and not worth a long fight. After all, another court battle would be expensive to the university in terms of both economics and reputation. But integrating the school would not be easy.

A 1962 study of integration at the University of Texas by the Religious Workers Association found that "the basic problem of the Negro student is to break through the monolithic concept too many whites have of the Negro student."[3] Not surprisingly, this burden rested on black students' shoulders. Yet the policies of the Board of Regents and university administrators, coupled with the attitudes of many white students, insured that black UT students would have difficulty finding a comfortable space for themselves on campus. By the late 1950s, however, white attitudes were beginning to change, as more white Texans began to question the morality of segregation. White students worked with African Americans to dispel the image of the "angry Negro" student as a troublemaker who had come to UT to fornicate with white coeds, thereby helping to make the University of Texas a more welcoming place for all its students.

Brown v. Board of Education and the University of Texas

Three weeks after the Court handed down its decision in *Brown*, the National Scholarship Service and Fund for Negro Students sent a postcard to the University of Texas registrar, H. Y. McCown, asking him to do three things: (1) send a copy of the school's latest bulletin; (2) put the service on the university's permanent mailing list so that the service would receive future bulletins as they were published; and (3) provide application and scholarship deadline dates. This inquiry prompted McCown to send a letter to university President Logan Wilson asking him to "take a new look" at the school's admission policy "with reference to Negro students." McCown believed that the university should adopt the same policy that the Texas commissioner of education had instituted—to continue maintaining separate schools for the state's black and white schoolchildren until a court said otherwise. Still, McCown also suggested that the university reevaluate its procedures for admitting black undergraduates in the wake of *Brown*. The current Board of Regents policy stated that the university would admit African American undergraduates only if Texas Southern University or Prairie View A & M (the state's two publicly funded colleges for African Americans) did not offer the students' desired course of study. This policy had kept black undergraduates from enrolling at the university. To continue to "exclude as many Negro undergraduates as possible," McCown suggested that the university adopt a policy that "required applicants for professional work offered at Texas Southern University or Prairie View to first enroll in one of the Negro schools and take at least one year of the academic work required for all degrees." This solution, McCown reasoned, would "keep Negroes out of most classes where there are a large number of [white] girls."[4]

This goal arose out of southern white men's desires to protect the "purity" of white women from the mythological "black beast rapist." Although the myth's roots go as far back as colonial times, this notion of the pure white woman and the "black beast rapist" became popularized during Reconstruction, when Congress began to give black men their civil rights with the passage of the Thirteenth, Fourteenth, and Fifteenth Amendments. The passage of these amendments frightened many white southerners, who believed that black men would now insist on having equal access to white women in addition to civil rights. According to historian Joel Williamson, this new black threat of freedom, coupled with the white myth of the black rapist, had to be kept in check at all costs, resulting in countless lynchings, many of which actually had little or nothing to do with sexual crimes. Moreover, believing that sexual relationships between blacks and whites hinted that the two groups were equal, white southerners passed laws prohibiting blacks and whites from intermarrying. Such antimiscegenation laws embodied the essence of southern whites' beliefs about race: that whites were racially superior to blacks and that any mixing of the two groups was bound to sully whites.[5]

Movies such as D. W. Griffith's *Birth of a Nation* helped to spread the myth of the black sexual predator throughout the South as well as to warn white southerners about what would happen if the two races mixed socially. Set during Reconstruction, the movie was based on Thomas Dixon's novel, *The Clansman: An Historical Romance of the Ku Klux Klan*, which sought "to create a feeling of abhorrence in white people, especially white women against colored men." In addition, Dixon wanted to "prevent the mixing of white and Negro blood by intermarriage."[6] Hailed as a masterpiece—President Woodrow Wilson hosted a showing at the White House—*Birth of a Nation* romanticizes the sanctity and virginity of white women, showing the Ku Klux Klan riding through a town, killing and intimidating African American men in an effort to protect white women's purity. While University of Texas administrators may not have ridden through Austin in Ku Klux Klan regalia, their policies suggest that they accepted this myth and subscribed to the idea that black men needed to be kept away from white women. Thus, these officials sought to prevent large numbers of black men (and especially younger black men who might have been more willing to challenge the racial hierarchy) from attending the University of Texas.

Also concerned about the possible admission of African American undergraduates after the *Brown* decision, the Board of Regents announced that black undergraduates would be admitted only after satisfactory completion of the freshmen prerequisites for their program at a tax-supported and accredited institution of higher education for African Americans in Texas. This new policy cleverly bought the state some time to figure out how it would implement (or circumvent) the law in *Brown*. The policy also served as a political ploy for Democratic Governor Allan Shivers in the 1954 gubernatorial election. Shivers, whose political allies included most of the regents and numerous prominent university administrators, wanted the state legislature to pass a resolution to "invoke and support interposition in order more effectively to fight desegregation and to help put an end to . . . creeping federalism."[7]

Perhaps to show his support for Shivers and the party's segregationist platform, in August 1954 McCown canceled the admission and invalidated the registration of the seven black male undergraduates he had admitted two months earlier. One of these students was John Hargis, an Austin resident who had completed his first year of coursework at Morehouse College in Atlanta, Georgia. The registrar informed Hargis, who had applied to UT to study chemical engineering, that he had not taken "pre-Engineering work" during his freshmen year. According to the registrar, Hargis had failed to take thirteen hours of courses required in UT's chemical engineering program as well as a six-hour course in American government and a six-hour course in American history. Because these twenty-five hours could be taken at Prairie View A & M, the registrar "regretfully" advised Hargis that his acceptance notice was "hereby cancelled." The university also revoked the admission of Marion G. Ford, a talented football player and honor student at Phillis Wheatley High School in Houston who had also applied to the chemical engineering department. After receiving the notice, Ford filed suit in federal district court to gain admission to the school.[8]

On May 31, 1955, the Supreme Court announced its follow-up decision in the *Brown* case, which addressed the implementation of its earlier decision that segregation was illegal. The Court ordered schools to integrate "with all deliberate speed." A week after the Court's decision in *Brown II*, UT President Wilson announced that the Board of Regents would meet on July 8 to "define the path the University will follow on undergraduate integration." "There can be no question about the general intent or meaning of the Supreme Court's decision," he told the *Daily Texan*, "but there are definitely some specific questions to be resolved." Law professor Corwin Johnson believed that integration at the university was inevitable, as he saw "no other recourse than admittance of Negroes" under the "edict handed by the Court." Black leaders also hoped that university administrators would follow the law in *Brown* and *Brown II*. Rev. M. C. Cooper, president of the Austin chapter of the NAACP, said that he hoped the Court's decision "would be carried out in good faith."[9]

University of Texas faculty and students had begun studying the integration of black undergraduates a year before the *Brown* decision. In the first of a series of student-faculty discussions held in the Main Lounge of the Texas Union, Dr. L. D. Haskew, dean of the College of Education, and Dr. Wayne H. Holtzman, associate professor of psychology, spoke about integration at UT and in the United States. Both professors believed that desegregation was a "social problem that's here to stay" and that those who worked to maintain segregation were "simply adding to the complexity of the problem." At a freshman coffee panel in March 1955, seven people—Emma Lois Smith, Sam Dickson, and Marila Spraggins of Huston-Tillotson College; Frank Cooksey, Virginia McDonald, and Dan Williams of the University of Texas; and Dean Page Keeton of the UT School of Law—examined how integration would affect the University of Texas community. Moderator Jack Lewis, the director of the Christian Faith and Life Community, argued that a "gradual acceptance of the Negro student in the classroom" would lead to a "deeper and richer understanding of the Negro." Improved understanding, Dickson and Williams pointed out, would lead to good race relations, since students of both races would be able to "observe another's habits and his contributions to the group." [10]

On July 8, 1955, the University of Texas Board of Regents announced that "all qualified students" would be admitted to the graduate school "regardless of whether the desired programs of study" were offered at the state's "Negro institutions." The regents also voted unanimously to abolish racial segregation at Texas Western College for the upcoming school year and at all other branches of the university system in the fall of 1956. With this edict, Texas became the first southern state to integrate all of its colleges and universities. The decision to integrate, said F. Lanier Cox, assistant to President Wilson, was a difficult one for the "nine good, conservative Texas" regents. Board of Regents Chair Tom Sealy of Midland, in West Texas, believed that "no legal difficulties" would arise over the board's decision. The year delay in integrating the University of Texas, Sealy told the press, resulted from budget problems and uncertainty regarding the availability of housing facilities for the additional students. Even with the delay, Sealy believed that the board's statement provided an "indication of good faith" and represented compliance with the Supreme Court's decree. [11]

Accompanying the decision to admit African American undergraduates to the University of Texas was a decision to set up an "enrollment restriction plan" for all incoming students that included a series of aptitude and subject matter tests (the first ever administered by a public school in Texas), along with "some other formula" by which prospective students would be required to reach certain standards. President Wilson attributed this decision to "inadequate funds and the mushrooming enrollment trend that has already developed." According to Wilson, the restrictions were "in effect a mandate from the legislature because not enough money was appropriated for the increased enrollment." The plan would alert university officials to the race of the applicant (a question the school could not legally ask), since students would take the test in segregated centers. Although these restrictions would inevitably keep some white students from enrolling in the university, the tests would also keep the number of African American students down without violating the law, much in the same way that poll taxes and literacy tests had legally reduced the number of African Americans who could vote in the South. [12]

Many in the university community reacted positively to the regents' announcement of the integration of Texas's colleges and universities. Dr. Judson Williams, dean of student life at Texas Western College, said that students and administrative staffers there "welcome[d] the ruling of the Board of Regents to end segregation and admit Negro students to the college this fall." The editor of the *Daily Texan*, a white male from East Texas, praised the regents as "judicious, humane and courageous in handing down their edict." "Their move," he continued, "will go a long way in promoting understanding . . . and in proving to the entire South that tolerance is workable." The editor also called on the NAACP to accept the year delay (in integrating UT) by "understanding the Regents" and meeting them "halfway." Arno Nowotny, UT's dean of student life, predicted that integration on the undergraduate level would create no problems since "few of them" would be admitted. Moreover, the fact that the African American graduate students who had attended the university had been "pretty high class, both morally and economically," strengthened Nowotny's belief that integration would go smoothly. The University Religious Council, an interfaith group of student religious organizations, expressed its "appreciation" regarding the regents' decision to admit African American undergraduates. Like most other campus religious organizations, the council believed that the policy of segregation ran "contrary to the teachings of Christ." Wrote the leaders of the Baptist Student Union, "We are therefore heartily in favor of the decision on integration made by the Board of Regents and pledge ourselves to a wholehearted implementation of this policy in every area of university life." Mary E. Post, a 1945 graduate of the university, wrote to the regents that she was "proud and pleased" about their decision. "It must be very gratifying to you," Post ended her letter, "to know that you are helping build a healthier, happier country."[13]

Not everyone, however, was happy with the regents' decision. A group of whites in Houston filed suit seeking a writ of mandamus to stop integration at the university, but the Texas Supreme Court refused to hear the lawsuit. Believing compulsory integration to be "unconstitutional," Governor Shivers urged UT administrators to "avoid haste in abolishing segregation." Attorney General John Ben Shepperd said that the state of Texas would "exhaust every remedy before complying" with the Supreme Court's decision because the immediate or too-sudden mixture of black and white students would be "rash, imprudent, and unrealistic." Four members of Congress from Texas and Texas Senator Price Daniel (who as the state's attorney general had fought *Sweatt v. Painter*) were among the eighty-one representatives and nineteen senators who had signed the Southern Manifesto, a document that declared *Brown* a "clear abuse of judicial power." The Dallas Sons of Confederate Veterans branch, upset that the Supreme Court had intended to "destroy" whites "by ordering their amalgamation through integration," vowed to do all in its power to preserve its heritage and to "resist the attempts of those who would destroy our civilization." The veterans' group called on the Board of Regents to "redeem" itself with the white people of Texas by "rescinding this tragic order." White Texan M. Barn accused the regents of not having "half as much self-respect, manhood and decency as a rotten skunk." If they did, Barn reasoned, the regents would never have consented to "allow even 1 nigger to enter the U." Said one University of Texas coed, "I've been taught for twenty-one years that Negroes should know their place—which is not in white circles. I can't change my attitude now." A parent of another University of Texas student said that he could not have his "son or daughter dancing on a dance floor or swimming in a pool with someone as black as the ace of spades and with a skull three inches thick."[14]

Many people wondered how white students and faculty at the university would treat black undergraduates. In 1954, Holtzman had polled five hundred male students and found that 26 percent of them favored doing away with segregation, while only 6 percent wanted it. Holtzman also found that students from West Texas were more likely to support integration than those from East Texas or the Gulf Coast; however, a poll taken a year later found that more than 43 percent of the student body did not favor integration. The University Student Assembly conducted a four-month survey of "official and semi-official adjuncts" of the main university in the spring of 1956, attempting to find out how white students and merchants near the campus would treat black undergraduates. The results showed that white students would "generally" accept the black students, as would most of the surrounding community. "We wanted to find whether Negro students will be accepted as students," said acting Student President Bob Siegel, and "this report indicates they will." The University of Texas Longhorn Band members and its director, Vincent DiNino, favored including blacks who met "the playing standards and impress[ed] our council with being the type of boy[s] to quietly and efficiently become strong band members.[15]

Many students believed that any potential uproar over the admission of African American undergraduates would be "second class" compared to the furor over Heman Sweatt's 1946 lawsuit to gain admission to the School of Law. Most students in the 1940s, a significant number of them World War II veterans, simply sought education as a way to improve their socioeconomic standing and saw Sweatt, himself a World War II veteran, as a troublemaker rather than someone who felt he had a right to attend any school to which he qualified for admission. Some of these students organized protests, burned crosses, and formed groups to keep Sweatt and other African Americans out of the university.

By the time the Supreme Court ordered Sweatt's admission in 1950, however, the tide was changing. Another civil rights movement was on the horizon as black and white protesters began fighting segregation through sit-ins, pickets, and other nonviolent demonstrations. African American World War II veterans began organizing civil rights protests to demand the same freedoms they had given to those in other countries during the war. And some white students began to challenge white racism through their poetry and music. Although people heard rumors that riots would break out when the first African American graduate students arrived on UT's campus, no riots ever occurred. Students in Austin and throughout the country were of a more liberal bent with regard to desegregation, which they often saw as inevitable, said Dr. C. W. Hall, director of the Wesley Bible Chair and Foundation. Many students seemed to agree with Texas's civil defense director, William L. McGill, who said of the Supreme Court's ruling, "It's the law of the land, isn't it? That's all there is to it."[16]

Some white Texans believed that UT students accepted integration because they were communists. Although a few students may indeed have been communists or communist sympathizers, college students at UT seemed simply more apt to accept the finality of the Court's decree. They knew, like other college students throughout the country, that the steps to desegregate American society needed to be taken calmly, lest hysteria result. To this end, in 1954 the National Students' Association unanimously passed a resolution calling for the desegregation of America's schools at all levels by 1955. That same year, the National Student Council of the Young Men's–Young Women's Christian Association passed a resolution urging that its members work, as college students, toward desegregation of enrollment, faculty, and administration in higher education, fraternities, and local churches. This plan to mix white and black students on the college level constituted the best plan for desegregating America's schools for several reasons. First, white college students would have the opportunity to sit in classes with black college students and discuss the "race problem" in the United States. Second, many white college students would have the opportunity to take anthropology and psychology classes that would challenge white supremacists' "scientific" explanations of Negro inferiority. Finally, college students in general were probably less likely to form or join groups that promoted the superiority of the white race because college campuses were often seen as bastions of liberalism.[17]

Before the first African American undergraduates set foot on campus, UT administrators gathered to determine how far integration would go on UT's campus. McCown worked with the director of the Texas Union to avoid problems at the

Union, which in the 1950s served as the center of student social activity. Because student groups held teas, receptions, and coffees there, university administrators wanted to take steps to limit the amount of social mingling between black and white UT students. The two men worried particularly about dances, because black men would have access to white women in a social setting, and consequently agreed that no more dances would be held. McCown also believed that university administrators would stand "on firm ground" in counseling African American students against participating in extracurricular activities, because these students' test scores indicated that they would "have difficulty meeting our academic standards." Thus, university administrators would be doing these black students a favor: "in fairness to themselves," they needed to "devote all their efforts to adjusting to the new situation." McCown believed that his plan for limiting the amount of interaction between black and white University of Texas students would be enough to keep most parties—the members of the Board of Regents, university administrators, and the citizens of Texas—satisfied that only a little bit of desegregation was taking place.[18]

In the fall of 1956, about 110 African American freshmen and graduate and transfer students as well as 18,000 other students enrolled at the University of Texas. Few protests occurred when the blacks arrived on campus, a sharp contrast with the fanfare that accompanied the admission of the first black undergraduate students to other colleges and universities throughout the country. At Lamar State College of Technology in Beaumont in southeast Texas, whites not associated with the school set up picket lines on the outside of the campus and later harassed two black students when they tried to attend classes. At the University of Alabama, President Oliver Cromwell Carmichael, with the backing of the Board of Trustees and the governor, encouraged turmoil on campus as students and faculty stood by while segregationists invaded the campus to demonstrate and riot against African American Autherine Lucy's admission. Six years later at the University of Mississippi, two National Guardsmen protecting African American James Meredith were killed when riots broke out.[19]

The first black undergraduates at the University of Texas found their reception mixed. While some enjoyed their experiences at UT, many did not. Austin resident John T. King said that his time at UT was "nothing but pleasant." Willie Jordan, who enrolled in the School of Architecture, said that he valued his experience at UT: "I still do respect almost all if not all of my architecture deans, professors, and classmates." He recalled that the first black students took an approach that "was not . . . angry."[20]

King's and Jordan's experiences, however, were not common. Most of the first African Americans on campus, like John Hargis, found UT to be "lonely and unpleasant." Edna Humphries Rhambo, the first black student to receive an undergraduate degree from the University of Texas, said that white students sometimes dirtied her chair and engaged in other forms of "petty harassment." Leon Holland said that his family warned him to be careful at UT, and when he got to campus, he thought it would be wise to heed their advice since he knew that some white students did not want to go to class with him and the other African American undergraduates. His wife, Peggy Drake Holland, recalled several incidents at the College of Business: white students often would purposely run into her, sometimes knocking her and her books to the floor. One evening, when Peggy Holland was studying in the business library, an older white man sat down across from her at a table and stared at her for a couple of minutes before writing something on a piece of paper and sliding it over to her. Holland did not read the note and quickly ran off, never again to study in the business library. Marion Ford, whose admission university administrators had canceled in 1954, returned to Texas to attend UT after two years at the University of Illinois because the "University of Texas was where I wanted to go," he said. However, Ford was not allowed to participate in intercollegiate sports as he had at Illinois, so he took twenty-one course hours during his first semester in Austin: "There was very little to do except study," he remembered. Little had changed from six years earlier when John Chase enrolled in the School of Architecture and experienced some hostility from white students and received hate mail with racial slurs. Chase knew and had a great deal of sympathy for Heman Sweatt: "If the case had been built on me, I would not have graduated, either."[21]

Toward the end of the first year of complete integration at UT, the Student Assembly established the Human Relations Committee to study the problems associated with integration and to analyze how these problems affected students, faculty, administration, and area businesses. The committee found that only two students had reported "probable" incidents of discrimination in the classroom: the Student Assembly investigated both incidents and resolved them "to the satisfaction of both parties concerned." The group also found that African American undergraduates had participated in student government and religious organizations. Although just two African American women and twenty-six African American men took part in intramural contests, these students participated without "any problems." "Good sportsmanship was in evidence at all times and there were no unpleasant incidents of any nature," wrote Dean McCown.[22] The committee also found that African American participation in extracurricular activities was "satisfactory" and that social functions had been integrated with "very little difficulty."

Holland enrolled in Army ROTC, while Hargis joined the student chapter of the American Institute of Chemical Engineers; served from 1957 to 1959 in the cabinet of the Wesley Foundation, a Methodist group; and became one of the first vice presidents of the University Religious Foundation. However, African American undergraduate students could not join any of the university-approved social fraternities and sororities, which had strict rules prohibiting the admittance of African Americans. As a result, African American students formed their own social organizations on campus or simply joined none at all. Many African American students felt that the university and its students never completely welcomed them. As black undergraduate Anthony Henry put it, "Negro students on the University campus" had been "desegregated, but not integrated." Other blacks were humiliated as much by the "overwhelming welcome" white students provided to blacks who joined various organizations as by overt acts of discrimination.[23]

For their part, university administrators remained wary of social integration even after blacks had been on campus for a year with no significant racial incidents. In the spring of 1957, deans, directors, and key student activities personnel met to discuss potential "integration problems." According to McCown's summary of the meeting, participants worried specifically about three "problem areas": (1) intimate social contact between black and white students (in labs, at dances, and in plays); (2) African Americans in positions to make decisions affecting white students (as teaching assistants, counselors, and graders); and (3) public appearances between blacks and whites where this relationship could offend (white) observers.[24]

Despite their attempts to follow the letter of the law, university administrators continued to work to maintain the racial status quo in areas not directly related to the classroom. Faculty members set up separate testing centers for black and white students and assigned white students in need of counseling only to white graduate students. At the Student Health Center, administrators segregated the bathrooms and nurses kept African American students in separate rooms, a policy that McCown claimed caused "no criticism." At the Texas Union, no "disturbing incidents" had occurred as a result of integration, but McCown feared the possibility of "mixed dancing" or of "Negroes appearing in public performances in talent shows." In 1961, when the English department requested permission to hire an African American woman as a teaching assistant, Chancellor Harry

Ransom indicated that although he knew of no written policy, the University of Texas "would not at present, nor, he thought for some time, employ Negroes for any kind of classroom work."[25]

The admission of African Americans to the University of Texas Medical Branch (which included a medical school and a school of nursing) offers a good example of the conflicting messages the Board of Regents sent to the citizens of Texas about how far integration would proceed at other schools in the UT system. The regents integrated the Medical Branch, located in Galveston, in the fall of 1949, a year before the Supreme Court ordered Sweatt's admission to UT's Austin campus. By 1961, twenty-four African Americans had enrolled in the School of Medicine, but only thirteen had graduated. African Americans were first admitted to the School of Nursing in the summer of 1950, and over the next eleven years, 350 African Americans enrolled. The campus also had thirteen African American nurses on campus, including one supervisor and two head nurses. The executive dean and director of the Medical Branch credited the "success of this venture" to the first five students, who, he said, had "resisted every effort of the N.A.A.C.P. to publicize their enrollment" and who had "conducted themselves in exemplary fashion."[26]

The reality of integration at the Medical Branch actually differed substantially from what these numbers would seem to indicate. During the first ten years after African Americans were admitted, black and white staff and students maintained Jim Crow seating in the dining hall, and the school maintained separate hospitals for its black and white patients. The white hospital boasted facilities far superior to those of the black hospital, which the state commissioner of health declared "crowded." Moreover, until the summer of 1956, the commissioner considered the obstetrical service and delivery room of the Medical Branch Negro Hospital "intolerable." Sterilizing equipment did not work properly, and over a six-month period three babies were born in the elevator when it became stuck between floors. In light of these facts, the regents approved renovating the Negro Hospital despite the exorbitant cost because doing so would allow for "full segregation" in the labor rooms, delivery suites, and in the newborn nurseries. Social integration at the school similarly fell short of the ideal. Several faculty members "raised an eyebrow" when African American couples attended the freshman class's traditional fall outing. Four members of the faculty who were "Texas-born" and "representative of familiar feelings of apprehension or caution on the problems of integration" subsequently endorsed a proposition that only students could attend undergraduate functions attended by both men and women.[27]

The slow integration of the Medical Branch mirrors in many ways the situation on the University of Texas campus. In the fall of 1961, regent Wales H. Madden Jr. wrote to the other members of the Board of Regents regarding desegregation on UT's campus. Acknowledging his "personal prejudices," Madden explained that he was not willing to accede to the "extremists who demand immediate integration." That said, Madden wrote that he was well aware that even a gradual plan of integration might not head off a lawsuit filed by African American students at the school. Fearing that a lawsuit would receive international attention and provide "headline material throughout the nation," Madden urged the regents to "review carefully our position, particularly with respect to the integration steps taken in other state-supported schools in the south and in Texas." While such a review might not be a defense in a lawsuit, Madden believed that it would offer valuable information regarding how the University of Texas measured up against these other schools. Placing the situation at UT into such a broader perspective would then allow the regents to continue dragging their feet on the integration process. [28]

In many respects, the University of Texas led most other Texas schools in terms of desegregation. Southern Methodist University in Dallas had not officially desegregated and had only a small number of African American students in its theology department. Texas Tech in Lubbock, in West Texas, had just integrated the preceding fall, and Baylor University in Waco and Texas A & M University in College Station had yet to integrate. The most conspicuous example of desegregation had occurred at North Texas State, which enrolled 202 black students in 1961—approximately the same number as at UT, although North Texas had a smaller student body. The dormitories at North Texas State were integrated, as were intercollegiate athletics. As for students at North Texas, President J. C. Matthews said that they had "worked out their own social problems quietly, and for this reason the administration has avoided all written rules." [29]

Such was not the case at the University of Texas, where the Board of Regents, with the cooperation and assistance of university administrators, set the policies that dictated how far integration would go on campus. Consequently, both entities continued to enact or recommend policies—both written and unwritten—that limited the interaction (and thus the integration) of African American students. However, these same entities sent conflicting messages to the citizens of Texas regarding just how far integration would go. As one regent wrote, "There is no plan (and in our opinion there should not be one) either for steady progress toward integration, or for firm resistance against it." All decisions with "overtones or incidental involvement," he wrote, "will be handled as before on their economic and professional merits." [30]

Many students, however, thought differently. African American students believed that they deserved equality on campus "not only because we are Negroes, but because we are students and . . . human beings with feelings." Some white students believed that because the University of Texas stood midway between the South and West in both location and racial attitudes, the administration had an "obligation" to promote policies that would advance positive relations between black and white students. "We consider arguments based on fears such as the possibility of interracial marriage or legislative reprisal to be invalid and unethical," wrote one prointegration group. Thus, while the regents used the small desegregation steps they had authorized as an evasive tactic to maintain the status quo with regard to integration, black and white students continued their fight to fully integrate the campus and its educational facilities.[31]

The absence of African American professors, instructors, and teaching assistants on the University of Texas campus served as yet another reminder that African Americans remained second-class citizens and were believed incapable of serving in positions of authority. By refusing to allow African Americans to teach on campus, the regents and university administrators not only gave credence to the belief that black people lacked the ability to serve in these positions but also strengthened the notion that white students could not and should not be put in positions subject to African American authority. University administrators and board members unquestioningly accepted this unspoken and unwritten rule; however, it was inadvertently challenged in the spring of 1961 when Associate Dean Leo Hughes of the Graduate School approved the appointment of a qualified African American woman as a teaching assistant in the English department. In the past, when African American students applied for teaching assistantships, the Graduate School would grant them university fellowships "as a means of avoiding an awkward situation." Because this particular student lacked the credentials to win a fellowship in an open competition, Hughes faced an unusual dilemma. He could award her a fellowship she did not deserve (and thus deny her "a chance to acquire the training and prestige that a teaching assistantship at the University of Texas represents"), or he could appoint her to work as a teaching assistant. Hughes chose the latter approach but consulted with UT President Joseph Smiley about the decision. Smiley resolved the "extremely delicate and complex" problem by simply canceling the appointment.[32]

The issue resurfaced a year later after an article in the *Negro Labor News*, an African American newspaper published in Houston, announced that African American Maxine Prescott had been appointed as an instructor in the UT School of Nursing at the Medical Branch in Galveston. Prescott, a spring 1961 graduate who had also completed state requirements to become a registered nurse, was to begin work in obstetrics in September 1962. After receiving a copy of the article from a "concerned white Texan," Regent A. G. McNeese Jr. asked the Medical Branch's director, John Truslow, about the matter, and Truslow confirmed Prescott's appointment. Even though the regents planned to bar even qualified African Americans from serving as instructors, Truslow believed that faculty selections should be based on "merit without regard to color." McNeese worried about the possibility that Prescott—or any African American, for that matter—might be sent to UT's campus in Austin to teach, thereby upsetting white Texans, who he said were already uncomfortable with the integration progress at the state's flagship university. McNeese's most pressing concern, however, was that Prescott's appointment broke all precedent, thus making it "more far-reaching than the appointment of one instructor in one school at the Medical Branch." McNeese feared that this appointment could lead to the dismantling of other racial barriers, especially the one that kept blacks and whites socially separate. Consequently, McNeese and the Board of Regents restated their policy, this time in a written memorandum, that African Americans were not to serve as instructors on any University of Texas campus, although they could continue to serve as research assistants.[33] Three more years would pass before the first African American received a teaching appointment at the University of Texas at Austin.

While the Board of Regents continued to work to maintain segregation, some white students and professors fought to eliminate racism on campus. Law professor Ernest Goldstein sent a letter to Harry Ransom, who had become UT's vice president, urging the school to "terminate the unwritten rules establishing racial criteria for use of drinking fountains, toilets, and the like." Students and faculty began challenging these customs as well as the unwritten bans on African American students' participation on intercollegiate athletic teams and in on-campus theater productions. After receiving a lukewarm response from Ransom, Goldstein circulated a petition among the faculty and student body that called for an end to these unwritten rules. The faculty overwhelmingly supported this effort, voting 308 to 34 in favor of the elimination of such barriers. In a letter to fellow regent Thornton Hardie, Wales Madden downplayed the significance of the faculty vote, arguing that he would not speculate on the outcome "if the entire faculty expressed an opinion on this matter." Madden also dismissed the significance of a student vote in favor of the petition, writing that students should be "congratulated" for "generating interest in voting on any referendum or election": when he was a student, it was difficult "to obtain broad student participation in campus elections." For Madden and the rest of the Board of Regents, however, the bottom line was that the University of Texas had "exceeded the dictates of the Supreme Court in the integration area." Moreover, the regents had voted unanimously on all matters related to integration at UT, securing the approval of the chancellor, the president, and all the vice chancellors. The university administration would continue to speak with one voice.[34]

In the fall of 1961, a Committee on Minorities, created by the Board of Regents in response to a petition by Professor Jerre Williams, began to work on behalf of African American students on campus. Originally intended to track the progress and plight of African American and other minority students on campus, the committee's work expanded to include pressing for equal treatment of African Americans by the UT administration and businesses on or near the campus. This shift in the committee's focus angered the Board of Regents, which did not really want to establish such a committee and whose goals were diametrically opposed to those of the committee.[35]

The committee's work became especially important in light of the regents' continuing refusal to enact regulations that would open all of the campus and its activities to African American students. Moreover, like their white counterparts in the North, University of Texas students increasingly began to question the principle of segregation and became more willing publicly to state their concerns. As sophomore premed major William Boyd argued in an editorial in the *Daily Texan*, integrationists' most important role was to "quell the fears of the segregationists." Boyd also believed that UT students should "shoulder the responsibility of integration" because "it is not a task to be passed on to our children." In 1945, the *Daily Texan* had received approximately twice as many letters in support of integration as opposed to it. In 1950, on the heels of the Supreme Court's decision in *Sweatt v. Painter*, only 5 percent of students polled opposed integration at UT. In 1961, the largest number of UT students to ever sign a petition voiced their support for integrating the school's intercollegiate athletic program. The committee understood that to succeed in its work, it had to latch on to this student momentum.[36]

Not all students agreed with the committee's philosophy, however. In fact, the 1961 Student Government election highlights the UT students' divisions regarding campus integration. The Student Party, a campus political group organized in November 1960, submitted a platform to the student body that included a statement very strongly supporting complete integration on campus. When asked about his position on integration, another candidate, Charlie Hayden of the Foundation for the Advancement of Conservative Thought (FACT) Party, stated simply, "I am an integrationist." Neither of the other two presidential candidates supported complete integration of the university. Chancy Croft of the Representative Party announced, "I don't favor immediate integration at this time. . . . I'm not for integration next month, or next year, or the next year. I think it should be reached eventually." Independent candidate Cameron Hightower believed not only that a majority of students opposed integration but also that some violently opposed it. "At least 50 per cent of the student body is not emotionally ready for integration," he told a *Daily Texan* reporter.[37]

The members of the Board of Regents believed that the students who favored integration were too boldly challenging the regents' authority and consequently began discussing whether to limit integrationists' work on campus. At their regular July 1961 meeting, the regents issued a statement directed toward the general faculty, the Students Association, and representatives of "other groups which had submitted petitions and resolutions concerning integration policies at the Main University in Austin." While acknowledging that not all board members agreed with the Supreme Court's integration decisions, the regents believed that they had proceeded "along this path" in good faith and would continue to do so "with all deliberate speed." Regent L. D. Haskew issued an even more determined statement, saying that there would be "no change in the segregated policy." In response to student pickets and petitions, Chancellor Logan Wilson said that students were "quite free to picket off campus in an orderly way as long as they wish. University policy, however, is not arrived at in response to this sort of action." Vice chancellor Harry Ransom agreed with this position. Calling the regents' decisions with regard to integration "the wisest ones available," Ransom issued a statement to the press asking the regents to wait six months before reviewing desegregation progress at the Austin campus.[38]

Student protests nevertheless continued that fall in the form of demonstrations, petitions, and sit-ins. Student leaders announced that these activities would continue until the regents agreed to treat all African Americans "like Americans, like students, like Negroes, who—if this nation is at all what it is trumped up to be—have the right to be free." Under the leadership of editor Maurice Olian, the *Daily Texan* continued to publish articles, editorials, and letters in support of full integration. In the eyes of the regents, however, the student paper was simply "maligning" and "down grading" the University of Texas and the Board of Regents. Hardie feared that the "continual repetition of these and similar statements" would adversely affect "the minds of former students and other citizens of Texas whose continuous support the University needs" and called on administrators to censor the *Daily Texan*. If doing so were not possible, Hardie urged the administration to encourage "right thinking" faculty to write letters to the paper in support of the regents' work or to get these faculty members to help "some of our fine students in the preparation of letters and statements" to the *Daily Texan*. Such a strategy, he hoped, would "abate the viciousness and the unfairness of these attacks." The next move, Hardie suggested, would be to use public monies to hire "competent public relations counselors to get the true picture to the public, the students and to the faculty" of the "great strides which have been made at The University under Dr. Logan Wilson and Dr. Harry Ransom." "Every Texan should be proud of the progress which has been made and is being made," Hardie wrote. [39]

But students continued to press for progress both on campus and in society in general. In February 1962, the Young Democrats, the University Religious Council, the Student Party, Students for Direct Action, and the university Young Men's Christian Association organized a drive to gather food, clothing, and money for more than four hundred evicted African American sharecroppers living in a tent city outside of Somerville, Tennessee. Dean Ed Price forced these groups to set up their collection booth on the Drag (a seven-block stretch of Guadalupe Avenue that runs in front of West Campus, the most widely used entrance to the university) rather than on the UT campus, where most groups set up their booths. Denying that racism and prejudice played any part in his decision, Price called the movement "a commercial endeavor" rather than a "legitimate charity." Students, however, believed that Price and other university administrators wanted to halt the work of all civil rights groups on campus. [40]

University of Texas students also worked with civil rights leaders trying to integrate the Austin Ice Palace, a newly opened ice rink in East Austin, a primarily African American and Mexican American section of town. Many students saw this segregated facility as a direct insult to the black people who lived in that neighborhood, but the owners argued that they would go out of business if they admitted African American skaters: "Integration is strictly a business matter, having nothing to do with the moral issue raised." UT students, however, refused to accept this reasoning and aided a group of African American mothers who had set up pickets outside the rink. In an unprecedented move, university administrators took a stand in the integration policies of an off-campus establishment. Sheila O'Gara, the director of the Women's Physical Education Department, canceled the physical education department's ice skating classes because of the Ice Palace's segregation policies. Said O'Gara, "The University is completely integrated in regard to classes. This is our policy, and any class offered must be integrated." This policy represented a dramatic shift from earlier University of Texas policies that mandated the cancellation of women's swimming and intramural swimming and wrestling to avoid close contact between whites and blacks. Although the rink's owners promised to admit African Americans registered for the department's ice skating classes, O'Gara refused to reinstate the classes.[41] At least one university administrator was implicitly admitting that segregation in off-campus facilities negatively affected black students' total educational experience.

The thinking of most University of Texas administrators and the Board of Regents, however, remained more in line with that of the many white Texans—as well as the legislature and the governor—who believed that desegregation had been achieved (or had gone far enough) on the UT campus. Wrote one white resident to President Wilson, "A firm 'no-fooling' policy is called for at Texas University. If the Negroes aren't satisfied to be getting all they said they were sueing [*sic*] for . . . then let them go elsewhere and good riddance of them." Although the University of Texas had been desegregated—black students were allowed to attend classes—it was not integrated. Board of Regents policies still kept African American students from participating in many campus activities and from joining some university-approved organizations, thereby keeping black students, as Anthony Henry noted, "from the general stream of University life." Nevertheless, the regents believed that no "substantial changes should be made in the immediate future" and instead pledged to "continue to move forward with due and deliberate speed," as they thought "advisable."[42] University of Texas students remained unsatisfied and continued their efforts to force open the university's extracurricular activities as well as businesses near the campus.

I believe that white youth should meet and cultivate friendship and association with Negro youth. . . . Too often in interracial education in the past the Negro student has been circumscribed in his activity to the atmosphere and life of the classroom and has been shut out of the rest of the program of the institution. They should not be confined to the sidelines but should be allowed to go all the way into the program of the University. —Dr. William H. Jones, executive vice president, Huston-Tillotson College, December 2, 1954

3 Desegregation on and off Campus

In the fall of 1963, African American UT student Ed Guinn walked into Raymond's Drugstore on the Drag to cash a check, a service the store routinely provided to UT students. But when Guinn walked in, the white man at the counter said that the store did not cash checks for Negroes. Guinn replied that the store had cashed checks for white students and thus should do so for him, but the man was adamant. Guinn "wasn't in the mood to be trifled with," as he said, and yelled "Bullshit!" at the man. Perhaps, Guinn later realized, the white man was shocked that a "young nigger would curse at him." In any case, the man reached across the counter and slapped Guinn. Aware of the racial implications of this exchange between an older white man and a young black man, Guinn called the police. "I was just so pissed that he thought he could slap me like that," Guinn recalled. "I didn't care that he was white and I was black and that it was 1963. He had no right to touch me." The police arrived, listened to both men's stories, and then arrested Guinn on an unpaid parking ticket. "Can you believe it?" Guinn said twenty-seven years later, laughing. "He slapped me, and I was the one who went to jail."[1]

This protest, although seemingly minor, was just one of the many in which Guinn would participate during his four years at the University of Texas. Like other UT students, he believed that very little had changed since the regents had opened the university to all qualified students. Eight years later, most campus-area businesses—restaurants, movie theaters, and barber shops—refused to serve African American students. With the tacit approval of the Board of Regents, administrators still refused to allow African American students to participate in intercollegiate athletics, and many university-approved organizations, such as fraternities and sororities, still refused to admit African American students as members. Nevertheless, university officials wondered whether they had gone too far in opening the campus and its activities to black students.

In the late 1950s, the University of Texas allowed African American athletes from other schools to participate in intercollegiate and interscholastic events on its campus yet prohibited UT's black students from playing on teams in those same events. Some black UT students protested this policy by attending home football games and cheering for the black athletes on the opponent's team. In 1955, prior to the school's complete integration, the UT Athletic Department had refused to invite any all-black colleges to the Texas Relays. That policy continued for the following year, a situation that posed a potential problem for the university, which was hosting the National Collegiate Athletic Association (NCAA) National Outdoor Track Meet. The NCAA invited all teams that qualified, regardless of the team's ethnic and racial composition, and university administrators allowed African Americans from other teams to compete.[2]

The prohibition against black students participating in athletics did not extend to intramural sports, perhaps because integrating these sports posed little threat of alienating the university's white alumni. Moreover, to keep African American students from participating on intramural teams would have probably meant eliminating intramurals altogether, because some university administrators interpreted *McLaurin v. Oklahoma* (1950) as including intramural sports. Administrators also feared that white students would protest such action, since intramural sports formed an integral part of many students' lives. Perhaps not wanting to give students and "liberal" faculty any reason to pounce on the current policies, university administrators decided to integrate intramural sports.[3]

However, university officials canceled two intramural sports, swimming and wrestling. It is unclear whether Dean of Students H. Y. McCown was aware of a 1933 Texas law that prohibited "Caucasians" and "Africans" from boxing and wrestling together, but he believed that wrestling, "a contact sport" should be "eliminated." After "carefully" considering the matter, Berry Whitaker, the director of intramural sports for men, agreed that wrestling should be eliminated "to avoid incidents." Similarly, swimming would have permitted black and white participants to see each other in limited clothing. More importantly, these sports would have facilitated the exchange of bodily fluids between black and white participants, a possibility that white segregationists feared because they believed that this kind of intimate contact threatened the white-dominated social hierarchy. Although McCown also planned to continue segregating the intramural teams by gender—thereby keeping black men from coming into contact with white women—such actions actually were unnecessary: intramural teams tended to be segregated by race because the organizations from which the teams derived were themselves segregated.[4]

These rules, like the laws white southerners passed during and immediately after Reconstruction, simply represented an extension of the fear, jealousy, hatred, and fanaticism that had ruled southern society since the end of the Civil War. However, many black and white UT students did not want to perpetuate this cycle of inequality and banded together with other like-minded people to bring the plight of black UT students into public light. Through protests, rallies, sit-ins, and other nonviolent demonstrations, many on- and off-campus activities became open to all.

The Barbara Smith Controversy

In the spring of 1957, Barbara Louise Smith was a nineteen-year-old African American music student in UT's College of Fine Arts. Born in Center Point, a small town in East Texas, Smith grew up singing in a Baptist church. In the fall of 1956, Smith had transferred from Prairie View A & M to the University of Texas to study with Edra Gustafson, a well-known music teacher. Smith told the *Daily Texan*, "For a long time I had been aware of the great need for better trained musicians for my people and felt that the University was the school in Texas that was best prepared to equip me for this work." To Smith, the purpose of integration was to learn from those with the best expertise and take this information back into her community. In October 1956 a faculty committee chose Smith, who many classmates believed had the best soprano voice in the class, to play the female lead in the school's production of Henry Purcell's opera, *Dido and Aeneas*. Based on Virgil's *Aeneid*, the opera offers a classic recounting of the tragic love between Dido, queen of Carthage, and Aeneas, the Trojan prince. Because the committee had chosen two white men—David Blanton and David Richards—to play the role of Aeneas, the opera would have an interracial cast. The opera's opening lines would prove to be prophetic: "Oh my sorrow. I am possessed with torment. Peace and I are strangers grown."[5]

Smith and E. W. Doty, the dean of the College of Fine Arts, immediately began receiving telephone calls threatening them and the university with harm if Smith performed with the white men. One such call to Smith's dormitory came from a state representative's wife, who, after asking if Smith lived at that residence, said she "better not appear on the stage." Doty refused to give in to the pressure, but during the winter, the controversy grew when Representative Jerry Sadler of Percilla, in East Texas, raised the issue in the legislature, contending that because the title characters are in love, the appearance of a black Dido and a white Aeneas would be "offensive" to many people. Sadler then threatened to vote against appropriations for the university. Representative Joe Chapman of Sulphur Springs in East Texas also objected to Smith's inclusion in the opera, arguing that the people of Texas "don't want mixing of Negroes and whites publicly and the University of Texas should not do it from that standpoint." Six weeks before the production was to open, UT President Logan Wilson instructed the College of Fine Arts to remove Smith from the cast; Smith, however, was not told of the decision until just a couple of days before the production was to go on.[6] Her removal touched off a storm of controversy and exhibited the lengths to which University of Texas administrators would go to keep African American students from being full members of the school. It also exhibited the university's fear of black bodies and interracial sex, and white Texans' obsession with protecting one of the South's greatest treasures, the white woman.

The parties involved recalled the events leading up to Smith's removal somewhat differently. Believing that it was "poor public relations to cast a Negro in a University production," Chapman said that he had called Wilson to discuss the matter but denied having threatened to vote against the university's appropriations. Chapman explained to a reporter, "I'm a Texas ex and he's a long time personal friend of mine. That was the first he heard about the Negro girl being in the cast. I didn't say anything about appropriations. We just talked about public policy and what would be for the good of the university." Chapman believed that he had the support of most university students, whom he described as "loyal, solid Texans." In Chapman's view, "starry-eyed, befuddled liberals" were "promoting agitation and following the Communist Party line by creating as much confusion as possible." Some of Chapman's opponents, however, wondered if qualifying as a "loyal Texan" meant, as *Time* magazine put it, "abandoning our religious heritage as Christians and Jews, and our political heritage as Americans."[7]

Wilson had a different recollection of events. In a statement released to the faculty just a few days after Smith's removal, Wilson said that in late March 1957 he had received word from McCown that "a Negro student had for some time been rehearsing the leading feminine role for the public performance of an opera." Wilson then called Doty, who confirmed this information. Believing that a mixed-race cast would have involved "an unprecedented step for us and one taken only lately by such organizations as the Metropolitan Opera in New York City," Wilson called a "conference of administrative officers." He subsequently decided that Smith's performance "would set back progress already made in the peaceful working out of a difficult and controversial problem." Thus, Smith had to be removed from the opera. The call from Representative Chapman, Wilson told the faculty, came after the committee had decided to remove Smith: "It was an administrative decision made by the administrative officers involved and in what was considered to be the best interests not only of the University at large but also of the student herself."[8]

Wilson's decision to dismiss Smith relied in part on black and white Texans' fears of miscegenation. Although white Texans usually applied this fear to sexual relations between black men and white women, a black woman playing the romantic lead opposite a white man still brought these fears into the forefront. About Smith's role, Wilson had said, "In any American university this would be regarded as venturous but in a Southern university it would inevitably be provocative of far-reaching consequences." Texas whites, Wilson believed, were not ready for social integration, let alone an interracial opera. "On basic social issues," Wilson had said in defending his decision, the university "is subject to the will of the majority of its citizens, insofar as that will can be interpreted by those most directly responsible to them." "The decision itself was made without either pride or apology," Wilson said in his concluding remarks. In essence, President Wilson followed Booker T. Washington's view of integration, with the races as separate as the fingers in all things social. The university had desegregated, which many white Texans thought disgraceful enough, but many people found a "white boy and a negro girl enacting those passionate love scenes," as Raymond Orr of Kerrville wrote to Wilson, "disgusting" and "downright vulgar." Continued Orr, "How I wish the people of Texas had the stamina and pride of race the fine old states of Georgia, Alabama, Mississippi, and Louisiana have." Smith's presence in the opera also played directly into the hands of those who believed that school integration was simply the first step in a massive mixing of the races. "You can not mix races one way without going all the way eventually," Mrs. Ferris Galbreath of Victoria wrote. One coed made the connections explicit: mingling of white and black students would lead to familiarity, which, in turn, "would lead to intermarriage, which would produce its unhappy product, the mulatto, who is respected by none and rejected by all."[9]

Most UT students believed that university administrators should not have removed Smith from the opera, arguing that she had a right to appear since she had fairly won the title role. Students expressed their disapproval of Wilson's decision in several different ways. Some, such as Charles Smith, wrote letters to the *Daily Texan*. Smith asked whether a "golden monument" could be erected on campus with the inscription "dedicated to the principles of liberty, justice, and segregation." More pointedly, Representatives Chapman and Sadler were hung in effigy, accompanied by a ten-foot banner reading "Demagogues—Chapman and Sadler." About five hundred students signed a petition that said in part, "As a group of interested students who are concerned about our campus' policies on integration, we would like to register our protest to the recent action taken in regard to the current opera production." The Alba Club, a Latin American organization on campus, adopted a resolution condemning Smith's removal. The presidents of two leading service organizations, the Cowboys and the Silver Spurs, recommended that students boycott *Dido and Aeneas*, while the Young Republicans and the Young Democrats adopted a resolution urging the investigation of "all cases of racial discrimination," including the Smith incident. Said the resolution, "The entire student body of The University of Texas is affected when any student is denied his or her right to participate on an equal basis in student activities."[10]

Other Texans, including university alumni, also expressed their disapproval of Smith's removal in a variety of ways. In an article in the *Dallas Express*, an African American newspaper, Marion Butts chided Wilson on his handling of the matter, wondering why UT's president did not know what was going on at his school as well as why he could not see the positive "Far Reaching Consequence[s]" of an African American female playing opposite a white male. Butts also called Smith's removal from the play "just another Southern weak" scapegoat and found it "surprisingly interesting to see it being used by a University President, who is suppose to represent truth, Democracy and orderly thinking." State legislators Elizio De La Garza of Mission, Menton Murray of Harlingen, Malcolm McGregor of El Paso, W. N. Woolsey of Corpus Christi, Bob Wheeler of Tilden, Bob Mullen of Alice, Oscar M. Laurel of Laredo, and Maurice S. Pipkin of Brownsville wrote to Smith to apologize for Chapman's behavior: "We want her to know that the person who caused her difficulty did not think for the entire Legislature—that he represented only his peculiar thinking." "It is most unfortunate," the legislators' letter continued, "that some people have lost their sense of values, are more interested in personal advancement and the applause of the folks back home than they are in Christian principles of right and wrong." Assembly Secretary Nancy McGoosby, who did not sign the letter and believed that the university needed to "go slow" as it integrated, said that she would like to "tell the gentleman from Sulphur Springs to go to hell." In a letter to university Vice President C. P. Boner, T. H. McKee said that he and his family were "appalled" at the university's decision to remove Smith. Furthermore, McKee said, if he "had his way, as a white citizen of southern birth," he would "close the doors of the State University at high noon today and keep them closed until that young woman was given the place at the head of her class in the drama production." Allan Metz personally attacked President Wilson: "If the newspaper reports are true . . . you are nothing but a contemptible craven and unfit to be janitor of the poorest one-room school in the most backward and degenerate county in Texas." One alumnus wrote that he was "deeply ashamed"; said another, "It makes me sick to my stomach."[11]

The University of Texas faculty, who Chapman believed were "raising hell" and "trying to get the rest of the cast to quit" unless Wilson reinstated Smith, had varying opinions regarding Smith's removal. Roger Shattuck, an assistant professor in romance languages, called for a faculty committee on integration that would "function intelligently and constructively" in facing issues that might threaten the university's complete integration. In a speech before the Faculty Council, philosophy professor John Silber called the university's lack of an official policy for the participation of African American students in social functions "unfair to our Negro students." He also wondered whether the university's policies with regard to segregation in matters outside of the classroom complied "with either the intent or the letter of the Supreme Court decision." Silber ended his speech by thinking about how university administrators had treated Smith: "It is not enough to say that we are without pride; I think we should be overcome with shame." R. H. Williams, professor of Spanish and Portuguese, condemned the action in a five-page typewritten report in which he stated, "The people of Texas and all other citizens are entitled to some kind of testimonial that the administration's attitude was not approved unanimously." In contrast, business professors Charles Zlatkovich and Joseph Bailey defended Wilson's actions, telling the Faculty Committee in June that as a state-supported institution, the University of Texas was compelled to conform to the desires of the majority of its citizens, who did not support an interracial cast. J. W. Reynolds, Glenn E. Barnett, and Clyde C. Colvert of the College of Education signed statements supporting Wilson's decision as "judicious."[12]

The Committee of Counsel on Academic Freedom and Responsibility had a more middle-of-the-road opinion of Smith's removal. In their official statement on the case, committee members announced that they believed that the University of Texas had accepted the Supreme Court's decision in *Brown v. Board of Education* in "good faith" and had succeeded "to a considerable degree" in integrating African American students. The committee conceded, however, that only "educational integration" had occurred at the university, although the goal of integration should be "full opportunity to participate in . . . both curricular and extracurricular" activities. In light of Texas's social climate in the late 1950s, however, the committee concluded that Wilson's decision to remove Smith was "wise."[13] The whites of Texas were simply not ready to see a black woman playing a romantic lead opposite a white man, even if that woman had the best voice in the school.

Many people commended Smith for her behavior during the controversy. An editorial in the *Dallas Morning News* praised her for refusing to "become another Autherine Lucy" and boasted that her graceful handling of the situation had done "much to help race relations." The *Daily Texan* commended Smith for maintaining "a personal dignity throughout the entire incident" and for being able to "see herself as not so much the central figure . . . but as a part of a larger pattern." African American Carter Wesley wrote in the *Houston Informer*, a black weekly, that Smith should be congratulated "for refusing to strike back or to show any resentment over the denial . . . of rights due" her. She was "too dignified and poised to fight in the gutter for honors [won] by . . . merit and worth, [even] if those who gave the honors were little enough to want to take them back for cheap reasons." Another *Informer* editorial posited that the Smith controversy would serve as fuel against die-hard segregationists who "have been mouthing that Negroes do not have the qualifications to go to school with whites." The writer also encouraged "the Negro community to discover the talents of the Barbara Smiths not only in music and art, but in science and technology and elsewhere." "When discovered, these talented Negro youths should be encouraged and supported to join Miss Smith and others like her in helping to bring truth and justice and fair play to American life, and in promoting the kind of excellence which Barbara Smith has displayed." Even Chapman gave Smith "a lot of credit" because she had "never complained."[14]

Smith at first hesitated to answer reporters' queries about her removal, simply saying that it had not occurred because of her singing abilities: "If it was my singing ability, I would never have been selected for the part in the beginning." After reporters pressed, Smith said that her first reaction was "one of great hurt": "I do not believe anyone who had been practicing a role for six months and who had any feeling for the role she was trying to interpret could react otherwise when the role was taken from her for any reason." Smith said that Wilson had told her that her removal was "necessary" to ensure her "personal well being" and that there was a possibility that her appearance in the opera would "precipitate a cut in the university's appropriations by the Legislature." Smith later said that her dismissal was "best for harmonious integration" and that the faculty committee that chose her to sing the lead in the opera "displayed striking naivete." Although shocked by her removal, Smith stated that if she were President Wilson, she would have done the same thing. "I believe [Wilson and Doty] want the same thing I do and are trying to achieve the most harmonious fulfillment of integration at the University." "I just want to go back to being a student," she said. [15]

The story generated national and international headlines. Moreover, in the immediate aftermath of the incident, Wilson refused to answer questions about it, thereby fueling the rumor mill and contributing to the story's stature. Most U.S. papers chided the university's actions as cowardly and racist. After reading about Smith's removal in the *New York Times*, singer and civil rights activist Harry Belafonte called Smith to let her know that someone was "in her corner." He offered to give her money so that she could study music "anywhere she chose." Although "thrilled to death" about Belafonte's offer, Smith said she wanted to stay at UT, where she had "found exactly what I wanted." She believed that she was getting the best voice training available anywhere, and except for this incident, she had been treated well in Austin. She did, however, accept financial assistance from the Belafonte Foundation of Music and Arts for her final two years at UT. [16]

Dido and Aeneas went on as planned, although only two performances rather than four took place. Smith's understudy, Martha Ann Kelly, who was white, played the role of Dido, and Smith attended on opening night. By all accounts, the opera was a failure. According to Bradford Daniels of the *Daily Texan*, "The opera was disappointing. Primarily, it lacked spirit." Kelly's singing "lacked force and imaginative styling," and Dido's lament, "When I Am Laid in Earth," was "most disappointing" because she "didn't sound like or appear to be a heartbroken woman." *Time* magazine reported that the auditorium was only half full for both performances and that from the flagpole in front of the university's Main Building hung a swastika flag with the words "No Comment" on it. White UT undergraduate James Prentice attended *Dido and Aeneas* "out of a general curiosity" but believed that the play was doomed as soon as the university removed Smith. "The actors, especially the one who had replaced Smith, were in a no-win situation," Prentice said, "because Smith had a beautiful voice and it would have been difficult to replace her. The committee that selected her for the role did so for a good reason." Like other critics of the play, Prentice found the production "pretty mediocre."[17]

Although most people soon forgot about the controversy, Smith said that "nightmares" of the incident haunted her for years. "The irony of all of this," she recalled later, "is that all I wanted to do was be a student in the classic sense of the word . . . and I was denied." Smith returned to the university in the fall of 1957 but admitted that she felt great pain at being betrayed by people "at the high echelons" whom she had trusted. The Music Building auditorium was packed for her junior and senior recitals, and some people even stood outside to hear her sing. Smith received a bachelor of music and applied voice degree in 1959, to which Rep. Chapman said, "I wish her all the success in the world. She is a great artist." She soon left Austin for New York City to study voice, drama, dance, and languages with funds from the Belafonte Foundation. Smith changed her name to Barbara Conrad to avoid confusion with another singer named Barbara Smith and continued to do well in her musical career, touring Europe and signing on with the Metropolitan Opera in 1981. In an ironic twist, Smith played Marian Anderson, the African American woman whom the Daughters of the American Revolution had barred from singing in Constitution Hall in 1937, in the 1975 ABC television production of *Eleanor and Franklin*.[18]

In 1984 Conrad returned to the University of Texas for the first time since her graduation to sing in Earl Stewart's production of his opera, *Al-Inkishafi* (The Awakening), based on an ancient Kiswahili poem. The performance marked "the end of an inner struggle and a new beginning" for Conrad, "a wonderful, exciting experience" that finally began to heal her wounds from 1957. The University of Texas also worked to heal these wounds. In 1985 Smith received the Distinguished Alumnus Award, and she returned to the university two years later as the recipient of the Texas Cowboys Centennial Lectureship. She also sang with the Austin Symphony in December 1990 to "focus attention on the importance of minority education and the function of the arts as a tool for education." She has subsequently returned to Austin many times and is now able to focus on her positive experiences at UT. "In spite of all you have read about that was not good," she said in a 1984 interview, "I had a lot of marvelous experiences and good friends in Texas."[19]

University administrators learned far different lessons, however. School officials saw the casting incident as a mere "complication" of the integration problem. "It will cause the students to be looking for incidents," McCown wrote, "and make the more liberal students to bend over backwards to make Negroes feel that they are accepted." McCown and other administrators worried that white students' acceptance of black undergraduates would increase the number of young black Texans who applied to UT. This prospect frightened McCown and other university administrators, who perhaps reasoned that these "more liberal students" might also accept the mingling of the races outside of the classroom and maybe even in the bedroom. This was as unacceptable to them as it was to many white citizens of the state of Texas in the 1950s. Many people might argue that the first years of "integration" at UT represented a success, since university administrators desegregated the university without allowing black students to integrate all facets of campus life. [20]

Desegregating the Campus and the National Civil Rights Movement

Many University of Texas students of both races began to question why integration was moving so slowly on the campus, especially in social activities. After moderate successes at integrating most businesses on the Drag, students next targeted a show produced by the Texas Cowboys, a men's honorary service organization founded in the early 1900s. As a sort of fund-raiser/pep rally, members of the Texas Cowboys put on a minstrel show every November, just before the annual Texas–Texas A & M football game. Like most minstrel shows, the Texas Cowboys' program featured white performers in blackface singing "black" music and mocking black southern dialect. Students first protested the minstrel shows in 1957, and in November 1960, a group of black and white UT students circulated a petition calling for an end to the shows. "This is not a protest against the Cowboy organization," said African American graduate student Claude Allen, "but only against that aspect of the annual show which does the damage." Other supporters of the petition believed that the show's negative depiction of African Americans contributed to "racial disharmony" on campus. [21]

A few days after students began circulating the petition, they staged a rally outside the Texas Union, carrying signs that read "Jim Crow is not funny" and "We protest Jim Crow campus humor." Picketers were met by supporters of the show such as UT student James Fritchiz, who said he did not understand the objections because the show was "all a joke anyway." "We just don't see why it's an insult," he said. "If they don't like it they don't have to buy a ticket." The Texas Cowboys issued a statement saying that the minstrel show was purely entertainment and was not intended to degrade the Negro race. Most students who wrote to the *Daily Texan* expressed similar attitudes. Changing the format of the minstrel show was, as one student wrote, "nothing more than a ridiculous form of censorship." Some students, including David Magrill, believed that the minstrel show should have been a source of pride for African American students: "Negro folklore and folk songs have a place in America's cultural heritage. You will find some of America's finest humor in shows of this type. This is nothing to be ashamed of."[22]

Other UT students understood, as Eric Lott argues in *Love and Theft: Blackface Minstrelsy and the American Working Class*, that minstrel shows had originated not in humor but in "the 'borrowing' of black cultural material for white dissemination" and in the pretense "that slavery was amusing, right, and natural." The Young Democrats endorsed the cause of the petitioners and asked the Young Republicans to join in the protests against the minstrel shows so that "equality of opportunity may become a reality and not just an ideal." In addition, the Young Democrats asked the university administration to withdraw its sanction from the event, believing that such an endorsement was irresponsible to "the 21 per cent of our citizens who were born Negroes." An editorial in the *Daily Texan* also endorsed a change in the show's format. Calling the Cowboys' minstrel show "a false stereotype of the American Negro," the editor argued that such a show should not exist at a first-class university. The writer continued, "People should be able to think about their fellow human beings without the crutches of 'typical' images." The editor also pointed to an important irony of the annual minstrel show—that a supposed "honorary organization dedicated to University service" would produce a show that contributed to "racial misunderstanding" on campus. The Texas Cowboys eventually offered a benign response to the controversy surrounding their shows. In a statement released to the *Daily Texan*, the Cowboys said that they were "unaware" that their annual minstrel show "presented an unfavorable stereotype of the Negro race on campus" and agreed to meet with black UT students to "ameliorate the situation amicably." Nevertheless, the minstrel show went on before "a sold-out crowd." The tradition finally came to an end in the fall of 1965, when the Texas Cowboys voted to discontinue the use of blackface. During that program, however, one Cowboy in blackface ran on stage only to be told that he was one year too late.[23]

Another common practice among campus social organizations around the country was the holding of "slave auctions" or "slave days" as a way of raising money for the groups or for charities. Members of a group such as a fraternity or sorority would agree to perform work for "buyers." However, a slave auction on a college campus—especially at the University of Texas, where whites had just recently admitted African American students yet systematically excluded them from some activities and buildings—served as another reminder of black students' second-class status. In 1960, the *Daily Texan* described an auction held on the steps of Theadorne and Pearce Co-ops for Women as a "humanitarian effort" that was "swarmed with slaves and bidders" whose "tumultuous shouts" could be heard "whenever a glistening husky or curvaceous woman servant stepped on the auction block." Roughly twenty men and between twenty and thirty women were auctioned off to high bidders for "servitude and duties ranging from garbage can scrubbing to serenading." The *Texan* reported that Martin "Princess" Spitzenberger went to Tom Cole for $2.00 after "a skillful demonstration of the art of stripping."[24] The *Texan*'s lighthearted tone in reporting the auction and the apparent lack of protests regarding the event represents yet another example of the racially insensitive culture that existed on the UT campus.

On March 9, 1962, Martin Luther King Jr. spoke at the Texas Union Main Ballroom before a crowd of twelve hundred people, most of them UT students but fewer than ten of them African American. In his speech, "Civil Liberties and Social Action," King announced, "Old Man Segregation is on his death bed. The only question is how expensive the South is going to make the funeral." King also told the crowd about two myths that existed about segregation: that neither time nor educational determinism could solve the problem of segregation. Ending segregation, King said, would require both legislation and education: "The law may not make a man love me, but it can keep him from lynching me." At the end of the speech, a group of UT students met with King to enlist his help in planning further nonviolent activities that might lead to total integration on the campus.[25]

By this time, King had risen to national prominence, and whether he was speaking or leading civil rights protests, his visits to most U.S. cities were big news. Not in Austin. Only the *Daily Texan* and the *Capital City Argus*, a black Austin weekly, covered King's appearance. The *Austin Statesman*, the *Dallas Morning News*, the *San Antonio Express*, the *Houston Post*, and the *Ft. Worth Star Telegram* ignored his speech. King's visit may have received so little press because even state and university leaders who recognized that integration constituted an important issue wanted to avoid the high-profile civil rights protests and negative publicity that had occurred elsewhere in the South. Thornton Hardie acknowledged as much in an October 1962 letter to his fellow members of the Board of Regents, university administrators, and university lawyers. Hardie had read that "certain of our negro students intend to get quite active on the subject of further integration, and may import Martin Luther King." Another King appearance would "undoubtedly stir up considerable controversy and much adverse publicity." Consequently, the regents needed to devise a plan that would enable them to avoid further integration as well as the sort of ugly scene that had occurred at the University of Mississippi just a few weeks earlier, where rioting had accompanied James Meredith's enrollment at the heretofore all-white school.[26]

The *Daily Texan* had kept students abreast of the events at Ole Miss, and as the situation escalated, UT students sought ways to show their support for Meredith. After much debate, the Student Assembly voted twenty-one to eight to send a telegram to the Ole Miss student body and the press and another to Meredith. The message told Meredith that the UT students "salute your courage and perseverance in facing overwhelming opposition to stand up for your constitutional rights. Your struggle is exemplary of the principle that individual rights can only be achieved through uncommon valor." Students also held a moment of silence on the Tower steps following the death of two National Guardsmen at Ole Miss. About 300 students participated in the demonstration, which, Student Assembly President Sandy Sanford described as "not a demonstration for James Meredith or against [Mississippi] Gov. Ross Barnett" but rather "evidence of our sympathy with Ole Miss students . . . and in favor of the constitutional process." UT students staged similar protests in solidarity with other civil rights campaigns in the rest of the country. In the wake of the violence that erupted in Birmingham, Alabama, during the summer of 1963 (including police and fire commissioner Eugene "Bull" Connors's attacks on peaceful civil rights protesters with fire hoses and attack dogs as well as a Sunday-morning church bombing that killed four young African American girls), roughly seventy students attended a "sympathy protest" in front of the Main Building.[27]

After the Student Assembly sent the telegram, UT students weighed in on the action. Some believed that the assembly was "acting out of its sphere." Others, like Judy Schiffer, felt that the telegram should have been sent because "Meredith needs all the support he can get": "Our support may influence others to carry on the job of providing education for everyone." Ed Dunagan, a radio deejay for KNOW, said that the station received about a dozen telephone calls after it announced that the telegrams would be sent. All of the calls, he said, opposed the action. Dunagan's findings seemed to contradict the results of the *Daily Texan*'s random sampling of fifty students, a majority of whom favored the sending of the telegram.[28]

The Student Assembly's public support for Meredith seemed to further threaten white southerners' comfort with the current state of racial affairs. Meredith's admission to Ole Miss—a school with a 114-year tradition of unrepentant racial and educational separatism—represented the fall of one of the last bastions of segregation. If integration could be forced in Oxford despite the united opposition of the school's students and Board of Regents and the state's governor and legislature, what was next? UT's administrators, Board of Regents, and alumni saw their greatest fear, miscegenation, on the horizon. "I pity . . . your children or your children's children and their spotted offspring," wrote alumnus T. S. Bailey to the *Daily Texan*. Moreover, Bailey and other whites believed that students' support of Meredith represented simply another example of northerners trying to impose their will on the South: "You're . . . just a bunch of misinformed socialistic thinking kids that belong up among the other Yankee degraders that are trying their damndest to literally shove the smelly negro race down the throats of the white Southerner."[29]

The violence in Oxford and elsewhere in the South led a small group of black UT students to reexamine the slow pace of integration on their campus. These students formed Negroes for Equal Rights, an organization advocating "non-violent agitation" at the University of Texas because satisfactory progress toward integration had not occurred there. Many white students worried that despite its professed commitment to peaceful means of protest, the new group's activities would precipitate the kind of violence that had occurred in other parts of the South. In addition, the white students argued that black students needed to be patient about civil rights because the realities of the situation at UT demanded "negotiation and compromise." "Segregation on the campus," they advised, "is better faced by peaceful negotiations with the powers that be than by any form of action which might be detrimental to the cause of" those who faced discrimination. The white students also wanted their black fellow students to continue working in interracial groups: even though white students could not fully understand "the racial sentiment against discrimination," it was not impossible for them to "feel philosophical, legal, sociological, or ideological antipathy toward it." "White cooperation and support should not be rejected."[30]

Negroes for Equal Rights rejected these arguments and continued its efforts without the help of white students. The group also shifted its focus from desegregation to political rights, matching the shift in focus of the Student Nonviolent Coordinating Committee and other national civil rights organizations during the early 1960s. One member of Negroes for Equal Rights, Booker T. Bonner, believed that students needed to focus their efforts on Governor John Connally, a conservative Democrat who had narrowly defeated incumbent Governor Price Daniel in the party's primary and then won the 1962 gubernatorial election. As the students knew, Connally had won the election in part as a result of the support of African American voters. Connally had subsequently made token comments about civil rights for African Americans, but his appointment of Frank C. Erwin Jr. to the Board of Regents worried many black students, who saw Erwin as "a die-hard segregationist who had fought integration tooth and nail . . . and who was personally responsible for keeping any civil rights plank out of [Connally's campaign] platform."[31]

In July 1963, Bonner staged a twenty-seven-hour sit-in in an effort to meet with Connally following Erwin's appointment and Connally's statement of opposition to President John F. Kennedy's proposed civil rights legislation. Connally finally agreed to a meeting with Bonner but backed out when other black leaders also arrived for the meeting. During the first week of August, Bonner organized a demonstration at the governor's mansion, located about eight blocks from the UT campus. Between fifty and a hundred protesters passed out handbills calling Connally a "Jim Crow governor of the worst kind" and "a segregationist [whose] record is one of exploitation of the thrust and hopes of Negroes." The handbill also called into question Connally's claims that UT was integrated, since the university's twenty thousand students included only about two hundred African Americans: "That's not integration, it's TOKEN INTEGRATION, the most famous segregationist obstructive tactic ever invented." Bonner and Negroes for Equal Rights then led an August 28 march from Rosewood Park in East Austin to the State Capitol that coincided with King's March on Washington. In Austin, six hundred African Americans endured 102-degree heat and sang "Tell John Connally we shall not be moved." Connally stayed in his office during the demonstration and later said, "Bonner apparently believes that progress on civil rights comes through demonstration. I do not."[32]

Perhaps agreeing with Connally, the Student Assembly focused its efforts on integrating all campus organizations by attacking segregated organizations' pocketbooks. In March, the Student Assembly suspended requests for blanket tax appropriations from the Athletic Council, the Longhorn Band, university choral organizations, and the Oratorical Association pending a review of their integration policies. The blanket tax was a fee that students paid that allowed them entry to certain events. The Student Assembly hoped that withholding funding would both challenge segregation and send a message to the regents as well. When asked about the Longhorn Band's segregation policy, band director Vincent DiNino said that although the band was not integrated, it did not have a policy of segregation. "In the past 7 years, nine Negro students have auditioned for the band, but none were accepted," DiNino reported. He attributed the students' failure to join the group either to their lack of the necessary academic standards or to their failure to follow up on their applications. "No applications for auditions by Negro students were ever turned down," DiNino said. Still, students generally believed that the real reason that the band had no African American members was that white UT alumni did not want to see black faces on the field during a football game in any capacity.[33]

Like the band, the choral and oratorical associations told the Student Assembly that although they had no black members, they would gladly accept qualified African Americans. Consequently, the Student Assembly focused on withholding funds from the Athletic Department, which steadfastly refused to recruit or play African Americans. Some students questioned the legality of suspending the blanket tax from the Athletic Department, while others wondered if anyone would buy the blanket tax if athletics were not included. The Student Assembly proposed a compromise under which it would sell two blanket taxes, one that included segregated organizations and one that did not, thereby enabling integrationists to avoid supporting segregated athletics. In the end, however, the assembly voted to allocate the Athletic Council's $8.65 appropriation per student as originally suggested by the Rules and Appropriations Committee, and all of the other segregated organizations received their original appropriations after promising to admit qualified students without regard to race. The band had already accepted an African American clarinet player for the next school year.[34]

Desegregating the Drag and Downtown Austin

During the 1950s and 1960s, the center of UT's student community was the Drag, seven blocks of Guadalupe Avenue located in front of West Campus that housed restaurants, theaters, barbershops, clothing stores, liquor stores, nightclubs, and the university Young Men's–Young Women's Christian Association (YMCA-YWCA). Because these establishments constituted such a vital part of campus life, efforts to provide African Americans access to the area were part and parcel of efforts to desegregate the campus itself. Moreover, segregation on the Drag reminded many students of the racial segregation that they saw in most other parts of Texas and throughout the South.

Many businesses along the Drag and in downtown Austin refused to integrate their establishments, with some proprietors claiming to fear the loss of white customers. Like other white southerners, business owners on the Drag believed that blacks and whites should not mix in such places as barbershops, restaurants, and theaters lest African Americans demand equality in other areas of society. The Barbara Smith controversy spurred black and white UT students to increase efforts to open the university and its surrounding community to all students. The larger civil rights movement was also expanding its focus beyond education. The Supreme Court had already declared school segregation unconstitutional and set forth enforcement policies. For more than a year, African Americans in Montgomery, Alabama, had refused to ride the city's buses until they were desegregated. In February 1960, students at North Carolina A & T College in Greensboro staged a sit-in at the local F. W. Woolworth's, a form of social protest that quickly spread throughout the rest of the country. White segregationists found sit-ins particularly threatening because they forced whites to have direct social contact with blacks—although the segregationists did not mind having blacks cook the food but just did not want to eat next to them. Moreover, the sight of lunch counter employees serving black and white customers side by side simply provided yet another reminder that white southerners were losing their power over blacks.

UT students chose restaurants as one of their first targets, noting other protesters' successes in forcing eating places to integrate. Although the university had integrated its on-campus eating facilities, African American students had a difficult time finding places off campus to get a meal, a particular problem on Saturday and Sunday nights, when the university closed its cafeterias. Black students had to travel to East Austin, on the other side of an interstate highway, to find a meal. According to African American student Donald Hill, most of the Drag's restaurants and entertainment establishments had a mantra with which UT's black students were familiar: "I am sorry, but we don't have facilities to accommodate Negroes." But as Hill asked, "If Negro and white students can eat in the University restaurants together, why should they be segregated on the Drag?"[35]

Efforts to desegregate Drag eating establishments had begun in 1952, when Sam Gibbs, a graduate student member of the assembly, sent letters to fifty-two restaurants and lunch counters within a seven-mile radius of the campus asking about their policy with regard to serving African Americans. Worried that economic reprisals would result, owners protested to the dean of student life, and Gibbs promised not to make public the results of the survey. Gibbs found that most owners adamantly opposed serving African Americans, although some said that they would "go along" when other owners adopted an open policy. As late as 1957, only one restaurant on the Drag (the Sweet Shop, a small candy and sandwich shop) served all African American students, while another served African American students only if a white person accompanied them. A 1957 report filed by UT President Logan Wilson's administration found that four restaurants on the Drag served African American students, although one provided only drive-in service. The Student Association Human Relations Committee tried to persuade university administrators to keep the central cafeterias open on Saturday and Sunday nights; when this effort failed, the committee recommended that the Student Association open a snack bar on campus, another suggestion that was never implemented.[36]

In the late 1950s, UT students organized the Steer Here Committee, which established a point system for restaurants. Restaurants earning at least eighty-one points on a hundred-point scale would receive a three-color "Steer Here" sign to place in the window. The committee originally based its ratings on sanitation, food quality, and fair price, but in 1960, in response to prointegration sentiment on campus, the committee began awarding twenty points to those restaurants that served African American students. Restaurants that did not serve black students could not earn approval. Shortly after the policy change, university students and local pastors began visiting the Night Hawk restaurant chain, and the combined efforts persuaded the management to agree to serve African American UT students after they identified themselves as such. The chain later agreed to serve "all Negroes without question who are otherwise acceptable as customers."[37]

The success of the sit-in movement elsewhere in the South gave UT students a new idea. Believing that direct action—coupled with legal suits and economic pressure—would force the hands of rabid segregationists, college students in Austin stepped up their attempts to integrate local restaurants. Beginning in the spring of 1960, students from the University of Texas, St. Edward's University, Huston-Tillotson College, and the Episcopal and Presbyterian Seminaries set up pickets in front of Drag restaurants that refused to serve African American students. "It'll at least make everyone aware that integration progress has been bogged down," said one UT student protester. In March 1960, at the first of three demonstrations, about thirty black and white students battled wind and cold to bring attention to the overall plight of black students at the University of Texas, passing out leaflets and carrying signs that said, "First class school. Second class students." The *Daily Texan* reported that the demonstration was "rather dull on the surface," although a "detectable tension" arose after a few boys made "nasty" remarks to one of the white students demonstrating. After the third day of picketing, students met with Chancellor Harry Ransom to discuss their concerns but described the meeting as "unsatisfactory." Students subsequently turned their full attention to desegregating Austin's lunch counters, especially those near the campus.[38]

Students later extended these protests to include the segregated lunch counters on Congress Avenue in downtown Austin. Led by Rev. William A. Clebsch, a professor of history at the Episcopal Seminary, an interracial coalition of students from four local colleges—UT, Huston-Tillotson, St. Edward's, and the Episcopal Seminary—gathered at the university Young Men's–Young Women's Christian Association (YMCA-YWCA) to plan protests and devise strategies to force the integration issue. In April 1960 students gave the owners of segregated lunch counters in and around the university campus one week to integrate their establishments after negotiations between business leaders and the Austin Council on Human Relations broke down. Students at the meeting believed that the time "for the more harmonious means . . . of solving the problem [was] fast running out." Clebsch said that if the businesses refused to integrate, students would employ sit-ins and pickets to secure the operation "of a free society." "We don't want" to resort to direct action, said one African American student, "but we are ready." The group also sent a letter to Senator Lyndon B. Johnson asking him to use the television station he owned in Austin, his regular newsletter to his constituents, his influence in the Austin business community, and his personal influence "to bring into practice the full human rights of all the citizens of Texas in all areas of their activity." UT's Young Democrats also wrote to Johnson to show their support of the interracial coalition. [39]

The group staged its first protest not on the Drag but on Congress Avenue between Fourth and Eleventh Streets, within walking distance of the Texas State Capitol, to draw media attention to the fact that Texas lawmakers—whom the citizens of Texas had charged with passing fair laws—patronized segregated lunch counters. Held on April 30, the first demonstration lasted for nine hours. Each hour a different group of thirty blacks and whites picketed the segregated lunch counters carrying signs bearing such slogans as, "I don't want it 'to go,' I want to sit down"; "We want more than a cup of coffee, we want dignity"; "Intelligently speaking, segregation is 'ridiculous' "; "Why pay for racism?"; "Is Austin Progressive? We Hope So!"; "Sit-Ins? It's up to you!"; and "Apartheid in Austin?" A few passersby heckled the protesters. Although none of the targeted restaurants closed during the first day of picketing, merchants including the Austin Hotel Coffee Shop, the Liberty Cafe, the Hickory Grill, and two Renfro's Drug Stores vowed not to open if the demonstration turned into a sit-in. A waiter at the Austin Hotel Coffee Shop said that the hotel's headquarters in Galveston ordered the shop to close its fountain should protesters stage a sit-in. In fact, the manager of the shop had already prepared a "Sorry the fountain is closed" sign. The owner of the Liberty Cafe ordered his manager to chain the door in order to "bar Negro students from staging a sit-in." Employees at the Hickory Grill and both Renfro's Drug Stores said they would close their lunch counters as soon as African Americans tried to sit down. Said one owner of a Congress Avenue restaurant, "If I can't stop them at the door and they sit down, I'm not going to serve them."[40]

The Austin community at least tolerated the first days of the protests. Police Chief R. A. Miles simply wanted to "keep from agitating the situation" and refused to comment on what his department would do if the pickets turned into sit-ins. Judge St. John Garwood, a former associate justice of the Texas Supreme Court, agreed to serve as chair of a biracial action committee charged with mediating an agreement between students and lunch counter operators. He urged the Austin community to give the committee a chance to broker an agreement between the two groups before the students began more direct confrontations. Austin Mayor Tom Miller had "no comment" on the pickets. In a statement issued after the first protest, the Austin Commission on Human Relations praised the group's "peaceable" actions yet recognized the problems managers of public eating establishments faced "in adjusting their policy to provide non-discriminatory service." The following week, the commission sent letters to all Austin ministers and lunch counter owners urging them to exhibit signs of "openness" to avoid "imminent demonstrations." Garwood attempted to persuade lunch counter owners to create a plan for integrating their establishments within a reasonable time frame. He told the protesters that the owners were worried that white customers would stop patronizing the establishments if they started serving African Americans. Said one merchant, "There are not enough Negroes to replace the whites that would refuse to eat with Negroes."[41]

But the protesters refused the requests for further patience, and two days after the first pickets, students staged their first sit-ins at twelve campus-area restaurants and lunch counters. Like other sit-in protesters around the country, students had been schooled in nonviolent direct action before the protest began. Their instructions included admonitions to be "courteous, not to laugh out loud, and not to strike back if physically attacked." About forty African American students sat-in at the F. W. Woolworth's on Congress Avenue, while an interracial coalition of students staged sit-ins or picketed at the H. L. Green and Kress lunch counters as well as other segregated establishments in downtown Austin and on the Drag. At the Greyhound bus station, five African American students sat at the lunch counter, where an employee told them that the bus station had a separate dining room for them. The employee reported that the students stayed for about thirty minutes and "caused no disturbance."[42]

As news of the sit-ins reached the University of Texas campus, students responded in various ways. The UT Student Assembly voted nineteen to four to endorse the "peaceful means of protest" shortly after the first sit-in began. However, according to assembly member Ronnie Boyd, an engineering student, the resolution did not represent "the majority view of the University." UT student Elmo Johnson wrote to the *Daily Texan* that the "sit-in, picket, and boycott [had] no more place in modern society than [did] the lynch rules of yesterday." To further the overall cause of the lunch counter sit-ins, a group of UT students formed Students for Direct Action (SDA), whose goals Chair Sandra Cason described as "publiciz[ing] the Negro's plight [and] throw[ing] the spotlight on individuals who are responsible for this plight."[43]

The University Religious Council (URC) passed out cards to incoming patrons at five segregated Drag restaurants. The URC asked patrons to hand the cards, which read, "I will continue to patronize this establishment if it is integrated," to the cashier. Students and business owners disagreed about the success of the program. The URC said that most entering patrons took the cards, while restaurant owners said that only a few students turned in the cards. UT student Egan R. Tausch mocked this protest by passing out cards on which he had written "Protect the Rights of Whites—Back Segregation." Tausch told a reporter, "Segregation is the right way to end this whole mess. Proprietors have a right to refuse admittance to whomever they want to."[44]

On November 29, an unknown person threw a handmade bomb through a window at the YMCA-YWCA as about twenty-five members of the URC gathered to discuss their card handout assignments for the upcoming week. According to the *Daily Texan*, the bomb "hit the [building's] window frame and fell into a stairwell below where it exploded." "Had the bomb exploded in the meeting place," Austin Police Captain Otto Ludwig said, several students "might have been killed." With the help of the FBI, Austin police uncovered the bombers—two male University of Texas students. One of the arrested men told the police that "he didn't have anything against colored people. He just didn't like the way they were going about this." A judge fined the two students two hundred dollars and sentenced them to thirty days in jail. Students connected with the URC and the integration movement vowed not to let the bombing interfere with their work. Said Brad Blanton, head of the URC committee, "This will have no effect whatsoever on our campaign. It most definitely will continue." And continue they did. The URC passed out thirty-eight hundred cards in less than a month.[45]

By the 1961 spring semester, the protests against the segregated restaurants and lunch counters on the Drag waned. The demonstrations were having some success despite the fact that business owners said that they felt that students were trying to tell them how to run their business. Bray and Jordan pharmacies announced that they would serve all customers regardless of skin color. Individual African Americans could receive lunch counter service at Woolworth's, although large groups of African Americans often could not. However, because Renfro's Drug Stores refused to integrate, students continued demonstrations against those establishments.[46]

With the sit-in protests generally having met with success but also stagnating, prointegration students planned their next move against Drag businesses that still refused to serve African Americans. The next target would be Drag barbershops. Concerned that African American students had to travel to East Austin to get haircuts, Student Assembly member John H. Strasburger, a law student, wrote a bill that directed the Grievance Committee to study the possibility of opening barbershops near the University of Texas campus to African American students or of establishing a new barbershop near the campus that would serve all students regardless of color. The assembly refused to vote on Strasburger's resolution, citing its "impracticality." In the fall, however, the Student Assembly voted sixteen to five to allow the Grievance Committee to "examine the possibility of integrating Drag barbershops." Another law student, Jim Johnson, opposed the bill, arguing that "the Student Assembly, as a legislative body, had no right to interfere with private businesses." Barbers and hairdressers located on the Drag said that their refusal to cut and style African American students' hair resulted in part from the fact that "Negro hair requires a different cutting process" and that they were not trained to do the job. "I'm proud of my work," one barber explained, but "I don't feel I could do a good job for a Negro customer."[47]

Simultaneous with the resolutions to integrate Drag barbershops, black and white UT students began protesting against the Texas Theatre and Varsity Theatre, which refused to allow black patrons to buy tickets to see movies. This problem was particularly egregious for black liberal arts students, whose professors often assigned the class to see films that could only be seen in movie theaters, yet no Austin theater permitted African American patrons. Led by the YMCA-YWCA group and SDA, students first targeted the Texas Theatre on the evenings of December 2 and 3, 1960. More than one hundred black and white students demonstrated at the theater on both nights. Each student would approach the box office and tell the cashier, "I would like to buy a ticket if everyone is being admitted"; after being refused, the student would walk to the end of the line to repeat this process. Shortly after the demonstration began, theater manager Leonard Masters closed the box office and began selling tickets just inside the door to "anyone who really wanted to see the show." Said one African American student, "I do want to see the show." Another black student waved a dollar bill and complained that it was his last one and that he couldn't get rid of it. Almost an hour after the second night's demonstration began, students returned to the YMCA-YWCA, where they decided to continue the protests and to discuss other ways of letting the officials at Texas Theatre know that UT students supported integrated theaters.[48]

Three days later, about 150 students braved cold and rain to continue the protests against the Texas and Varsity Theatres. The demonstrators now included more than just UT students—three coeds from Trinity University in San Antonio, an Austin couple with their baby, and high school students from Austin who had read about the demonstrations in their local newspapers joined the protests. Protesters repeated the box office tactic from the earlier demonstrations and sang Christmas hymns to call attention to the hypocrisy of the white business owners and managers, most of whom professed to be Christians. In addition, URC members handed theater patrons cards that read, "I will continue to patronize this establishment if it is integrated." Ticket taker Thistam Castaneda estimated that 70 percent of the patrons who entered the theater handed him the cards.[49]

As the protests continued, various segments of the university community weighed in with their opinions. UT faculty and teaching assistants sent a letter to the *Daily Texan* expressing "their agreement with the objectives of students now seeking to integrate theaters on the Drag." Members of the Department of Germanic Languages wrote to the paper to express their opposition to "arbitrary discrimination against members of the University community by private business enterprises." The cabinet of the university's Wesley Foundation believed that it was imperative that "Christian students" take a stand and support or participate in the demonstrations against the two theaters. UT students Clifford Bennett, Donald Hill, Donald Mathis, and Chester Helms urged others to "help put an end to the absurdity of racial discrimination . . . through sit-ins, stand-ins, programs of positive patronage, or whatever means practicable." Another student, Leon Holland, explained that he participated in the Drag protests because "it was just time to bring segregation to an end, especially to places so close to the University." While almost all Drag business owners opposed the protests, one businessman who had integrated his establishment said that "if the demonstrations accomplish what they are after, they are worthwhile." Even former First

Lady Eleanor Roosevelt recognized the work of UT student demonstrators, sending a telegram in which she wrote, "I admire so much the stand which the students at The University of Texas have taken."[50]

Opposition to the demonstrations also arose. Led by University of Texas students Mike Cavy, Bill Melnnis, and Stanley Timmins, a dozen or so counterprotesters appeared at the theater, with most claiming to oppose only the demonstrations, not integration. Believing that Drag businesses should have a right to "make [their] own decisions in such matters as whom to serve," members of the Foundation for the Advancement of Conservative Thought (FACT) also opposed the protests. During one demonstration, some white teenagers drove by in their car and shouted at the white protesters, "Does your mother know you're out here with Niggers?" One of the theater managers wanted to "take steps to prevent" the demonstrations, while another believed that the students were simply "a bunch of kids" who "haven't grown up yet." He continued, "I thought the University gave them enough homework that they wouldn't have time to tell a private businessman how to run his business." Some businessmen and members of the state legislature accused the student demonstrators of having been influenced by communism. Another senator from Normangee in East Texas introduced legislation to outlaw sit-ins.[51]

No organized demonstrations against segregated Drag theaters took place during the Christmas break. However, when the students returned to Austin in January, they resumed their efforts with the assistance of students from the Canterbury Association (an Episcopal student group) and from Huston-Tillotson College. To their other tactics, protesters added pickets, carrying signs that said, "We will not support segregation" and "Your money spent here supports segregation." One protester carried a sign with a quotation attributed to Dr. Blake Smith, pastor of the University Baptist Church: "Racial segregation is a betrayal of Democracy, an affront to human dignity, and an insult to God!" Tensions at the demonstrations rose as the theater managers became more forceful with the picketers and opposition to the demonstrations became more vocal. At a demonstration at the Texas Theatre, protesters claimed that the manager pushed them away from a roped-off area near the box office. At another demonstration, the police arrested two youths and charged them with aggravated assault for shoving, pushing, and spitting on picketers and tearing up their antisegregation signs. The demonstrators commonly encountered segregationists who drove by the theaters and shouted such things as "Keep them niggers out!" and "Nigger lovers!"[52]

This former petroleum building held the "Basement" Law School of the Texas State University for Negroes, 1947.

All photographs courtesy of the Center for American History at the University of Texas at Austin.

Heman Sweatt stands in a registration line at the University of Texas at Austin after the U.S. Supreme Court, in a unanimous decision (*Sweatt v. Painter*, June 1950), ordered his admission.

African American students stage a protest at all-white Kinsolving Dormitory, October 1961.

Black and white University of Texas students on the Drag (a stretch of Guadalupe Avenue near campus) protest the slow integration process.

W. Astor Kirk, a professor at Austin's Tillotson College. Kirk threatened to sue the University of Texas after the school allowed him to take graduate classes but segregated him within the classroom.

University of Texas students picket at a movie theater on the Drag.

University of Texas students protest continued segregation at movie theaters on the Drag.

African Americans protest the University of Texas's segregated admissions policies.

A demonstrator protests segregated lunch counters at the Liberty Café on Congress Avenue in downtown Austin. A sign on the door says, "We reserve the right to refuse service to anyone."

The Negro Association for Progress petitions for a black history course, November 1968.

On one occasion, three black UT students—Robert Bell, Lewis Woods, and Don Hill—attempted to buy tickets at downtown Austin's Paramount Theater. Bell and Woods pretended to be Egyptian students, while the lighter-skinned Hill pretended to be a student from Hong Kong. Pretending to be the only one of the trio who could speak English, Hill walked up to the box office and bought tickets for himself and his foreign friends. After the three men entered the theater, however, the usher refused to let them take their seats. Hill explained that they were not black but foreign students, and the man said, "But some of the other theaters have been having trouble with integrationists. And if we let dark-skinned foreigners in, we might make a mistake and let a Negro in." He sent the three "foreigners" away. The trio then went to the Texas Theatre, where Hill again attempted to buy tickets. The cashier explained that there was a "strange phenomenon called segregation which exists in our democracy." He made the trio promise that they were Egyptian and Chinese but then decided not to allow them in after consulting with the manager. The three men then went to Varsity Theatre. After they spoke a "few words of gibberish," the cashier sold them tickets, and they went in and watched Alfred Hitchcock's *Psycho*.[53]

This demonstration shows how subjective race can be and is. It also shows how southern whites had created a system of behavior that "served to reinforce the supremacy of the white race and the inferiority of the black." Thus, these "dark-skinned foreigners" were accorded the privileges of whiteness and allowed into the movie theater. In other words, these southern whites treated what they thought were dark-skinned foreigners as honorary whites, yet when they thought these same "dark-skinned foreigners" might be mistaken as "regular" southern Negroes (by "real" southern Negroes), these whites treated them as second-class citizens. This, of course, was to prevent these Negroes (especially those college students) from getting "too uppity." This racial etiquette, as historian David Goldfield calls it, produced a "stage Negro" who whites thought knew how to behave. In fact, many southern whites fancied themselves as experts on African Americans' feelings and behaviors. Hill, Bell, and Woods operated under this trope. They were, in many ways, turning what Stanley Elkin called the "Sambo" personality on its head. While the black students were "puttin' on ole massa" by pretending to be foreigners, the white managers thought they knew what and who blacks were.[54]

Students continued the protests in front of the Drag theaters for the remainder of the spring term. Many people, including supporters of integration, questioned whether the stand-ins should continue since they seemed to have little effect.

SDA President Chandler Davidson believed that the issue of whether the stand-ins were working was immaterial because the protests were "keeping Austin aware that the theatres exclude Negroes" and also a "very effective means of installing morale." UT student Byron A. Bassell Jr. suggested that both the theater owners and the demonstrators could save face if the theaters established Jim Crow seating, allowing African Americans to sit in a separate section within the theater. In the fall, the students negotiated agreements under which the Texas Theatre and Varsity Theatre would be open only to African Americans for sixty days and then would be open to everyone. [55]

The success of the theater protests served as a springboard for other issues affecting African American students on campus. In March 1963, students representing a variety of campus organizations met to plan a campaign on behalf of a city ordinance that would have made it a misdemeanor to refuse service to anyone because of race or color. The students decided to set up pickets and hold stand-ins in downtown Austin as a way of publicizing the need for the ordinance. The first protest began on March 9 at the Paramount Theater when an African American student attempted to buy a ticket to see a movie. After he was refused, about seventy-five students walked up and down Congress Avenue, mostly in front of the Paramount and State Theaters, for three and a half hours. One employee of the Paramount, a UT freshman, briefly joined the picketers but was then told to return to work, which he did. Ten minutes later, however, he walked out in street clothes, saying, "I just did not feel that I could work there against my principles." Charles Root, the manager of the Paramount, remained defiant in his stand against integrating the theater, arguing that it would be integrated "only when the rest of the Austin business district is ready." The following weekend, two more civil rights demonstrations took place in downtown Austin. Forty members of the Southwest Student Action Coordinating Committee held a stand-in at the Paramount and State Theaters as part of a statewide protest against the Interstate and Loews Theaters, two segregated movie chains. Later that afternoon, members of the Campus Interracial Committee picketed and handed out literature to people on Congress Avenue about an antidiscrimination ordinance to be considered in April by Austin's new City Council. [56]

After making little headway toward integrating the Paramount and State Theaters, students turned their efforts toward downtown restaurants and eateries. Members of the Congress on Racial Equality held a sit-in at the Piccadilly Cafeteria, but assistant manager Benny Thurman remained adamant, simply telling one of the protesters, "The colored do not eat here." UT students then set up pickets in front of the Hillsberg Cafe, Sunset Grill, Robert E. Lee Grill, and Plantation Restaurant. The demonstrations at each place followed the same pattern: approximately fifty white students would occupy tables and booths inside the restaurant while approximately thirty-five black students picketed outside. Each white student would order a cup of coffee or a cold drink and sip it slowly during the duration of the sit-in, thus keeping the restaurant from making any money. Shortly before the restaurant was to close, the white students would pay their meager checks and join the black protesters outside, where the group would sing "We Shall Not Be Moved," a theme song of the civil rights movement. These demonstrations were not without confrontation. On one occasion, more than a hundred white hecklers gathered around the protesters in front of the Plantation Restaurant. An ambulance driver passing by shouted at the protesters that he was "going to get me some niggers." And at a demonstration in front of the Robert E. Lee Grill, picketers were doused by a washtub of water poured out of an upper-floor window.[57]

To gain support for the city ordinance against discrimination, members of the Campus Interracial Committee held a parade on the Drag to celebrate "the Death of Uncle Tom whose only comment on life for 300 years has been 'Yah sir.'" Students hoped that such a parade would show white Austin residents that "a new Negro" existed. "This new Negro," they said, "is a dynamic person who demands to be recognized as a human being, who demands an end to racial discrimination." The parade had mixed results. Few African Americans participated, thereby making the white students seem "over zealous" to some observers. A truck in the parade ran out of gas, and the wind ripped apart a sign calling for the end of lynchings. Nonetheless, organizers believed that the parade was a success. They argued that the fact that the Austin City Council allowed the parade to happen and that Austin police officers provided protection for parade participants showed that the city recognized the students' right to protest segregation. Moreover, parade supporters believed that the number of people who stopped shopping to watch the parade was not insignificant.[58]

Students' efforts to integrate the city of Austin slowly paid off. While prointegration university students staged sit-ins, stand-ins, and pickets, the Austin business community moved ahead with a gradual—and quiet—plan of integration. A restaurant on the Drag opened its doors to African American students who could produce proof of having paid the blanket tax. A barbershop agreed to hire one barber to cut African American students' hair if students would refrain from publicizing this development in the local newspapers. Representatives of three hotels near the university agreed to house African American guests of the school. And in 1963 the city passed an ordinance prohibiting race- or color-based discrimination by businesses and restaurants.[59] With the city officially open to all Austin residents, students again turned their attention to making the University of Texas a welcoming place for all students.

Black Fraternities and Sororities

Fraternities and sororities have been on college campuses for 250 years. White male students organized the first Greek letter society (later known as a fraternity) at William and Mary College in 1750 because they felt the need to be able to relax and recuperate, to enjoy the friendships formed on campus, and to learn those things that they felt could not be taught in the classroom. Similar to fraternities, the first white sororities offered young women a way to fight boredom, to enjoy closer friendships, and to assume some role outside the heavy demands and dull routine of classroom work. These early fraternities and sororities were usually open only to those from wealthy, privileged families fortunate enough to benefit from a good education. These organizations later became more social in nature, although some, like Delta Upsilon, were founded to promote "the great objects of social and literary improvement."[60] None accepted the few African American students on campus as members.

In the early 1900s, increasing numbers of African Americans began attending colleges and soon began forming their own Greek letter organizations, which served as a haven from discrimination and prejudice, especially for African Americans at predominantly white colleges and universities. The first two black fraternities were Alpha Phi Alpha, established at Cornell University in 1906, and Kappa Alpha Psi, established at Indiana University in 1911. Since the acquisition of a college education was sometimes dangerous, futile, or even impractical, black fraternities and sororities held their members to strict academic standards to insure that educational opportunities did not go to waste. Like white fraternities and sororities, the black organizations made membership exclusive and had a secret-society culture replete with rituals, oaths, and symbols. Unlike their white counterparts, though, black fraternities and sororities served a more utilitarian purpose for their members—they allowed African American students to form communities on what were often hostile white college campuses. Moreover, black fraternity and sorority houses frequently constituted the only on-campus housing available for African American students.[61]

Although many national fraternities and sororities opened membership to African Americans during the 1950s, those at UT remained segregated. Dean of Men Jack Holland believed that "no problem" existed in this area because fraternities had a right "to select their own members on whatever basis [had] been used in the past." Moreover, because of discrimination clauses in the constitutions of most white fraternities and sororities, the chapters claimed that they could not integrate without the permission of their national organizations. By the 1960s, some white University of Texas students began publicly challenging this position, noting that the University of Michigan and other institutions of higher education had passed regulations prohibiting fraternities and sororities from discriminating against potential members because of their race. Students began writing to the *Daily Texan* to urge UT's fraternities and sororities to remove restrictive clauses in their constitutions and by-laws. [62]

Despite claiming to have nondiscriminatory selection policies, UT's campus honorary societies also excluded African American students. As late as 1963, no African American had been invited to join the two men's service groups, the Texas Cowboys and the Silver Spurs, although the Silver Spurs had nominated an African American student for membership during the 1959–60 school year; he fell two votes short of election. The women's honorary societies fared only slightly better. In 1961 Donna Guess became the first African American chosen for membership in the Orange Jackets, an honorary society for junior women, and in 1962 the first African American woman joined Spooks, another campus honorary society. Nevertheless, most African American female students remained excluded from these two prestigious service organizations. This exclusion from many aspects of UT's academic and extracurricular events made it difficult for black students to feel as if they were a part of the school. "No matter how you try going to pep rallies and things," said Huey McNealy, an African American student from Houston, "you can't get any real school spirit, especially when you think about everything that is denied you." [63]

One of the most distressing aspects of the University of Texas campus in the early 1960s was the difference in attitude that many white students held about foreign students versus African American students. Donald Hill, a black English major from Houston who was "light enough to pass for white," said that he had "quite an advantage" on campus because white students often thought he was a foreigner. "Funny how a foreigner has more rights around here than an American citizen," Hill continued. All aspects of the campus were open to the foreign student. This phenomenon was not (and still is not) uncommon. White Americans have, throughout the history of this country, consistently elevated (and often welcomed with open arms) the newly-arrived (white) immigrant over the native African American. [64] Such was the case on the University of Texas campus. While the Board of Regents, university administrators, and white students rarely protested the presence or inclusion of Mexican American and other nonwhite students, they vigorously and sometimes aggressively fought to limit the presence and inclusion of African American students. Their protestations made black students feel their blackness at all times.

This extreme discrimination and isolation that many African American undergraduates faced on the University of Texas campus in the late 1950s led some black students to organize Greek letter societies. The dean of men and the dean of women supported these efforts in the belief that there were certain advantages to "concentrating the social activities of *these students*." The underlying message was clear—if black students had their own organizations, they would not need or want to socialize with white students. The Desegregation Commission, which had been formed to study the first days of undergraduate integration, recommended that a study be conducted into the possibility of establishing "all-Negro fraternities and sororities" on campus or that a meeting on the subject be arranged for Greek Week. Three years after the first black undergraduates were admitted, a group of African American transfer students who had been members of Alpha Phi Alpha at other schools began talking about forming a campus chapter of the fraternity. They contacted Dr. Thomas Cole, the fraternity's southwestern regional vice president, and visited Dean Holland to discuss the matter. Following Holland's advice to "make haste slowly and carefully," the men formed Alpha Upsilon Tau, a prefraternal colony of Alpha Phi Alpha. The purpose of the group, according to its charter, was "to promote the general welfare and social security of male students who are and who may later become members of APA, Inc." Officially open to all students regardless of color, the all-black UT chapter required that any member be "a bona fide student at The University of Texas" and "socially desirable." Members also had to demonstrate "scholastic competence by maintaining at least a 'C' " average. In 1960 the national fraternity installed the group as an official Alpha Phi Alpha chapter, with twenty full members and six pledges.[65]

While black sororities at UT served a function similar to that of black fraternities, women's groups also provided a unique social bond forged out of their experiences as black women on a campus that treated them badly for being both an African American and a woman. The sororities also served as an important source of leadership training for black women, who generally could not get such opportunities in black organizations that included men and who often were barred from joining white groups. Beginning in 1958, two national black sororities, Delta Sigma Theta and Alpha Kappa Alpha, began working with university administrators to establish chapters on UT's campus. Writing to UT's dean of women, Dorothy Gebauer, Alpha Kappa Alpha President Ethel LaMay Calimese asserted that the chapter would "maintain a superior standard for scholarship ('B' average) and for character" and that the women would do "all in our power to promote amiable relations with the other fraternal organizations" on campus. Gebauer agreed and wrote to Dean of Student Life Arno Nowotny that the two sororities would "strive to make a superior contribution to the University." That same year, Delta Sigma Theta formed an interest group under the name the Delta Club (later known as the Delta Torch Club) with twenty-three members, and Alpha Kappa Alpha organized the Vine Club (later the Ivy Leaf Club) with fifteen members. Before they could become official sororities, both organizations had to gain approval from the Student Organization Maintaining Houses Committee and the dean of student life, members had to maintain an overall minimum grade point average of 1.25, and the national groups had to give final approval for the establishment of UT chapters.[66]

The Vine Club needed only one year to fulfill the university's requirements, and in 1959 Alpha Kappa Alpha officially established a UT chapter. When the Student Organizations Maintaining Houses formally approved the Delta Torch Club's petition to become an established chapter of Delta Sigma Theta, the University of Texas had three Greek letter organizations for African American students.[67] Despite their lack of sorority or fraternity houses, their small memberships, and the fact that they were on academic probation, these organizations made it easier for black students to form their own communities outside of those formed in all-black dormitories and cooperatives.

A December 1960 article in the *Daily Texan* highlights the importance of black fraternities and sororities in African American student life on the predominately white and racially hostile University of Texas campus. "One Big 'Cannot'—a Negro Student's Life" began with the three attitudes that many white students had toward the two hundred black students on campus—indifference, perfunctory courtesy, or sour looks. African American students also lamented the fact that white students rarely talked with them before or after class and that discussions of race in the classroom caused discomfort. In 1961, black students could not participate in campus drama productions or intercollegiate sports or enter some Drag businesses. They had to use segregated bathrooms in Memorial Stadium, where the University of Texas football team played its home games. McNealy accurately summed up the situation of the typical African American UT student when he said, "You name it, we can't do it."[68]

Like the African American students who chose not to join the Greek system, those in fraternities and sororities endured numerous slights on campus. Because the National Panhellenic Council did not allow African American members, the three black UT chapters were not members of the campus Interfraternity Council or Panhellenic Council and consequently formed their own governing body. African American Greeks were usually excluded from parties at white fraternity and sorority houses. In one instance, however, a white sorority inadvertently invited the Alpha Phi Alpha men to a party at their house. According to the fraternity's Carl Huntley, the chapter had just been recognized in 1960 when the invitation arrived, and the men knew it was a mistake: "The white girls probably thought it was a new white fraternity." To see how "these white folks would respond," the Alpha men decided to attend the party, arriving "fashionably late" and dressed in their finest clothes. The fraternity members were not surprised to receive a "lukewarm" greeting at the door and walked around the room sipping tea and eating cookies while trying to strike up conversations with anyone who would talk with them. Most of the white fraternity members and almost all of the sorority women refused to even acknowledge the presence of the black men. Feeling that they "had made their statement," the Alpha Phi Alpha members stayed for "about an hour" before leaving with little fanfare. They knew that they were unwanted at the party and that they were committing a very serious social taboo, but they believed that their presence was simply the first step of many in integrating the UT Greek system.[69]

However, their attendance at the party did little to improve the relationship between white and black Greeks on the University of Texas campus. The African American fraternities and sororities remained excluded from the university's Panhellenic association until 1966, and the debate about whether the Greek system should be forced to integrate continued. Beginning in the 1950s, students called for white fraternities and sororities to voluntarily integrate: if they remained unwilling to do so, protesters asked that the UT administration step in and force the white fraternities and sororities to "do what was morally right." In one debate on the subject held in November 1963, Bruce Maxwell, a former UT student and leader in the Austin integration movement, stated his belief that it was "the responsibility of the University to desegregate the system, but it was the responsibility of the individual to desegregate his mind." Johnny Musselman, president of Sigma Alpha Epsilon, disagreed. Although he believed that segregation was morally wrong, he argued that fraternities and sororities had the "right as Americans" to discriminate. Moreover, Musselman believed that the integration of fraternities and sororities went against "natural law." "Types of people hang together," he said. "If you're going to have people that are going to work together, live together and accomplish things, you're going to have people who come from similar backgrounds."[70]

Many members of the Board of Regents and university administrators were members of segregated fraternities and sororities and generally seemed to agree with Musselman. When Commissioner of Education Francis Keppel warned the university that it could lose federal funds if it continued to permit a segregated Greek system following passage of the Civil Rights Act of 1964, Dean Holland made it easier for white fraternities to sidestep the law by permitting them to hold rush off campus. After selecting new pledges, the fraternities could return to university facilities since "any possible discrimination had already occurred."[71]

In spite of Holland's ruling, the Interfraternity Council opened rush to black UT students for the fall of 1964; however, many more years would pass before any African Americans participated in rush activities for white Greek organizations. Black fraternities and sororities continued to grow on UT's campus. In December 1969 the Omega Psi Phi fraternity established a chapter on UT's campus.[72] Into the 1970s, the black Greek system continued to serve as a valuable resource and retreat for UT's African American students, especially as tensions between white and black students on campus increased. At the dawn of the twenty-first century, the Greek system at the University of Texas at Austin remains essentially segregated, although a few fraternities and sororities have accepted members of both races.

In October 1961 coeds living in dormitories were advised that Negro guests would be obliged to go directly to the room of their hostess and close the door. They were not allowed the use of the dining room, drinking fountains, or toilet facilities. [Local civil rights attorney Sam Houston] Clinton likened this ruling to the instructions on a monopoly card—"Go to jail; go directly to jail; do not pass go."
—Carolyn Coker, "Social Policies Come to Light," *Daily Texan*

4 Dormitory Integration

On a cold December evening in 1963, twenty-five members of the Campus Interracial Committee staged an "orderly" demonstration in front of Kinsolving Hall, a women's dormitory that had opened a few years earlier to ease the overcrowding in women's housing. The new dorm was the pride of the University of Texas, and its most famous resident was President Lyndon Johnson's daughter, Lynda, although she had moved out of the dorm shortly before the demonstration. According to William Spearman, chair of the committee, the group had nothing against Lynda Johnson, who "was forced to live under a segregated system just like [us]." The students' demonstration, said Spearman, was intended to bring attention to the fact that "the University has taken all steps but one necessary for total integration."[1] Dorms and cooperatives remained segregated.

On November 8, 1961, three students—Leroy Sanders, Sherryl Griffin, and Maudie Ates—and two of their fathers filed suit to force the university to integrate its dorms. Four days later, the Board of Regents voted to fight the case and allow the courts to settle the issue. The lawsuit came after a fall semester of student protests against the university's segregated housing policies: African American male students who wanted to live on campus could reside only in San Jacinto Dormitories D and F and one wing of Brackenridge Dormitory; African American female students could live only in the Almetris Co-op and the Whitis Co-op.

The struggle for desegregation of state universities in the South usually began with the demand for registration and access to the classroom. However, many civil rights activists saw integration of the classrooms as only half of the fight. After federal courts had mandated reforms and made maintenance of classroom segregation legally impossible, the second and generally more obscure effort to desegregate student living accommodations and access to other campus facilities began. The debate's rhetoric invariably became laden with the long-standing taboo against interracial cohabitation—whites' fear of "sharing of sleeping and bathing facilities and the intimacies inherent therein" with African Americans. Moreover, if black women lived with white women, black men might visit black women, thus, some whites reasoned, endangering white women.[2]

The history of the desegregation of the dormitories, residence halls, and rooming houses at the University of Texas at Austin is a long story of optimistic declarations, sporadic protests, and reluctant concessions. The Board of Regents needed twelve years to order the integration of university living facilities, and the victory for the students was, in the end, rather anticlimactic. The Board of Regents' declaration that they would "let the courts decide" about integration left a leadership vacuum, and students and faculty who wanted to fully integrate the university stepped into that vacuum.

Negro Housing, 1950–1958

In the early 1950s, the University of Texas faced a serious housing shortage. The number of students had increased dramatically following the end of World War II and continued to increase every year with the advent of the GI Bill and other government programs. In addition, veterans returning from the Korean War greatly outpaced enrollment expectations. Although the Supreme Court had ordered the University of Texas to admit Heman Sweatt and other African American professional and graduate students who could not do their work at other Negro state schools, the Board of Regents kept the university's housing facilities closed to African American students. African American students lived off campus—many in East Austin and some in privately owned dormitories near campus, although most of these facilities prohibited African American residents. The university Young Men's Christian Association and the Christian Faith and

Community, a religious organization, opened their doors to all students regardless of color, and African American students could live in student cooperative houses (co-ops), although no black students applied before 1958.[3]

Almost three years passed after the Sweatt decision before the university made plans to provide housing for African American students, and these plans came only after John D. Davis II, an African American assistant professor at Marshall College, applied for admission to one of the university's dormitories. The university asked Judge Scott Gaines, a recent addition to the Board of Regents, to give an opinion, and he informed the university that "under the decisions of the Supreme Court," admission to the dormitories could not be refused "on the ground of race or color." Gaines also added that should such a case involving the issue of dormitory admission reach the U.S. Supreme Court, the "Negro student would win." UT President Logan Wilson then appointed a committee to make policy recommendations concerning the housing of African American students. Committee members Carl V. Bredt, associate dean of student life; Jane Greer, director of women's residence halls; and Helen Deathe, director of men's residence halls, felt that it would not be "good administrative practice" to attempt to house "colored and white students in our regular dormitories" since the two races would be "thrown together for all dormitory life, including bathroom facilities, social rooms, seated dining room service and the like." Although the committee acknowledged that full integration might someday be required, members believed that for the time being the university should make provisions "to house Negro students in comfortable and desirable facilities" to avoid forcing the two races together "in areas of dormitory-student life that may not be acceptable." Meeting on January 28–29, 1955, the Board of Regents approved housing male African American students in San Jacinto Dormitories D and F and McGinnis House and black women in the residence at 2515 Whitis Avenue. The regents later approved additional housing in Cliff Courts for African American men, an action that, according to Vice President C. P. Boner, "probably saved" the university "some embarrassment" because some "more liberal student leaders were considering Negro housing as a popular cause to espouse."[4]

The proprietors of private dormitories that housed university students seemed more open to the idea of integrated housing. According to the final report of the university's Desegregation Committee, two directors of men's dormitories said that they would consider applications from black students, and two other directors said that if the university desegregated on the undergraduate level, they would consider housing applications from black students on the same basis as those of white students. One director of a women's dormitory said that its board of directors would decide on the admission of African Americans; a second director said that the dorm was associated with a church and consequently would aid in integration "in every way [it] can"; and a third director simply stated that the dorm would accept black students. A fourth director, however, said that because of "the policy set by its sponsoring group, [the dormitory] could not accept Negroes." Rooming houses mimicked the attitudes of the university's administration: as one director stated, "While educational opportunities should be equal, social facilities should be separate."[5]

On July 8, 1955, more than a year after the Supreme Court's first *Brown v. Board of Education* decision, the UT Board of Regents adopted new "admission policy recommendations": "Beginning with the fall semester of 1956, the University would . . . admit qualified applicants on all levels without reference to race." Although the *Texas Observer* reported a few days later that the regents would be developing a plan for integrated housing, they never formulated such a plan. In a joint news statement issued a year later, chair of the Board of Regents Tom Sealy and President Wilson stated that except for Whitis House and San Jacinto Dormitories D and F, "all other University owned and operated housing continues to be available to white students only."[6]

Some integrated housing units had existed prior to 1956. In a statement to the *Daily Texan*, President Wilson remarked, "In the past, white and Negro students have lived in the same housing unit, but the white students live there on a voluntary basis." Writing to Graves Landrum, UT's business manager, Director of Auxiliary and Service Activities F. C. McConnell noted that the university had "housed Negro and white students together in one of the San Jacinto Dormitories" each semester since June 1, 1953. The university had tried to keep "this problem" from developing by "giving students who live[d] there full information." In spite of the university's misgivings, "there [had] been little or no trouble on the racial question." In 1959 an African American student noted that Dormitory D had been "integrated," with "six Latin Americans and a Japanese American among the Negroes."[7]

In the fall of 1956, the university accepted 101 undergraduate African American students—63 men and 38 women. Men who had no family or relatives in Austin had the option of living in San Jacinto Dormitories D and F or in "hutment" housing called Cliff Courts. The San Jacinto Dormitories were temporary "barrack-type residences" across the street from the football stadium. None of the San Jacinto Dorms had air-conditioned rooms. Cliff Courts were privately owned group apartments in East Austin, a considerable distance from campus. The thirty-three "prefabricated structures" had been shipped from New Orleans and built in about two hours each. Each apartment had a single room with no cooking facilities, save for an occasional illegal hotplate. Like the San Jacinto Dorms, Cliff Courts had been built to accommodate the post–World War II increase in students, but the owner had expected the dorms to last for only three years. However, university administrators concluded that Cliff Courts would serve as a temporary housing solution for African American men: as such, little was done to fix them up. Leon Holland lived there for one summer and recalled that they were "pretty shabby."[8]

A committee organized to study housing initially contemplated not designating alternative housing for African American men if the owner tore down Cliff Courts. However, an African American lawyer approached Margaret Post, the owner of a house for white university men at 2607 Wichita, and offered to pay her three years' rent in advance for a three-year lease. Her house sat between the Chi Omega sorority house (a white sorority) and another private white men's residence. According to the dean of student life, the university's failure "to provide adequate housing for negro students will increase the possibility of negroes initiating plans of their own," possibly putting black men in close proximity to white women. Furthermore, if the committee designated any other dormitory for African American men, the Division of Housing and Food would need to contact all white students to "advise them that negroes would also be housed in the unit." The university believed that such a plan would "cause much confusion" and "probably would get people to talking and cause some publicity and direct attention to the situation." In the end, the owner of Cliff Courts did not destroy the building, and it remained a university-approved residence until 1960.[9]

In the first five years after UT began to integrate, no African American woman lived in a university dormitory. Moreover, only one African American woman had ever lived in a private dormitory. Albertine Bowie, an African American law student, applied to live in the Christian Faith and Life Community, located at Wooten Hall at Nineteenth and Rio Grande. An Episcopal minister highly recommended her to live in the dorm, and when a vacancy came open on November 1, 1954, the students and staff "unanimously recommended her immediate admission to fill said vacancy." The Executive Committee of the Board of our Faith and Life Community, which consisted of Deans W. R. Woolrich, Page Keeton, Margaret Peck, and Arno Nowotny as well as several other laymen and ministers, unanimously recommended that Bowie be admitted at the beginning of the spring semester because to admit her mid-semester might "prove embarrassing."[10]

Bowie's admission to the dorm led J. B. Dannenbaum, a consulting engineer from Houston whose daughter attended the university and lived in Wooten Hall, to write to President Wilson, Governor Allan Shivers, and Dean Nowotny protesting this "most unwise action." He believed that this "experiment in race relations should not be permitted" because it would "endanger the future of our children [and] of the great institution which they all love." Dannenbaum later met with Wilson; Jack Lewis, the director of the Christian Faith and Life Center; and Rev. Jack Carter, the Episcopalian minister who had recommended Bowie for admission, to encourage them to revoke Bowie's admission. Nevertheless, the board decided to move forward with her admission. Dannenbaum then wrote to Regent Leroy Jeffers to see if something could be done to "prevent this breakdown in living standards." When nothing could be done, Dannenbaum withdrew his daughter from the dormitory. According to Nowotny, this small step toward integration represented an attempt to change the university's segregation policy "quietly, naturally, and without publicity."[11]

When the university realized that the privately run cooperative at 2515 Whitis Avenue would not accommodate all of the university's African American female students, administrators arranged housing for some of these women at Eliza Dee Hall, located in East Austin on the campus of Huston-Tillotson College, approximately two miles from the UT campus and owned by the Methodist Church's Woman's Division of Christian Service. The dorm's twenty-five UT student residents received transportation to the university in a station wagon. Students paid fifty-two dollars per month for their room and two meals a day. University administrators praised the dorm's management in a 1956 memorandum: "Under the wise and moderate guidance of the supervisors in the dormitory, these students have adjusted to a new campus situation in an adequate manner."[12]

Eliza Dee provided adequate if remote housing for African American female students for two years, but the State of Texas slated the building for demolition during the summer of 1958 to make way for a new highway. The university had to find alternative housing, yet integration of existing women's dormitories was still not an option. In a handwritten note to himself, Vice President Harry Ransom mused, "At the present time we are somewhat vulnerable, but my solution would not be to move toward limited integration in the women's dorms. We will run into a tough social spot if we integrate our women."[13]

The only other university-approved housing available to African American female students in 1956 was Whitis Dormitory (also referred to as Whitis Hall), a virtually condemnable property with a great deal of structural damage and outmoded electrical work and plumbing. This building housed only eight students, who did not share rooms but had access to common living room facilities.

University officials originally planned to operate Whitis on a nonsegregated basis, and during the 1955 summer session, the university received applications from five white and three black students. By the fall of that year, however, Whitis housed only black women.[14]

Peck, the dean of women, pleaded with university administrators to remedy the housing shortage for African American women in light of Eliza Dee's imminent razing and the clearly inhospitable conditions at Whitis. Peck urged the university administration to guarantee more private housing, improve Whitis Dormitory, or encourage the Methodist Board to build another dormitory. Furthermore, Landrum believed that the university needed to make available some facilities for African American female students to avoid "encouraging a suit." In response to these concerns, Ransom waived the Board of Regents' rules on construction and contracting so that a new cooperative for African American women might be ready for the fall of 1959. On March 14–15, 1958, the Board of Regents authorized "the repair and remodeling" of Whitis Dorm and the "repair, remodeling, and construction of an additional facility at 2506 Whitis," the site of a former university staff dormitory, to house twenty-eight women. A report of the Special Committee on Student Housing indicated that this facility was intended to be the first integrated university housing: "The house is available to all applicants and is not a residence exclusively for Negro women." In addition, a new Eliza Dee Hall was built on the Huston-Tillotson campus, housing both Huston-Tillotson and UT students.[15]

Sometime in the mid-1950s, university administrators banned African American students from visiting the white women's dormitories. At a September 1956 dormitory meeting, a housemother informed her white female residents that "no Negro students are to be allowed in the dormitories as guests at any time." Dorm resident Robbie Thomas wrote to the editor of the *Daily Texan* to protest a policy she believed forced "prejudice on all of us." Thomas wondered why the university found it necessary to "keep its colored students from so much as setting foot in the door of its dormitories" even though it had opened the doors to its classrooms. Furthermore, Thomas pointed out the hypocrisy of the university's policy—African American women were allowed in the dorm, but only as maids who swept the floors, made the beds, emptied the trash, and did "the other dirty jobs of a living establishment."[16]

Although President Wilson said he did not recall the Board of Regents instituting a policy banning African Americans from the white women's dorms, he believed that the ruling was "entirely in accordance with the Regents' basic policy . . . that Negro students will be integrated at the University of Texas at the undergraduate level for educational purposes but will be segregated for residential purposes." In a "Residence Hall Bulletin" printed sometime before 1958, the university formally outlined its policy regarding visitors of the opposite race: Negroes could not use the social and dining areas of the women's residence halls (except for Whitis Dormitory) and did not have overnight privileges in these dormitories. Students could invite African Americans of the same gender to their rooms as personal guests but were expected to respect the rights of their fellow residents at all times.[17]

In early May 1958, administrators decided that it would be in "the university's best interests to provide some housing for married African American students." H. Y. McCown, the dean of student services, recommended that the university set aside for African Americans two duplexes in the married students' housing complex. The two suggested duplexes were "well removed from the larger apartments which have children playing outdoors," thus posing "no problem from a public relations standpoint." As was often the case, the university's main concern was not equal housing per se but avoidance of negative publicity and keeping "rabble rousers" at bay. The university's move to provide housing for black married students came too late for some. Dr. June Harden Brewer, one of the first African Americans to apply for admission after the *Sweatt* decision, knew that living in university-operated housing was not an option. She and her husband lived in a house in East Austin near Huston-Tillotson College.[18]

In the fall of 1958, the university opened its "combination dormitory and co-op" for female African American undergraduate and graduate students at 2506 Whitis. The facility housed thirty-two women but had no air-conditioning or washer and dryer. Although the school owned the building, the co-op leased the house and purchased the food and other furnishings. Residents and others soon came to call the new facility the Almetris Co-op, after their housemother, Almetris Marsh, who had previously served as the housemother at Eliza Dee. Almetris served as the "key social outlet" for many of UT's blacks in the late 1950s and into the 1960s. Marsh made a concerted effort to provide good, hospitable housing even though she received very little help—financial or otherwise—from the dean of women or any other administrative office. Marsh seems to have taken very seriously university guidelines suggesting that "fresh paper, well-kept floors, and a light, cheerful interior . . . constitute a direct contribution to the mental and physical health of the student, since they tend to elevate his spirits and promote his general health." She also took very seriously her role as housemother, keeping a scrapbook with photographs of the house's Thanksgiving dinners, the women's invitations to dances and parties, and notices of residents' special achievements or successes. Marsh, an expert seamstress, also made one woman's wedding dress. Trudie Preciphs recalled Marsh as "youthful" and stated that she "kept up parties because she knew we needed them." Peggy Drake Holland said that Marsh watched closely over the women living at Almetris and spent a great deal of time teaching them how to "get along in the system": "She mothered and tried to protect us," Holland recalled.[19]

Because white students generally excluded African American students from participating in campus social life, Marsh's parties and dinners represented one of the few university-oriented activities that her charges could attend. These events caught the attention of a group of white university students who claimed to be members of the Ku Klux Klan. The Klansmen sent the Almetris residents a letter threatening that if the parties continued to "giv[e] the niggers entertainment," "immediate action" would be taken. Because there were so few African Americans on campus, the KKK said, the group could "kill all yall few niggers at U.T. with one nice bomb." In another racist incident, some unknown students drew a white hand and a black hand with blood on it on the pavement in front of the Almetris house.[20]

Ironically, the high quality of life at the Almetris Co-op provided university officials with an excuse to avoid designating other housing for African American women. Ransom wrote in 1959 that the university was "so far out ahead of the others [in desegregating] that I seriously doubt that we would be selected . . . for a test case" by the National Association for the Advancement of Colored People. Furthermore, he believed that "the Negro girls" were "much happier in Almetris than in a predominantly white dorm. Reasons: social life, activities, and togetherness."[21] Such a view ignored the horrendous conditions at Whitis House. Moreover, the university severely underestimated the power of the *Daily Texan* and several student groups to force changes in housing policies.

Negro Housing, 1959–1960

The *Daily Texan* began publicizing the inadequate housing situation for African American students in early 1958. On May 16, two days before the end of the spring semester, the paper ran a series of articles about integration at UT. One article, "Integration Report: Housing, Eating, Recreation," noted that segregated dormitories "have tended to remove Negro students from the main stream of University life." Donald Hill, an African American student, believed that the "crux" of the problem was the fact that black students did not have the "right to choose." "The white student," he said, "can move into better housing if he is financially able, but the Negro must live under those conditions because the

University has so ruled."[22] The university's housing policy bred discontent and made it difficult for Hill and other African Americans to feel like true students at the University of Texas.

Despite the inadequate housing situation for black students, President Wilson believed that there was "no discrimination [at UT] which really impedes educational opportunities." In the future, said Wilson, the university would "move ahead with due deliberation" regarding integration on the campus. Wilson and other administrators failed to recognize (or acknowledge) that the university's housing policies tended to produce what the *Daily Texan* called "a feeling of hostility toward the University administration" among all students, white as well as black, and that the poor housing facilities "kept many Negro students from attending the University."[23] In addition, by keeping the women's dormitories segregated, the university ensured that "Negro men [would not be brought] into the reception rooms" and thus kept white female students safe.[24]

UT student Bud Mims believed that the university should not simply remain content. In a *Daily Texan* editorial, he argued that the university needed to make "every effort to move onward, to progress." All university-owned and -operated dormitories needed to be integrated within the next few years. And, until full integration was achieved, Mims argued, the university should provide black students with a greater variety of living places in both cost and quality.[25] Mims's attitude reflected a growing sentiment among white university students and some *Daily Texan* staff that something needed to be done about black students' on-campus housing situation.

In the fall of 1959, a chorus of complaints about the housing situation for African American students hit the university and the *Daily Texan*. A group of ten black students presented their concerns before UT's Grievance Committee. These students pushed for integrated housing facilities near campus as a way to bring relief to "inadequate housing for Negro students." Students focused particularly on the conditions at Whitis Hall. Gwendolyn Jordan, a Whitis resident, described the facilities in that dormitory as "shocking" and "beyond repair." Barbara Horn, another Whitis resident, believed that aside from the "horrible appearance" of the building, it was a "definite fire hazard, and to make the matter worse, there isn't a fire extinguisher in the building." Most Whitis residents said that they were not accustomed to living conditions like those at the university and believed that African American students had actually chosen not to go to UT because they could not find adequate housing.[26]

The Grievance Committee hearing coincided with the *Daily Texan*'s publication of an article written by Jerry Conn, "Negro Housing Shows Crickets and Discontent." In the article, one black male student who spoke "above-average

English" expressed his dissatisfaction with the quality and availability of housing for black students on campus. He noted that after sending in his application, the university sent him a card listing all of the men's dormitories. However, someone had crossed out all the white dormitories, leaving only the poorest facilities open for African American males and poor whites. The student believed that this practice was unfair, since he could afford to pay the higher fees and live in a better dorm. "If [money] was the only thing keeping me out of Moore-Hill Hall [a white dorm]," he said, "I'd move in next semester."[27]

Black university women, according to Conn, faced "double housing trouble: quality and space." The two university-approved dorms for black women, Whitis and Almetris, were full. Moreover, Whitis was in terrible shape. The waiting room, Conn wrote, had a "somewhat marred coverless floor" with water-stained wallpaper. The furniture was old and loosely covered with upholstery in poor condition. Bare light bulbs hung from the bedroom ceilings. The kitchen contained an oven with the door barely on its hinges. The plumbing in the bathroom was such that crickets came in at night—students laughed as they spoke about having to clean out "seven crickets before bathing each morning." When asked about the conditions of Whitis Hall, F. C. McConnell, director of food and housing, dismissed the article's complaints, commenting, "There is nothing horrible about that house. Just repaper and paint it and it will be in fair shape."[28] But the university did neither.

The publicity about Whitis did not end with Conn's article. In a letter to the editor of the *Daily Texan*, Anne Jonah, a member of the Grievance Committee, wrote of finding "dreary, loose and stained" wallpaper on her visit. Furthermore, the building was "old and hazardous," and the eight girls had only a narrow stairway from which to exit. To solve the cricket situation, which Jonah described as "no joke," housing officials had stuffed newspapers under doors. The kitchen, she said, was "appalling." The refrigerator, according to Jonah, was "tiny and ancient. There are no sinks—washtubs serve." The kitchen was so small that only one student could cook at a time. Because Whitis had no dining room, many of the residents ate standing up. The women entertained their visitors in what one resident described as the "utility" room. Moreover, while other women's dormitories had green grass and flower gardens, Whitis's backyard was simply mud. "The dreariness," Jonah wrote, "is shocking." Shortly after these articles and editorials appeared, university officials added a single fire extinguisher and a new sofa to the common room. These were followed by "a record player and improved kitchenette facilities," which, administrators claimed, made Whitis Hall "more attractive."[29]

The entire Grievance Committee sincerely attempted to catalog the problems of housing for African American students. Using the university's minimum standards for approval of student housing as a guide, the committee compiled a long list of infractions: Whitis Hall (1) did not meet the minimum standards for approved housing set by the University of Texas; (2) had inadequate kitchen facilities and no dining room; and (3) "exemplifie[d] the fact that housing established under the 'separate but equal' rule [did] not assure that the original establishment [would] approach or match an 'equal' standard." Student body president Frank Cooksey presented the committee's report to the Board of Regents, and the board responded through Vice President Ransom that the Student Association must not ignore the other pressing housing problems that foreign and married students faced as well as fraternity and sorority petitions for study space in university dormitories.[30]

In 1960 Ransom formed the Committee on Minority Groups to facilitate student communication with the Board of Regents. Roger Shattuck, a French professor, understood too well the regents' unwillingness to do anything about integration, writing to Ransom, "The University has [recently] tended to react to developments in [integration] rather than to anticipate and try to guide them." The committee comprised four students and three faculty members, and unlike many of UT's other study committees, this one took its mission seriously, inquiring into matters technically beyond its charter and making politically impossible but morally important recommendations. In its conclusions regarding housing, the committee recommended integrating Whitis Dormitory and Carothers, a dormitory for white female students; making air-conditioned rooms available to African American men; ending all "opt-in" segregation dormitories, in which residents could choose whether to maintain segregation; and granting each student access to all dormitory lobbies and dining halls.[31]

Perhaps in response to some of the concerns of both the Grievance Committee and the Committee on Minority Groups, the university spent thirty thousand dollars during the summer of 1960 to renovate Whitis and to open Section D of Brackenridge to African American men. (African American students referred to this dormitory as "Section D for Darkies.") Renovations to Whitis included new flooring and carpeting, the addition of one and a half baths, new plumbing and lighting fixtures, and electrical rewiring. In addition, the university built a fire escape from the upper floors, completely remodeled the kitchen, installed water fountains, brought in new furniture, and painted the inside and outside of the house. Joan McAfee, a resident of Whitis before and after the university remodeled it, said that the living room was "a great improvement of the old house," as were the fully equipped kitchen and laundry room and clothesline. "Maybe this doesn't sound like much," said McAfee, "but after living in the old house last year, we realize this dormitory is much better. Of course, we can't compare a repaired old house with Kinsolving and the other University-owned dorms."[32]

In December 1960, UT's business manager, Graves Landrum, admitted that "air-conditioned space [was] not yet available" for African American men; however, since some white men also lived in San Jacinto Dormitories and Brackenridge Hall and all the rooms were the same age and had the same care, Landrum argued that "Negro men had equal facilities with white men." Cooksey believed that it was "impossible to maintain separate but equal housing" and argued that it was not enough for the university to buy new houses or to remodel old ones to "maintain separate facilities for Negro students." Nevertheless, the Board of Regents clearly indicated that it planned "no substantial changes in the immediate future with regard to integration at the University." African American Ed Dorn lived in Brackenridge for a year before moving into College House, an integrated off-campus co-op with what Dorn described as a "group of intellectual thinkers." Residents of the co-op invited speakers who spoke about such issues as the civil rights movement and the capisimo movement, which raised money for César Chávez. Not many African American UT students participated in this housing experience.[33]

However, both black and white students were becoming louder in their demand for dormitory integration. Kinsolving Dormitory, the newest women's dormitory, quickly became a symbolic battleground for students opposed to segregation. In April 1960 four white students invited two black students to eat at Kinsolving. Although they held guest meal tickets, the black students were refused service. When the manager of the women's residence halls, Jane Greer, asked the black students to leave, some white students stood to leave with them.[34]

Despite evidence that many students in the mid- to late 1950s did not oppose segregation, demonstrations appear to have deeply divided students. During the cafeteria confrontation, "no gesture of any kind was made to ease tension. The people in the serving line looked as though someone had dared to cross sacred ground; . . . it was amazing that not one person showed any kind of amiability." One member of the group declared that the general atmosphere in the dining room was "reserved—almost hostile" toward the black women. A few students wrote to the *Daily Texan* to express their disgust regarding the "Kinsolving incident." Student Linda Maxwell questioned the university's legal right to choose who could be guests in white women's dormitories: "Does the

University have the omnipotence of selecting those whom we may invite as guests into our 'home'?" Carlos Dominquez thought about the "Christian" women who lived in Kinsolving and remained silent. He wondered what those who remained in the dining hall said for grace: "Was it ' . . . and spare us from the blacks, O Lord,' or perhaps, ' . . . and we thank You for giving us courage to manifest our humble intentions so righteously.' Hypocrites, take shelter."[35]

Although most students remained silent about the university's segregation policies, a small group of students and faculty became more vocal in demanding complete integration of the campus. In the spring of 1960 the Faculty Senate overwhelmingly approved a resolution calling for the desegregation of the dormitories. In March 1960 an organization known as "The Group" set up protest pickets and created prointegration pamphlets to bring attention to the university's "insufficient" integration policies in housing, theater, and athletics. After four days of demonstrations, Cooksey and four of the protesters met with President Wilson in a closed-door session that protesters called "unsatisfactory." The cabinet of the university's Wesley Foundation passed a resolution stating that it supported a policy of total integration and that through its Social Action Committee it would attempt to "make students aware of the various facets of the integration problem." The Lutheran Student Association endorsed a plan that would support recent integration moves on campus and across the nation. Also in the spring of 1960, the university Young Men's–Young Women's Christian Association held a discussion on the moral effects of segregation. In the end, only a small number of students actively participated in the demonstrations, and many students and administrators probably agreed with UT student David McDonald that the groups clamoring for integration simply represented "rabble-rousing, subversives who were clearly in the minority."[36]

Negro Housing, 1961

Prointegration protests and demonstrations heated up in the fall of 1961 following a statement by the Board of Regents that integration at the university had "gone far enough" and that further desegregation "would be against the sentiments of a majority of Texans." The regents had the support of UT alumnus John T. Malone, who wrote to Thornton Hardie of his "wholehearted" agreement with the regents' stand: said Malone, "Most of the ex-students and people of Texas are behind you in your position." The most widely publicized and controversial protests again occurred at Kinsolving Dormitory. The October 1961 wing meeting incident focused student anger and impatience with the administration's and the Board of Regents' insistence on maintaining the status quo. At the beginning of the fall term, student advisers in each wing of Kinsolving had held introductory meetings for new residents and told freshmen that (1) there were to be no black males in the lounges of white women's dorms; (2) white women should not invite black women to their dorm; (3) if a white woman invited a black woman into the dorm, they were to go directly to the white woman's room and shut the door; (4) a black man could enter the dorm only to deliver a message or food; and (5) black women could not use the drinking fountains or restrooms in white women's dormitories. As news of these new rules spread, prointegration leaders circulated a new petition calling for the end of segregation, declaring in part that they intended to "ignore the racist rules you are attempting to force upon us." Six thousand students signed the petition in only two days.[37]

For several days, university officials responded only with deafening silence. When students asked about the new dormitory policy, several administrators claimed to know nothing about it, though no one in the administration denied the counselors' statements. A few days after the story broke in the *Daily Texan*, counselors placed bulletins in the common rooms of all the university dormitories that explained that in dorms other than Whitis, "the social and dining areas . . . and overnight privileges . . . are not available to Negroes. Students . . . may invite other girls to their rooms as personal guests, but are expected to respect the rights of their fellow residents at all times." One adviser told her charges that although the official rules permitted African Americans in the dorm, "it is inadvisable to invite them." Students and alumni protested the new policy, which clearly indicated that the university was finally admitting what it had been denying for years—African American students were second-class citizens on its campus. As one student told the *Texas Observer*, "There seems to be almost a calculated attempt here . . . to cut off Negro students from any kind of social contact with whites—even to the point of its being taboo [for an African American woman] to study with a white girl in one of the dorms."[38]

The first of several Kinsolving protests began on October 12, 1961. Three girls from Almetris and one white student from another dormitory entered Kinsolving and rode the elevator to the fourth floor, where they visited two dorm residents. The six women then went to the television area and watched *My Three Sons*. None of the other Kinsolving residents said anything to the mixed-race group as the six women drank sodas, smoked cigarettes, and watched the show. The women "did everything they told us [blacks] couldn't do," Almetris Marsh Duren later recalled. "It's obvious," one of the black women said, "that this rule about Negro visitors is just a scare technique, and the dorms don't even intend to enforce it."

Another protest involved a black woman walking up to the desk of Kinsolving, asking to see a particular resident, being turned down by the white person at the desk, and then walking outside, only to have another black woman repeat this scenario. Following similar protests at both white and black dormitories, Dean of Students Glenn Barnett warned that university students who used the public areas of segregated dormitories "may be subjected to immediate disciplinary probation without appeal if they violated properly constituted authority."[39]

The most controversial protest occurred on October 19. A group of about fifty African American students gathered in the lobby of Kinsolving around 7:15 in the evening. According to the *Daily Texan*, the protesters "chatted in bunches; played 'Green Fields,' 'My Funny Valentine,' and other jazz tunes on the piano; read magazines; and studied." When Natalie Townes, the north wing residence counselor, asked the students to leave, they refused. Townes then left to call for help; when she returned, she asked the students to give their names. Most students refused, while others gave such false names as Elizabeth Taylor and Jackie Robinson. An hour after the sit-in protest began, the students left. "We have to go study," one African American student explained. The group then traveled to Almetris Co-op, where they sang "Texas Fight," the school song heard at football games. When later asked why she had participated in the Kinsolving sit-in, one black student replied, "We hope to show the University and the board of regents that Negro students refuse to be treated as sub-human."[40]

This demonstration might have remained a minor incident if not for the administration's handling of the situation. Shortly after the protesters left Kinsolving, Peck and McConnell arrived at the dormitory. The two spoke with Townes and wrote a report of the incident, which they forwarded to UT President Joseph Smiley. University administrators decided to speak with all the girls in Whitis and Almetris, beginning each meeting by reading a statement by Smiley: "It is clear that on Thursday evening, October 19, violations of University rules and regulations occurred. Investigations by the proper authorities are in process, and subject to the results of these investigations, appropriate disciplinary action will be taken." Administrators then asked each student whether she had participated in the protest at Kinsolving and whether she was willing to name names. To both questions the students answered "No comment" or "Fifth Amendment."[41]

After officials received word that another demonstration would occur, they decided to summon every black student living in a university dormitory or co-op to the Office of the Dean of Student Life. The administrators again asked the students whether they had participated in the protest at Kinsolving. Students who answered "No" were dismissed. Students who admitted participating were placed on disciplinary probation until the end of the semester. Students who refused to comment were told that "failure to answer yes or no as to your participation will subject you to disciplinary probation." Officials interviewed a total of forty-four women and forty-nine men, placing fifteen women and eight men on disciplinary probation. The administration gave these students no opportunity to appeal their penalties to the Faculty Disciplinary Committee, as was the custom. Students placed on probation were prohibited from engaging in extracurricular activities; a second offense would mean dismissal from the university.[42]

Later that day, President Smiley issued a statement urging university students to "continue to keep constantly in view the greatest good of the University." He asked students to end the dormitory protests so that the university could "get on with [its] real business—the training of the intellect in a wholesome academic community." As news of the disciplinary action spread, students and faculty mobilized to protest. Groups of mostly white students rallied in support of the demonstrators' actions. The faculty hastily circulated a resolution, eventually signed by 125 faculty members, calling on Chancellor Ransom and President Smiley to "revoke all rules and regulations governing the conduct of students in University dormitory and eating facilities according to racial criteria." After a week of protests, student leaders met with administration representatives and agreed to a one-week "cooling off" period before staging further demonstrations.[43]

The protests resumed seven days later. Students held "read-in" demonstrations—called "The Moment of Truth"—on the lower terrace in front of the Main Building every day between 10:50 and 11:00 a.m. Participants silently read the inscription on the building, "Ye shall know the truth, and the truth shall make you free." A hundred students demonstrated in front of Kinsolving and Whitis, singing "We Shall Overcome" and having their pictures snapped by personnel from the university's Traffic and Security Division and Fire Department. Students also collected money to send a telegram to Vice President Lyndon Johnson to express dissatisfaction with the university's segregation policy and to urge him to "take initiative" in setting the pace for equal rights.[44]

Leroy Sanders, et al., v. Harry H. Ransom, et al.

In early November 1961, Houston Wade, a graduate student and leader in Students for Direct Action, announced that the group was seeking to hire a lawyer to file suit against the University of Texas to force the university to admit two black students to currently segregated dormitories. Ernest Goldstein, a professor of international law at the School of Law and a member of the Committee on

Minority Groups, advised the students in their efforts. On November 8, three black students and two of their fathers, with the help of local civil rights lawyer Sam Houston Clinton, filed suit against Chancellor Ransom, President Smiley, the Board of Regents, the director of housing, and the managers of the residence halls. The plaintiffs asked the court to take jurisdiction under authority of the Fourteenth Amendment to the U.S. Constitution and to order the desegregation of all university dormitories because the university's dormitory segregation policies denied them and other black students "their rights, privileges, and immunities as secured by the Constitution and the laws of the United States."[45]

In an open meeting three days after Clinton filed the lawsuit, the Board of Regents stated, "With reference to student housing, we wish to say that in view of the filing of a lawsuit . . . we deem it improper to comment or take action at this time on this question pending final decision by the court." After determining that the suit to integrate the dormitories "involved questions of great importance to the students, the parents, and all citizens of our state interested in the University's welfare," the regents subsequently decided to refuse the services of Will Wilson, the state's attorney general, and hire its own attorneys—Houston's Leon Jaworski, president of the State Bar of Texas and the American College of Trial Attorneys; Austin's Frank Denius; and Austin's Edward Clark. Supporters of integration saw this move as the board's attempt to maintain segregation at all costs.[46]

In another controversial move, the board issued a press release warning the general faculty of the School of Law that "any member . . . who directly or indirectly assists the Plaintiffs in this suit would be guilty of disloyalty to his employer and subject to dismissal or other disciplinary action." Although many people believed that the regents had aimed this statement at Goldstein, he thought that the statement was "directed at the entire faculty." Goldstein admitted that he had previously spoken to a group of faculty and students who supported integration but said he told the group that they could expect to receive only "moral support." Law students circulated a petition protesting the regents' method of notification, believing that their actions constituted "an affront to the dignity and integrity" of the law faculty. Writing to Hardie, the law school's dean, Page Keeton, regretted that "there was some feeling that this was an improper means of communicating a direction to a particular faculty regarding proper conduct on their part."[47]

The Board of Regents then announced new rules under which the administration could fire a tenured professor on vague grounds. The board convened in Austin to ask Goldstein to appear to face unspecified charges. Gus Hodges, a UT law professor, informed the board members that if they insisted on Goldstein's appearance, the entire law school faculty would resign. The regents backed down. Shortly after this showdown, Vice President Lyndon Johnson invited Goldstein to his ranch for dinner. While strolling around the ranch, Johnson asked Goldstein about the incident. Goldstein recalled that Johnson "knew who the key faculty members were and where each of them stood. . . . He knew who was sincere but powerless as well as who was insincere."[48] Goldstein would continue his work to desegregate the university's dormitories.

The University of Texas's stance in this integration suit had repercussions beyond its campus. In May 1962, the American Institute of Chemical Engineers canceled its annual meeting at the university because one of its engineering societies objected to using segregated facilities. The national meeting of Tau Beta Pi (the engineers' equivalent of Phi Beta Kappa) had already been moved out of Austin in protest of the university's dormitory regulations. In June 1962, Bill Moyers, associate director for public affairs for the Peace Corps, announced that the university's action in the integration suit was "the catalytic agent" in the Corps's decision not to award a $257,513 contract for a training program in Brazil to the university. Moyers believed that the Peace Corps should not be represented by students and faculty from a university that fought so hard to maintain segregation.[49]

The university's lawyers planned to argue that because only three thousand of the university's twenty-one thousand students (just over 14 percent) lived in university dormitories, dorm residence did not constitute a part of the education system and thus was not covered under *Sweatt v. Painter, McLaurin v. Oklahoma,* and *Brown v. Board of Education.* "If it was," the lawyers asked, "we would be forced to the conclusion that 86 percent of the students are being discriminated against." The attorneys cited a 1933 Ohio State Supreme Court case in which an African American woman was denied enrollment in a home economics class because it would require residence in the home management house, which was closed to black female students. The Ohio court had decided that living in this house was a "social privilege" and thus unenforceable by law. If, however, the courts did decide that dormitories constituted part of the educational process, the lawyers intended to argue that the University of Texas was "proceeding in good faith and with all deliberate speed," as evidenced by the fact the university had desegregated all its other facilities. "I don't think anybody can quarrel with the good faith and deliberate speed the University has shown in integrating," commented Franklin W. Denius, one of the university's lawyers.[50]

In response, Clinton filed a brief that stated that the university's dormitories were a "public facility" and the fact that not all students could receive rooms did not diminish it as such. Clinton also showed that the university's literature contradicted its contention that dormitory life was not a part of the education system. Under the heading "Student Services," the *Information for Prospective Students* handbook stated that "all education is not gained within the classroom." Moreover, the *Manual for Residence Hall Counselors, Resident Hostesses, and Sorority Chaperones* quoted the managers of the women's dormitories, Esther Lloyd-Jones and Margaret Rust Smith, as believing that "through the housing program the college or university has a method for controlling experiences and influences that affect all phases of student development." UT alumna Jean Kamins Knaiger agreed, writing to Ransom that residence halls and dining halls constituted "perhaps one of the most significant parts of my education."[51]

The dormitory lawsuit languished with few significant courtroom developments because both sides refused to settle. Outside the courtroom, however, the university was quietly changing its policies. At its November 1962 meeting, the Board of Regents announced that dormitory residents could have African American guests of the same sex and that they had the same privileges as residents in all areas, including the living and dining rooms. In May 1964 the plaintiffs filed a motion to dismiss the case on the grounds that one of the three plaintiffs had graduated, one was married and had withdrawn from the university, and the third expected to graduate at the end of the current semester.[52] Although the lawsuit had ended, the university's problems with the dormitories had not.

Negro Housing, 1962–1965

In the fall of 1964, after news of the suit's dismissal became public, Jack Holland, director of student personnel services, wrote to the vice chancellor for academic affairs that "the first question asked of this office" was "What will you do about housing?" Parents and students were inundating Holland's office with questions about the continuing shortage of on-campus housing as well as the status of integration. The main concern of Holland and many others in the university community was to what degree UT would be responsible for facilities, services, sanitation, and integration of privately owned off-campus housing. In 1964 the Student Assembly passed a resolution requesting that the university approve only privately owned houses whose owners did not discriminate, although the measure exempted fraternity and sorority houses.[53]

On May 15, 1964, the Board of Regents voted six to one to completely integrate all university facilities, including dormitories, the following fall. The resolution exempted housing not on campus or otherwise "occupied by The University," but the regents had at last made an unequivocal statement from which they could not back down. "I'm very pleased," regent J. Lee Johnson told the *Austin American-Statesman* after the vote. "I've felt very strongly that this is the best thing for the University, and the right thing to do." The regents' actions made the University of Texas the first school in the South to integrate from "classroom to dormitory, from stadium to faculty, from band hall to scholarship awards." A year after the regents ordered the integration of the dormitories, former chair W. W. Heath boasted that "integration without incident" was the success of which he was most proud during his years on the board. "The problem," said Heath, "was to integrate in the manner laid down by the Supreme Court, and we did exactly that." When the regents announced their decision to integrate fully in 1965, Hardie concluded his statement by observing that desegregation of the University of Texas had occurred "without troops, marshals, violence or bloodshed."[54]

Because the regents changed their policy just three months before the start of the fall term, university administrators agreed to allow those applicants who objected to integrated housing to voice their complaints to the university, after which time "a final decision can be made in reference to refund of the deposit." That summer, the first black and white roommates lived together in Blanton Dormitory. According to Jane Greer, no problems arose and other residents made no comments. Many Texans, however, voiced their discontent regarding the integration of the dormitories, the last vestige of segregation on UT's campus. In a letter to the Board of Regents, whom she called "political cowards," Louise Chilton Bryan wrote, "Classroom mixing is offensive enough—but mixed eating and sleeping quarters are so unthinkable that they are disgusting and nauseating." Addie Barlow Frazier of Dallas wrote to Heath to ask if the regents had "lost all of their racial integrity."[55]

Private living facilities, however, remained largely segregated. Jack Holland, Ira Iscoe, and Margaret Peck proposed creating a list of integrated private housing so that African American applicants for the fall of 1965 would be able to find places to live. Such a list would serve another purpose—it would enable white students who objected to living with African Americans to avoid integrated facilities. Even though the creation of the list was illegal, the Student Off-Campus Housing Commission made it available in the fall of 1965. The list included twenty-two integrated facilities—dormitories, rooming houses, and apartments—for men and fifteen for women. Nevertheless, African American students had a difficult time finding private off-campus housing. While the owners of Grace Hall, a private dormitory for women; Kirby Hall, a dormitory operated by the Methodist Church; and Halstead Co-op opened their doors to African American students, the owners of Miss Texas, La Fountainbleu, Heflin Manor, and University Arms did not. In addition, most white real estate agents steered African American students toward housing on Austin's East Side, a long walk from campus that involved crossing an interstate highway. Black students who approached white landlords about housing near campus often were told that no apartments were available or that applications were not yet being taken for the fall, even though signs in the front yard indicated otherwise.[56]

Even after the official desegregation of the dormitories, most university living facilities continued to have de facto segregation. One black senior spoke of being assigned to live with a black freshman: "We have nothing in common," the woman said, "except our both being Negroes." In the same dormitory, another black freshman lived alone in a double room even though three white women were living in temporary housing in the facility's basement. When asked about this situation, university administrators claimed that there was no policy forbidding black and white students from sharing a room; however, officials also did not "force a Negro to live with a Caucasian or force a Caucasian to live with a Negro." When a white student requested a black roommate, a university administrator called the parents of the white student to make sure that they approved of the interracial pairing; no such phone call was made to the black student's parents. As late as 1972, the university also kept dorms segregated by asking future residents to indicate their race on housing contracts. The university housing contract now reads, "It is the policy of the University to assign roommates without regard to race, creed, or nationality."[57]

Although officials now considered the University of Texas fully integrated, many people still wondered what should happen next. Black students still had limited opportunities on campus, and many black parents hesitated to send their children to the school for fear that they would not be welcomed. One prominent sign of African Americans' second-class status at UT was the school's intercollegiate athletic teams, which remained effectively closed to black athletes. Efforts would now shift from tackling written segregation policies to those that remained unspoken.

Be it resolved by the Board of Regents of The University of Texas that there be, and is hereby, established with reference to the use and control of all public buildings of The University of Texas, including, particularly, Gregory Gymnasium and Hogg Auditorium, the following policy, to-wit: None of such buildings shall be used for any public meeting or entertainment attended by members of the Caucasian Race and the Negro Race, until and unless definite arrangements shall have been made in advance of the meeting or entertainment to segregate completely the members of the Caucasian Race and the Negro Race to be seated in the audience. The administrative officers of The University of Texas are hereby charged with the responsibility to enforce strict compliance with this policy. —Board of Regents policy adopted September 29, 1944

5 Black Integration of the Athletic Program

History was made in the spring of 1962 at the Texas Memorial Stadium. During the annual Texas Relays track meet, spectators could sit wherever they wanted in the stands, without regard to race. In addition, all-black schools were for the first time permitted to compete. Previous university policy set by the Board of Regents had permitted African American athletes to enter only as members of integrated teams or as individual competitors. A crowd of twelve thousand watched Coach Stan Wright's runners from Texas Southern University win five relay crowns while "smashing exalted records to smithereens, establishing new standards, and striking new pages in the annals of sport history." Ray "Jackrabbit" Saddler led the Tigers, running 46.0- and 46.3-second heats in the 400-yard dash. At the end of the meet, a group of sportswriters unanimously named the Texas Southern Tigers the meet's outstanding team. "In a standing ovation," one of the sportswriters wrote, "the huge audience roared its thunderous approval with unanimous cheers and applause."[1] Many observers thought that the Tigers had written a great success story—they had proved that African American athletes could compete with and defeat white athletes. Yet no

African American athlete participated in the Texas Relays as a member of the University of Texas's track team because of a Board of Regents' ruling that barred black students from participating in intercollegiate athletics.

The Board of Regents' prohibition was complicated. Because intercollegiate sports often constituted the most public face at UT—the face by which many people, for lack of any other knowledge, judged the school—the regents worried that allowing black students on university teams would "violate the spirit of the [white Texas] community." So while the regents allowed African American students to join the university's intramural teams, board members and university administrators offered at least six different reasons on as many different occasions why intercollegiate sports at the University of Texas could not be integrated: (1) the student body would not accept the change; (2) the university had a binding "gentleman's agreement" with other Southwest Conference (SWC) schools not to integrate athletics; (3) the university should not be the first to integrate its intercollegiate teams when some schools had not even integrated their student bodies; (4) segregated housing and eating facilities posed too great of a problem for teams traveling; (5) no good African American athletes were also good students; and (6) recruiting of good white athletes would suffer. The regents also privately worried about losing the moral—and, more importantly, financial—support of white alumni, whose donations helped to supplement improvements to the school and athletic department. Thus, university administrators decided that it "would be in the best interest of colored as well as white students to take account of long-established traditions in this region" and to maintain segregation in extracurricular activities, including intercollegiate athletics.[2]

The exclusion of African Americans from the playing field was not unique to the University of Texas. By 1961, among the SWC's eight schools, only the University of Texas and the University of Arkansas had integrated their classrooms. Southern Methodist University (SMU) and Texas Christian University had integrated only their graduate programs, and Baylor, Texas A & M, Rice, and Texas Tech remained completely segregated. Although the UT regents had admitted African American students in 1956, not all aspects of the campus were open to them. Black students were prohibited from joining, among other activities, the band, chorus, and all university-approved fraternities and sororities; and they were not allowed to even set foot inside most university-owned dormitories and cooperatives. The exclusion of African American students from intercollegiate sports, like the exclusion of black students from other parts of campus life, received a philosophical rationale that combined social Darwinism with fears of intimate social contact between blacks and whites, fears of black success on the playing field, and fears that an integrated playing field might be particularly vulnerable to "race-mixing."

The 1950s

Although disturbing to white Texans, the admittance of Heman Sweatt and other African Americans in June 1950 did not constitute cause for alarm in terms of the playing field. First, the University of Texas admitted African Americans only to its graduate and professional schools; such students were not eligible to play on UT's intercollegiate sports teams. Second, the South's unofficial rules of integration prohibited blacks and whites from competing and sweating together on a field of play—doing so was seen as downright inflammatory. Consequently, southern schools carefully scheduled their games, making sure not to play any school that might have an African American athlete. If, however, a southern school did play a team with a black player, an unwritten "gentleman's agreement" called for the team with the black athlete to keep him at home or not to play him, even on its home court.[3] The University of Texas asked its opponents to abide by these rules.

The university was so insistent on maintaining segregation on the playing field that administrators refused to allow C. B. Shepherd, an African American graduate student, to use the school's track facilities at Memorial Stadium to train for the 1953 Texas Amateur Athletic Union track meet. When Shepherd approached head track coach Clyde Littlefield about using the track, Littlefield at first said that the "facilities were too crowded." After noticing that the track was not crowded during the team's practice, Shepherd again approached Littlefield, who this time said that Shepherd could not use the track because of a regents' ruling that forbade "the use of state-owned athletic fields by both Negroes and Caucasians." The Social Action Commission of the Wesley Foundation, a Methodist student organization, took up Shepherd's case. The commission could find no Board of Regents ruling that prohibited Shepherd from using the track, nor could it find one that forbade graduate students in general from using any university athletic fields. In a strange twist, Chancellor James P. Hart sided with Shepherd, arguing that the athletic department's contention that the track was too crowded was insufficient considering that only one man wanted to use the track and that under *McLaurin v. Oklahoma*, the university was bound to "let Negro students have the same use of our athletic facilities as other students." Hart even argued that Shepherd's use of the track would not "raise any difficulties." In a special item at its May 29 meeting, the regents voted to authorize African Americans to use the gymnasium, the track, and the field at Memorial Stadium as well as other athletic facilities on the same basis and "subject to the same rules and regulations as other students in the University."[4]

By all accounts, the Supreme Court's decision in *Brown v. Board of Education* the following year shook the South like nothing since the Civil War. Segregationists especially worried about the playing field, where an American mythology insisted that brotherhood and sportsmanship (and, they feared, the races) mixed. Said Georgia State Senator Leon Butts in 1957, after submitting a bill to that state's legislature to ban interracial sports competition, "When Negroes and whites meet on the athletic fields on a basis of complete equality, it is only natural that this sense of equality carries into the daily living of these people." Not all whites in the North and West agreed with this thinking. Unlike white southerners, who felt threatened by the presence of black athletes, white Americans in the North and West, as *Sports Illustrated* writer Jack Olsen noted, could "compartmentalize [their] attitude[s] toward the Negro, to admire his exploits on the field but put him in the back of the bus on the way home."[5] Accordingly, white coaches in northern and western schools slowly began recruiting black athletes, especially after Jackie Robinson's successful 1947 integration of Major League Baseball.

Consequently, as more northern and western schools had African American players on their teams, southern schools found it increasingly difficult to schedule contests only against other all-white squads. This problem arose for the University of Texas in the fall of 1954. The UT football team was scheduled to play Washington State College (now Washington State University) at Texas Memorial Stadium on October 2. The Cougars had Duke Washington, an African American running back. No African American athlete had ever played football in UT's hallowed stadium because of a 1953 regents' policy that prohibited the "participation of Negroes in football games." After speaking with administrators at Texas and Washington State, UT athletic director Dana X. Bible decided that the university would neither cancel the game nor ask the Cougars not to play their African American athlete. Both teams would simply ignore the regents' policy. "Whether Washington State College plays the Negro boy here will be regarded by the University of Texas as their business and not ours," wrote Bible in a memo to the regents.[6] That "Negro boy" did play in that October 2 game, with few objections from the spectators. In fact, after Washington ran seventy-three yards for a touchdown, a "sizable part of the crowd gave him a standing ovation."[7]

This was a much tamer response than that received when Marion Ford, an African American honor student and fullback at Phillis Wheatley High School in Houston, announced his intention to try out for the UT football team. The University of Texas had accepted Ford to study chemical engineering shortly after the Supreme Court's 1954 *Brown* decision but before the regents had met to decide how the ruling would affect the university and its policy of accepting only those African American undergraduates who could not pursue their course of study at one of the black state-supported colleges. After Ford told a reporter for the *Houston Chronicle* of his plans, that reporter contacted Leroy Jeffers, a member of UT's Board of Regents. The newspaper reporter also contacted Bible, who said that he "did not care to comment" and that the matter was "one for policy determination by the Administration and the Board of Regents." After a brief meeting of the regents, university administrators, and Governor Allan Shivers, a former UT student body president and future regent, the university registrar wrote to Ford and four other African Americans whom the university had accepted, canceling their admission. Ford believed that the university did so because of his announcement that he intended to try out for the football team. "I was a victim of southern discrimination," Ford said. "I was not interested in living in their dormitories or becoming socially prominent with the Caucasians," he continued. "I simply wanted a chance to get the best formal training in my state, Texas." Ford's claims may have some credence. In his acceptance letter to Ford, Registrar H. Y. McCown wrote, "I hope that you will do well in the University and that you will get over your inferiority complex and the idea that you are being discriminated against." Ford at first refused to accept the university's decision as final and threatened to file a lawsuit but eventually dropped the matter and decided to attend the University of Illinois. Texas's whites were ecstatic that Ford would not be playing for the football team, seeing his possible tenure as a "really serious affront to our social welfare." "Surely the majority of Texans," Dr. J. L. Shanklin of Kerrville, Texas, wrote, "does not want to accept racial equality, nor do they want to foster a situation that will surely lead to social and sexual homogeneity."[8]

Following the Ford controversy, the University of Texas Board of Regents again voted to restrict the activities of African American students in certain nonacademic areas, most notably in intercollegiate sports, "in deference to the climate of opinion operative at the time." Integrating college sports in the 1950s posed a particularly difficult problem for the regents. Before the 1940s, whites prevented African Americans from participating in segregated sporting contests by calling attention to so-called genetic defects in African Americans. As Elmer A. Carter noted in a 1933 *Opportunity* article, "The Negro in College Athletics," whites believed that "the Negro was deficient in the qualities of which athletic champions [were] made. . . . That rare combination—stamina, skill, and courage—it was commonly believed was seldom found under a black skin." In the 1950s, however, some whites slowly changed their minds about the intellectual and physical capabilities of black athletes, even wondering if black players might not improve teams. At the same time, African Americans began to see sports as a way to improve the relationship between the races, an idea that threatened the rigid racial divisions between blacks and whites. "Athletics is the universal language," an article in the Howard University newspaper declared. "By and through it we hope to foster a better and more fraternal spirit between the races in America and so to destroy prejudices; to learn and to be taught; to facilitate a universal brotherhood."[9] This type of thinking troubled many southerners. Consequently, most white Texans were not ready or willing to have this experiment come to their flagship university, though they might be willing to watch African Americans compete as members of other school's teams.

In December 1955, the regents voted, without publicity, to "get the word to key people in intercollegiate athletics that the clause 'participation is limited to white schools,' be eliminated from invitations sent out for participation in athletic contests, such as the Texas Relays." This new policy was to take effect during the 1956–57 school year—not coincidentally the same year the regents voted to admit African American undergraduates to the university.[10] In September 1956, university officials gathered to discuss how this new policy might affect the athletic programs. At the time of their meeting, no African American student had inquired about trying out for the football team; however, administrators worried that a black student might want to try out for track, where "Negroes supply many outstanding athletes." Even though track is a noncontact sport, officials feared that a black runner might cause problems with public opinion; consequently, they again agreed to prevent African American athletes from joining any intercollegiate team.[11]

To head off any problems that might arise at athletic events because of the admittance of African American undergraduates, university administrators met in advance to establish a new seating policy. The previous policy had allowed for limited integrated seating at Memorial Stadium, since some African Americans bought their tickets through the Ex-Students' Association, which said it "could not afford to differentiate between whites and coloreds." Under the new policy, (1) any student, regardless of race, would be entitled to a seat in the student section; (2) African Americans holding tickets in the visiting section would be permitted to sit in that section; (3) African Americans who obtained tickets through the Ex-Students' Association would be permitted to sit wherever that ticket indicated; (4) all African Americans presenting tickets at the gate would be permitted to sit wherever their tickets indicated; and (5) African Americans who bought tickets at the gate would be sold a ticket in the African American section of the stadium. This approach, the men believed, would "reduce substantially the possibility of Negroes sitting among the white spectators in the West stands [where the general public sat] and thereby creating a situation of possible ill feeling or even violence." One unpleasant situation did occur when Joan McAfee, an African American student, sat next to a white woman and her son at a UT football game. "Every time I got up to yell for the team," McAfee recalled, "she yanked her son close to her so that I wouldn't happen to touch him." It was the last UT football game that McAfee ever attended. [12]

The university's policy could not, of course, prevent racial incidents from happening at other school's stadiums. African American UT student Lovie Williams had bought two tickets to UT's football game against Baylor University in Waco. Williams's tickets entitled him to seats on the 45-yard-line, near other UT students, but Baylor officials forced Williams and his date to sit in the "Negro section in the end zone." After the game, Baylor officials moved quickly to minimize the amount of negative publicity that would certainly arise because of the incident. Baylor President W. R. White wrote to UT President Wilson to apologize for Williams's treatment: "Those immediately involved [in the incident]," White explained, "acted upon the general mores of the community. They did not realize that they faced a completely new situation." He assured Wilson that such incidents would not occur in the future. To show that Baylor was a progressive school, White pointed out that the university constantly had mixed groups on campus without incident. "We had some Negro musicians who sat in a concert last Friday evening," he noted. In response, Wilson expressed regret at this "unfortunate occurrence" and said that he could find no way to blame White or Baylor University since no one could anticipate "every contingency . . . in this whole difficult area." In the end, however, the UT administration took steps to insure that such "an unfortunate misunderstanding" never occurred again. Before away games, university administrators notified authorities at the host schools that African American students attended the University of Texas and that "there is a possibility that some of them may draw tickets in the University of Texas student section." University administrators then asked if the other institution had any objections to the African American students sitting in the UT student section. [13] Although this procedure was merely symbolic—the university could not prevent black students from acquiring tickets in the student section of an away team's stadium—it represents one of the few instances in which UT administrators went out of their way to protect the rights of the school's black students.

In 1956 Marion Ford transferred to UT to continue his studies in chemical engineering. A week after a UT football game against the USC Trojans—a game in which African American Cornelius "the Chocolate Rocket" Roberts ran for 251 yards on twelve carries—Ford approached UT football coach Ed Price about trying out for the team, even though Ford would have had only one year of eligibility. "I was a cocky son of a bitch," Ford remembered, telling Price that the team needed Ford to win. Price responded, "Listen, Son, it's out of my hands. The policy is just too strong." "It would have been a good stroke for Texas," Ford said, "a beautiful opportunity for a premier university to forge ahead and a hell of a rallying point. After that, I became totally disinterested in athletics and went straight academe." Two years later, Louis Fontno, an African American civil engineering student, inquired about playing basketball at UT. He soon found out that there was no hope. "If you are an athlete and have been accustomed to playing the game, you can understand how we'd feel," he said. "Athletes are supposed to be challenged," he continued. "I don't think that real athletes would mind playing with a Negro." One year later, another African American student met with athletic director Ed Olle about trying out for the freshman basketball team. As in previous such instances, Olle told the young man that the university "had no authority to permit integrated participation in intercollegiate athletics" and that integration was impossible because "of long-established traditions in this region."[14]

Also in 1958, another African American student, Clinton A. Givans, wrote to Bible about trying out for the UT football team. A native of Texas, Givans had been drafted into the U.S. Air Force after one year at Tillotson College (now Huston-Tillotson College). Givans said he wanted to attend the university because there were "no Negro schools that rate[d] as high as the University of Texas in subject matter or intercollegiate athletics." Givans assured the administration that his intentions were noble. "I do not wish to make any national scandal or bring any bad reputation upon the school by a matter of racial segregation," Givans wrote, "but I really want to get a chance to try to make the varsity squad of the football team." Bible responded to Givans's letter in typical southern fashion, refusing to take responsibility for the school's racist policies: "In 1958 . . . we have football games scheduled with Georgia and Tulane, neither of which will permit its team to play against integrated squads. Furthermore, our Conference has not taken any action along this line. And it is our plan to continue to schedule teams in the South and Southwest. So the picture is most uncertain at this time."[15]

Following this exchange of letters, Dean McCown wrote to UT Vice President C. P. Boner asking that the university "establish a policy concerning Negro participation in intercollegiate sports, particularly football." Again, the university reiterated its position that blacks would not participate in intercollegiate sports for the foreseeable future.[16] The regents and university administrators were especially concerned that football at the University of Texas remain segregated. UT fans saw football as their major league sport. For any home game, tens of thousands of white fans filled Texas Memorial Stadium to watch their white sons and brothers run up and down the gridiron with the pigskin. Many of these whites saw the Texas football team as a bastion of white supremacy that could not be tainted by a black athlete. Football offered memorable examples of competence and vitality, just as it represented one of the principal measures of institutional prestige. Almost as important, those in charge of the University of Texas did not want to risk alienating white alumni whose donations helped make the university and its athletic program one the best in the South if not the entire country.

The university's desire to generate favorable publicity and its desire to maintain segregation on the campus came into direct conflict when the National Collegiate Athletic Association (NCAA) selected the University of Texas to serve as host for its national track and field meet in 1958. The NCAA's selection of Austin as the site of this event represented the first time "the big intercollegiate meet had been assigned to a site south of Lincoln, Nebraska." However, because the host institution was responsible for providing accommodations for the visiting squads, Bible and other university administrators faced a huge problem—African Americans were not permitted to stay in any university-owned facility. Housing black athletes somewhere off campus was not an option, because coaches liked to keep their squads together "for the sake of unity and proper team spirit." And even though the number of black athletes in attendance at the meet would be few, the university had to "weigh the favorable publicity that [would] result from a national athletic event involving a number of outstanding athletes . . . against an exception to [its] housing regulations." Bible and Boner decided to ask the regents if Moore-Hall and Simkins Dormitories would be available for integrated occupancy. After weighing the negative publicity that the university would certainly receive if it segregated the black athletes at the meet, the regents agreed to make an exception to its policy that "Negro students or Negroes attending a conference [could not be housed] in permanent University dormitories."[17]

The superior performance of black athletes at the NCAA track meet and around the country made some Texans, including at least one regent, rethink the university's ban on black participation in intercollegiate athletics. In 1958 board member Sterling Holloway wrote to UT President Logan Wilson outlining the reasons for allowing African American students to participate in varsity track and cross country at the University of Texas. First, the university was losing potential track stars. "Texas high schools are turning out Negro graduates with outstanding records in track and field sports whose talents are not now available for our University teams," Holloway wrote. Second, and more important, Holloway wanted to help the university "take [its] place with the great universities of the nation and of the Western world." The University of Texas would never achieve its rightful place, Holloway argued, as long as African Americans were prohibited from participating in something as basic as intercollegiate athletics. He wrote, "Provincialism, of which total exclusion of Negroes from athletics is an expression, is not the hallmark of a university destined to play a crucial role in the intellectual life of the free world." Nevertheless, Holloway knew that his experiment with race mixing could go only so far. He acknowledged that the university needed to pursue its course in "moderation," to take into account "the deep-seated emotions of those of variant points of view." The citizens of Texas might be able to handle seeing black athletes in track and field, Holloway reasoned, because "no bodily contact is involved and . . . only the effort or performance of the individual is the measure of excellence." During this period of perceived black hypersexuality, any sport that involved bodily contact was likely to "whip up the jaded nerves of the tired, dissipated or calloused spectators . . . to stimulate the fiercer emotions." The regents decided at their September 1958 meeting not to adopt Holloway's suggestions because they believed they could not integrate intercollegiate athletics "without antagonizing" the other schools of the Southwest Conference.[18]

One year later, McCown, now a dean, surveyed the head coaches of the basketball, baseball, football, and track teams to ascertain their feelings about African American participation in intercollegiate sports. Baseball coach Bibb Faulk said that he "definitely" did not want any African American players. "They will not fit into his set-up," McCown wrote in his report. Basketball coach Harold Bradley told McCown that although coaching African Americans would not be a problem, under present conditions he preferred not to have them on the team. Football coach Darrell Royal told McCown that African American players created problems. According to McCown, Royal was "quite pronounced in not wanting any Negroes on his team until other Southwest Conference teams admit them and until the housing problem is solved or conditions changed." Track coach Clyde Littlefield also did not want black runners on his team. All four coaches shared concerns centering on housing and recruiting: they did not want to house their black and white athletes in separate places, yet they also found it "unthinkable to assign a Negro and white student as roommates." Moreover, because no other Southwest Conference team had integrated, the UT coaches worried that integrating "would be ruinous in recruiting." "We would be labelled Negro lovers and competing coaches would tell a prospect: 'If you go to Texas, you will have to room with a Negro.' No East Texas boy would come here," the coaches told McCown. McCown suggested that the university "sound out other institutions informally" to get some idea "of their attitude" on the integration question. In the end, though, McCown recommended that the university continue its "delaying tactics" because he believed that "neither the school nor the public was ready for integration in intercollegiate athletics."[19]

The 1960s

In 1960, Holloway again asked the regents to reconsider his suggestion to allow African Americans at least to participate in track and field events at the University of Texas. Holloway said that most of the UT athletic coaches were more willing to consider allowing African American students to try out for the university's intercollegiate teams, although the coaches worried about "a possible embarrassment to the other schools in the Southwest Conference." Holloway's apprehensions went beyond the SWC, however; he was concerned about the world's image of the state of Texas after Rafer Johnson, an African American decathlete in the 1960 Summer Olympics, had publicly disparaged the state. Johnson, whose picture had appeared on the cover of *Time*'s August 29, 1960, edition, had said, "I don't care if I ever see Texas again. . . . There's nothing about it I like. If my family had stayed in Texas, I not only wouldn't be representing the U.S. in the Olympic Games—I wouldn't even have gone to college." At UCLA, Johnson had been a model leader and student. He was a star on the basketball team, had a B-minus grade point average in physical education (after switching his major from predentistry), was the first African American member of Pi Lambda Phi fraternity, and served as student body president during his senior year. Johnson's success, Holloway argued, proved that African American students could compete—and could compete well—in intercollegiate athletics at the University of Texas. He chided the other regents for "sticking [their] heads in the sand and refusing to face the facts of changes that [were] taking place not only in the South, not only in the United States, but in many nations around the world."[20]

Holloway also wrote to M. T. Harrington, the chancellor of Texas A & M and a UT alumnus, to ask how that school would react if the University of Texas had African American athletes on its teams. He reminded Harrington that track and field was a noncontact sport and that when the gun was fired to start an event, each man knew he was his own man. Holloway believed that the one real obstacle to overcome involved possible embarrassments to other Southwest Conference schools and in the problem of room and board for black athletes competing away from Austin. Harrington responded to Holloway's claims in a short and succinct manner: it would be embarrassing for all concerned if "Negroes were members of track teams of the University of Texas when they participated in events on the campus of the A. and M. College."[21]

Holloway's proposal to integrate track and field was fairly radical in light of the lack of racial integration that had occurred to that point at other southern schools (and many in the North, for that matter). At the University of Florida, administrators said they visualized no problems with regard to integrating athletic squads and participating in intercollegiate athletics, yet very little integration had taken place at the school. The president of the University of Georgia, which was under a court order to integrate, said that the integration of athletic squads had not yet become an issue. The president of Louisiana State University said that he would "find a good excuse" for prohibiting African American students from participating in intercollegiate sports. "To be specific," he said, his institution "does not favor whites and Negroes participating together on athletic teams." The University of Tennessee, unlike most southern schools, had made significant progress toward integrating its athletic programs. There, university policy was "both to admit qualified and interested Negro athletes to [its] teams and to play other teams with Negro members." The University of Oklahoma had also taken significant steps to integrate its educational, housing, and intercollegiate athletic programs. In 1958 the university had given Prentiss Gautt an athletic scholarship, making him the first African American athlete at a major southern school. Gautt helped the Oklahoma Sooners defeat the Longhorns in the 1959 Sugar Bowl, making a great play at the end of the game that led Don Weedon, a UT football player, to say to another Longhorn player, "It's plain. We've got to get us some niggers." School officials said that there was "little or no murmuring of disapproval on the part of the alumni or anybody else." By 1961, the University of Oklahoma had about ten African American students on athletic scholarships in football, basketball, track, and wrestling and several more on the squads but not on scholarship.[22]

The success of Junior Coffey, former all-state athlete in football and basketball at Dimmit High School in Dimmit, Texas, led some students to more directly challenge the university's ban against African American participation in intercollegiate sports. Coffey, who went on to play fullback at the University of Oklahoma, led the Sooners to a 35–17 victory over UT in the 1961 Cotton Bowl. As a high school senior, Coffey had indicated that he would like to play for the University of Texas: "I'd stay here if I could play for a Southwest Conference school. . . . I like Texas. I have seen them play a lot and I like their method of playing." Coffey received scholarship offers from Oklahoma, Kansas, Washington, Nebraska, Ohio State, and Iowa—but not Texas. "I guess they know what they are doing," Coffey said of the Southwest Conference, "but they're losing a lot of good Texas boys."[23]

Recognizing the need for direct action in integrating intercollegiate athletics, students and faculty began speaking out and organizing protests and petition drives against the rule prohibiting black athletes from UT's teams. In April 1961 the Student Association's Human Relations Committee studied objections to integrated university athletic teams, concluding that a noncontact sport such as swimming or track could be integrated in the next school year provided that a "qualified Negro athlete can be found." The Executive Board of the Campus Interracial Committee held a petition drive in support of athletic integration. After gathering the signatures of three thousand UT students, the committee delivered the petition to the Board of Regents. The Student Assembly conducted a survey of UT students and found that 74 percent of them favored integrating athletics while only 19 percent opposed it; the assembly subsequently voted twenty-three to zero to petition the regents to adopt a policy that allowed qualified athletes of any race to participate in the university's intercollegiate athletic program.[24]

On May 9, the General Faculty Council issued a statement calling for the university to "proceed with racial desegregation of all its facilities and activities in the manner prescribed by the Supreme Court's language, that is, 'with all deliberate speed.' " In September, students submitted to the regents a petition with six thousand signatures in favor of athletic integration. The regents ignored the document, saying, "We haven't even had a chance to read it." That October, students held the first campuswide referendum on integrating intercollegiate athletics, putting to a vote the question, "Do you favor allowing participation of capable athletes of all races in the University's athletic program?" The referendum drew the largest vote in the university's history—5,132 for athletic integration, 3,293 against it—and received coverage from both United Press International and the Associated Press. The results also attracted the attention of the vice chair of the Board of Regents, W. W. Heath, who stated on KTBC radio that the regents planned to ignore the referendum at their upcoming meeting, since "only about 20% of the student body voted in favor of integration." "To me," the station quoted Heath as saying, "that would indicate a great majority of students are satisfied with the situation."[25]

Apparently feeling threatened by student action against the university's policies, the regents called for the investigation of Claude Allen, a white graduate student and teaching assistant in the English department. Department Chair Mody C. Boatright interviewed three students in Allen's class and found that they knew his views on integration because of his out-of-class integration activities near campus but that he had never tried to impose these views on his students. The regents were particularly concerned about Allen's assignment that his students write an essay arguing for or against capital punishment or the integration of football. Most students chose to write about football and opposed integration, and none felt that their grade had been affected. After Allen mentioned the regents in a negative light during a discussion of the assignment, the board summoned him to appear. Allen said he felt safe, although at one point he thought he would be fired. Nothing, however, ever came of the matter.[26]

In general, the regents and university administrators agreed that it was best to not proceed with integrating athletics "until a majority of the schools in the Southwest Conference had voted in favor of permitting negroes on Southwest Conference teams." Therefore, coaches would not ask African American students to try out for their teams, and if an African American student did ask to try out, the offer would be declined. Moreover, although ticket sales to football games by mail and by drawing would continue to be handled on a nonsegregated basis, African Americans who bought their tickets at the box office would continue to receive seats in the Negro section. In November 1961, the regents released a statement declaring that they did not "intend to take any unilateral action which would disturb the excellent relations existing between the University of Texas, T[exas] A. & M., the University of Arkansas, Rice Institute, Texas Christian University, Southern Methodist University, and Texas Tech." Statements such as these led Maurice Olian, the UT student body president, to join with the student body presidents of SMU, Texas A & M, Baylor, Rice, Texas Christian University, and Texas Tech in signing a resolution urging that "capable athletes of all races be allowed to participate in the conference sporting events."[27]

Such actions likely failed to faze the regents, but they did move slowly to open sports activities to African Americans. In the spring of 1962, they announced that all-black schools would be allowed to compete in the Texas Relays, a small concession that did not carry over to other UT teams, especially football, the university's most cherished sport. Regents Wales Madden Jr. and Sterling Holloway continued the fight to integrate athletics. "My position was that we ought to go ahead and integrate all aspects of the university and it was not very warmly received," Madden recalled. Holloway was so adamant in his fight to integrate intercollegiate athletics at UT that other regents referred to him as agitator. "But if you are so branding everyone who is concerned about justice and obedience to the law," Holloway replied, "I am pleased to be included in that category."[28]

On November 9, 1963, the regents unanimously voted to desegregate all student activities at the University of Texas, including varsity athletics. This historic ruling made Texas the first SWC school to integrate its intercollegiate athletic program. According to Bertha Means, an African American schoolteacher and longtime civil rights activist in Austin, this vote did not come "out of the blue." In May 1963, Means said she called Frank C. Erwin Jr., then a new member of the Board of Regents, and asked him when the university planned to integrate its athletic program. Means was particularly concerned about the track and field program, because her son was a track star at Austin High School, and he wanted to run track at the University of Texas. Means said that Erwin promised her that he would do something about the situation, and six months later he made good on his promise.[29]

A few days after the regents' announcement, athletic director and head football coach Darrell Royal announced at his weekly press conference that the University of Texas athletic council would soon meet to discuss the specifics of integrating the school's athletic programs. "Certainly it's too late for this season," Royal said. Council chair Myron Begeman told the press that the start of athletic integration was not a matter that could be decided overnight. "We are not doing any recruiting now and won't be until after the holidays," he said. A week later, however, Royal claimed, "Any bona fide student who is qualified academically and athletically is welcome to try out for any of our athletic teams." Nonetheless, Royal said that no coach would be immediately recruiting African Americans, although the department would eventually "recruit those that we feel will fit into our program." Asked if he was currently interested in recruiting any specific black players, Royal replied with a simple "No."[30]

SMU followed UT's integration announcement with one of its own: Negro undergraduates at the school who were also athletes were welcome to try out for the school's intercollegiate teams. Said SMU athletic director Matty Bell, "There are no immediate plans to recruit Negroes but if there are any boys who are real good students and outstanding athletes, our coaches can feel free to recruit." The school also said that it would welcome playing against UT and other integrated squads, considering that it had been doing so since 1937. "We would certainly play against any integrated team in the Southwest Conference. This is no new decision for us," Marshall Terry, SMU's director of public relations, told the press. Administrators at Baylor University, Texas Tech, and the University of

Houston, a non-SWC school, announced shortly thereafter that they too would be integrating their athletic programs.[31]

The regents' decision received mixed feedback. As was to be expected, white Texans reacted most strongly to the integration of athletics. Retired Air Force Captain Seaborn Jones wrote to UT Chancellor Harry Ransom that the athletic department would "never be the same with integration" because "many young students will stay away." Moreover, Jones called on the administration to "ease up on integration" until it was possible to "stop it entirely." Ira Carroll of Trinity, Texas, wrote to President Joseph Smiley, "It is bad enough for the school to be integrated on any level, but when it comes to lodging and playing together I assure you and the Board of Regents that I will do all in my power to see that they never enter Texas University." Some alumni, however, welcomed the regents' decision. E. J. Schutze wrote that he was pleased that the action "took place without undue pressures and unfavorable publicity." He continued, "The University of Texas has shown courage and leadership when it might have been easier to wait for some other school to take the lead." Not surprisingly, the *Daily Texan*'s editors overwhelmingly supported the move to integrate athletics and looked to its possibility of improving race relations: "An 80-yard touchdown run by a fleet Negro halfback will do wonders in dissolving racial antipathy."[32]

Now that athletics had officially been integrated, many people began to wonder who would become UT's first African American athlete. Like other African Americans who were the first to integrate some of America's segregated institutions, the first black UT athlete would have to be of outstanding caliber. "The first boy who plays for Texas will really have to be something special to do anything for his race," a Texas coach said. "He must be a fine athlete as well as have the ability to take jibes and ridicule." This first black athlete would likely not be a football player, because the university did not want to risk losing the support of wealthy white alumni, many of whom were not quite prepared to watch black and white men rolling around together on the football field after a pigskin. Such a sight might suggest a certain equality between the races that they believed could lead to race mixing. These whites consequently believed, as Rogers Mielly wrote to Ransom, that the university had a responsibility to "discourage such close relationships in athletics" because they would "undoubtedly result in negroes marrying white women, and tainting the white race that thru the years had made considerable progress." Mielly and others worried that a black football player at the University of Texas—especially an outstanding one—would eventually be absorbed into the school's "social life" and be "placed on a pedestal before young [white] women at dances, and other social events which in due course bring on marriage." Ransom tried to assuage Mielly's fears by telling him that both the regents and Coach Royal had no plans to find a black football player simply to promote miscegenation. Simply stating this as a fact seemed to be all that was necessary to insure that miscegenation would never happen. "We are all aware of the problems which confront university students in the social aspects of their career at the University," Ransom wrote, "including relationships which participation in athletics involve."[33]

In late November, James Means, Cecil Carter, and Oliver Patterson spoke with UT track coach Jack Patterson (no relation to Oliver) about trying out for the team. On December 3, 1963, Means and Carter became the first African Americans to participate in workouts at UT after the official integration of athletics. Coach Patterson seemed encouraged by the runners, telling a reporter that since the two had gotten a late start he would give them "a little more opportunity to show their wares." "I'll have to trim the squad to 40 eventually," he continued. "If there's any prejudice shown at all, it will be in favor of these boys." On February 29, 1964, Means and Patterson competed in a track meet on the Texas A & M campus, thus becoming the first African American athletes to compete as University of Texas Longhorns. Patterson eventually quit the team, but Means stayed on and in 1965 became the first African American varsity letterman at the school and in the SWC. His experiences were, in general, positive: "I didn't have any problems, nothing sensational. . . . [O]nce a restaurant in Lubbock wouldn't let us go in and we had to go somewhere else," Means recalled. "Maybe I wore rose-colored glasses in those days because if people were saying derogatory things, I didn't hear it. No telling what their real response was back in the coffee shop."[34]

On May 22, 1965, Jerry LeVias of Beaumont, Texas, signed a letter of intent to play for Hayden Fry and his SMU Mustangs, putting himself in line to become the SWC's first African American football player. Coach Fry told reporters, "I hope this signing will open the door for future Negro student-athletes in the Southwest Conference. . . . The conference has been losing too many fine athletes in the past. I hope we can keep them in the state now." The news especially worried schools in the Big Ten, Big Six, and Big Eight Conferences, all of which regularly recruited the athletic talent that came out of Texas. One newspaper source estimated that the state had ten thousand black football players, none of whom had previously had the opportunity to play for an SWC school. LeVias at times found playing in the SWC quite difficult. In his first scrimmage on the freshman squad, LeVias scored several touchdowns before a frustrated defensive player blindsided him, breaking several of LeVias's ribs. LeVias rarely played that year because of his injury, and the next year he found that the rest of the SWC, including some SMU players, were not happy to be on the field with an African American. In what Fry described as one of the milder threats he received, an SMU alumnus threatened to withdraw his support from the university if LeVias played. Against the Rice Owls, LeVias heard a white fan shout, "Welcome to the Southwest Conference, nigger." After losing to SMU, Texas Tech Coach J. T. King said that the only way to defend LeVias was to "put a 'white's only' sign over the locker room." University of Texas fans also were not kind to LeVias: during one game, several UT players spit on LeVias, and one player told him, "Go back to your nigger mama."[35]

The addition of African American players to the University of Texas football team seemed to rest on the shoulders of head coach Darrell Royal, who had said in 1962 that he "had no objection to integration of intercollegiate athletics as such." Royal, however, worried about its effect on recruiting, claiming to fear that other schools would use UT's integration in recruiting efforts "with the white boys and their parents who might object to such a system or prefer to live, socialize and play with white boys." Few African Americans participated on UT's intercollegiate athletic teams, and as late as 1967, no UT coach had ever recruited a black athlete. In May 1967, members of Negro Association for Progress (NAP), a university group, converged on Royal's office to protest discrimination against African American athletes. Although Royal was not in his office, assistant basketball coach Leon Black was, and protesters met with him to discuss why no African Americans had been recruited. Black claimed that talent and physical makeup rather than discrimination created the problem: "We have to recruit for height," Black told the students, "and there are no really good tall Negro boys in the state." Black also told NAP that prospective African American athletes often lacked at least one of the three qualities necessary to play for a University of Texas intercollegiate team: character, intelligence, and ability. "We've gone after several boys, and [the Admissions Office] will not let them enroll." Royal, for example, said that he had tried to recruit John Harvey, but he could not gain admission.[36]

After meeting with Black, NAP members met with track coach and assistant athletic director Jack Patterson and repeated their complaint: "Why can Texas Negro athletes get into other colleges and universities but not into the university?" NAP members acknowledged that the university's standards were high but pointed out that other SWC schools with similarly high standards had recruited African American athletes. University athletic officials "claim that they don't know where Negro athletes are," Grace Cleaver, president of NAP, told the *Daily Texan*, "but the University of Houston and other schools, not only find Negro athletes—but recruit them." Texas Christian University, for example, had two African American basketball players, one of whom was "a top notch student." In recruiting athletes, former Texas Christian basketball coach Buster Brannon said, "we go looking for good players in white, Negro, and integrated schools. . . . We don't particularly care what color they are, or what school they attend." Said former SMU assistant football coach Chuck Curtis, "I'm sure there are a percentage [of Negroes] who can't pass the tests, but there are many who can." Patterson, however, remained steadfast in his claims, telling NAP to "show us any student who can meet the qualifications and we will be glad to consider him." Royal also blamed the absence of black recruits on African American athletes' inability to meet minimum university standards: "Contrary to popular rumor, the athletic department cannot get whoever they want in," Royal told NAP.[37]

That year, Sam Bradley of San Angelo signed a track-basketball scholarship, becoming the first African American to earn an athletic scholarship to UT directly out of high school. In February 1968, Royal finally recruited and offered a scholarship to an African American athlete, linebacker Leon O'Neal of Killeen, Texas. "He's a fine young man and a fine athlete," assistant coach Bill Ellington said of O'Neal, who also played basketball and baseball. "We viewed films on him, and he has an excellent record." Nonetheless, O'Neal faced a huge challenge. Although the football team had one other African American, E. A. Curry, he was not on scholarship and was not a very talented player. "He had a good personality, but he just didn't have the athletic ability," All-American Chris Gilbert said of Curry. Thus, African Americans throughout the state of Texas saw O'Neal as making a breakthrough in achieving equality at the University of Texas and in other areas of their lives. If O'Neal could succeed on the playing field and in the classroom, they reasoned, other African American athletes might have the opportunity to play football for the University of Texas. Unfortunately, O'Neal left the school a year after his arrival.[38]

In 1969, the University of Texas football team won a national championship with no black football players on its varsity roster—the last time an all-white team won a national championship. Many observers say that that dubious distinction still bothers Royal, whom a 1987 book quoted as saying, "What can I say? There were other all-white teams. They just didn't win the national championship." But in the view of Charles Pace, a 1972 UT graduate and a founding member of NAP, if Royal had not wanted an all-white football team, he would have recruited black football players and helped them stay on the team: "He was the athletic director and head coach, and we figured that if he had control over which white athletes came to the school, then certainly he could find some black athletes to come to the school as well." Charles Miles, a UT graduate who helped to recruit African American athletes in the early 1970s, agreed, stating that Royal "was in a position really to put some pressure on the people upstairs. Blacks felt he was carrying out mandates. They felt [after 1963] he should use that influence." However, according to Bill Little, UT's current assistant athletic director, the problem was not Royal but the Board of Regents and white alumni, who put a great deal of pressure on the university to keep football segregated and who had substantial say in the hiring and firing of the football coach.[39]

Darrell Royal is a very complicated figure, and observers are continually reevaluating his tenure at UT. In the late 1960s and early 1970s, many people saw Royal as the classic racist. On the surface, he seemed to refuse to recruit black athletes, claiming that they could not meet the difficult standards of admittance to the university or that they were simply not good enough to play for the University of Texas. Both of these reasons are quite weak, especially in light of the numerous black football players who left Texas for successful careers on other schools' teams. Others, certainly including Royal himself, say that he is not a racist: "I never have been anti-black and I've never mistreated any person, regardless of whether he was poor, or black, or whatever. . . . But until a few years ago, I didn't express my concern about the inequities which existed. I was just unconcerned, and I feel badly now that I was," Royal said in the early 1980s. Royal's wife, Edith, used to take "a little blind, black youngster to football games," and his supporters ascribe the action to him; Royal also "quietly" served as a trustee of all-black Tillman University in Tuscaloosa, Oklahoma. His supporters also cite an incident that occurred when Royal was coaching the Edmonton Eskimos, a Canadian Football League team: some white players began directing racial slurs at three African American players, and Royal called the white players aside and "chewed them out." Still, many people believe that Royal "missed the greatest opportunity in the history of UT to be perhaps the first major university in the South to recruit blacks," instead choosing not to do so and saying that he had "different ways of doing things." Royal's reluctance to recruit African Americans solidified the black community's image of him as a racist. Even football players described the coach as a "racist trying to change." The East Austin black community accused Royal of several injustices, including intentionally playing Donald Ealey and Julius Whittier at positions that kept them from reaching their potential and suiting up Curry simply to ridicule, exhibit, and embarrass him.[40]

Before they left UT, O'Neal and Curry helped to recruit Whittier, an African American lineman from San Antonio, Texas. Whittier's presence and success on the football team and in the classroom—he would become the first African American to letter in football at UT—showed that the presence of black athletes at UT would remain a reality. However, in 1970, as the University of Texas football team was looking at another national championship, two stories again called into question Royal's racist beliefs. On January 12, writer Bob Greene quoted Royal as having told several African American coaches attending a college football convention in Washington, D.C., "The black coach has not reached the point where his coaching is scientific as it is in the major colleges." Royal claimed that the story was a "vicious lie" and denied having been in attendance at the meeting. Royal, in fact, had the perfect alibi—he was in Austin at the Longhorn football banquet accepting the Associated Press national championship trophy from former First Lady Lady Bird Johnson. Royal considered filing a lawsuit but decided against it: "All I wanted was for the mess to be cleared up—and I wanted to keep on coaching. If I had been ready to get out of coaching, I would have taken 'em on. I felt like they really needed to be punished for that—and I still do, but it's too late now," Royal said some years later. [41]

The second article, James Toback's "Longhorns and Longhairs: The Setting Is Texas; The Issue Is Football, Blacks, and Hippies," appeared in the November 1970 issue of *Harper's* magazine. Toback interviewed five African American football players, all of whom believed that they were not playing football at the University of Texas because of Royal and lingering racism. One of the black athletes said that Erwin, the chair of the Board of Regents, "don't like black folks and he *loves* that Texas football team; so he wants to keep it lily white." Another said that Royal "don't have no use for no *nigger*. He wants a 'colored' boy. A proper Christian, a Boy Scout. And you won't find many of them around anymore, even in Texas." Toback asked Royal whether it was important to him to have black players on the team, and Royal answered, "No. . . . Listen, I know a lot of black people think I'm a racist. But what am I supposed to do, run around denying it? That's incriminating in itself." [42]

Royal admitted that both stories hurt his recruiting of African Americans. Assistant football coach Bill Ellington said that "a lot of people" sent Greene's article to potential black recruits in an attempt to lure them away from UT and onto other campuses. The year the article appeared, only one of fourteen African Americans recruited by UT decided to attend the school. "Most blacks around the state feel that Texas is the epitome of racism," said Bill Lyons, a former basketball player. "Recruits that will come are going to have to be stars so that people will identify with them. Not just one or two, but three or four." Dean Banks, chair of the Student Committee to Facilitate the Recruiting of Minority Athletes, said that Royal and his staff were dealing openly with the racial issue. Ellington was working with the committee and with Melvin Sikes, an African American professor of educational psychology, to "assure the best possible awareness of the overall social situation of black athletes." "It's going to take a coordinated effort to get black athletes just like it is to get whites," Ellington added.[43]

Two years later, a five-part series on the university's racist image among the state's African Americans again highlighted the problems Royal and his staff faced. At the time the articles appeared, the Longhorn football team had only six black players, with none on the thirty-nine-man freshman team because no African Americans had chosen UT the previous year. Roosevelt Leaks, a sophomore running back from Brenham, Texas, said that the people in his town hated his decision to attend UT, fearing that he would not get a fair chance to play. He also admitted that he had found some prejudice on the coaching staff: "Yes. It's here. . . . What more can you expect? . . . There's gonna be prejudice wherever you go to school." The other African Americans on the team—junior halfback Lonnie Bennett, sophomore linebacker Fred Perry, senior tight end Julius Whittier, senior halfback Donald Ealey, and senior defensive end Howard Shaw—also said that some of the coaches were racist, although none of the players gave specific examples. "Nothing out in the open. Just their overall attitude," Perry said.[44]

Because the black players had no tradition with the University of Texas—their fathers had not played for the school and they had not grown up cheering for the Longhorns—they felt no connection to the school, unlike their white counterparts. Bennett showed this distance when he decided to remain seated during the playing of "The Star Spangled Banner" and "The Eyes of Texas," the school song. Asked his reasons, Bennett simply said, "I don't know why. I guess I was in a rebellious mood or something." Whittier agreed with Bennett's protest, saying, "Since when have we seen orange . . . red, white and blue doing us a favor?" Royal was outraged at what he saw as Bennett's disrespect to the school and the flag and at Whittier's subsequent statement. "How can [Whittier] say that the orange has done nothing for him? He's been here on scholarship. He's been exposed. He's getting an education preparing himself where he can do something to contribute to his race. . . . I don't know whether the blacks can accept the fact that they are really wanted by the administration, by our regents, by our coaches, by everyone," Royal said.[45]

Today, white alumni and students alike accept African American athletes on their teams. Many African Americans argue that this acceptance is not really genuine but results from whites' realization by the 1970s that UT could not win without black athletes. Earl Campbell, who won the Heisman Trophy in 1977 and went on to a storied career with the Houston Oilers, also helped to change many African Americans' image of UT football. Every one of Royal's successors as UT's head football coach has had to rely on black talent to produce winning teams. Perhaps to make his black players more appealing to white alumni, current head coach Mack Brown does not allow black players to braid their hair into cornrows or wear dreadlocks, although he did suspend this rule for Heisman Trophy winner Ricky Williams, who played at UT from 1995 to 1999. Black athletes speculate that this rule is in place so that white alumni will not associate the black University of Texas players they see on the football field with the "ghetto thugs" they see on television and hear about in rap songs. Players believe that Brown may be attempting to "whiten" his black players by forcing them to cater to the fears of the white alumni as a way to make them feel safe about cheering for black players. Donnie Little, UT's first black quarterback, who played from 1978 to 1982, believes that even today, some white alumni only reluctantly accept black athletes. This is not surprising, considering many white people's objectification and love of the African American as an athlete but not as a man: "Athletics is really the only place an African American can show that he is a man. He can't do it on the job because he doesn't always get the best jobs," said former UT linebacker Brian Jones.

Nevertheless, the situation has improved for UT's black athletes. In 1985 Leaks became the first African American selected to the Longhorn Men's Hall of Honor in its twenty-eight-year history. Fourteen other African Americans have since been honored, including Henry "Doc" Reeves, a trainer, masseur, and doctor for the UT football team from 1895 to 1915. Today, the football team is more than 50 percent black, and African Americans make up the majority of the team's stars, including African American quarterback Vince Young. His performances in the 2004 and 2005 Rose Bowls solidified his status as one of the most talented black athletes in UT football history and brought the 2005 NCAA National Football Championship trophy back to the University of Texas some thirty-five years after the first black athlete joined the football squad.[46] Integration has arrived in all the other major sports, although only the women's track team has an African American head coach, Beverly Kearney. UT's next giant step will be hiring an African American as the head coach of one of the school's showcase athletic programs.

Man was not born to solve the problem of the universe, but rather to seek to lay bare the heart of the problem and then to confine himself within the limits of what is amenable to understanding. The question to ask is not whether we are perfectly agreed, but whether we are proceeding from a common basis of sentiment.
—Johann Wolfang von Goethe

6 Desegregation from 1964 to the Present

In April 1964, Volma Overton—president of the Austin branch of the National Association for the Advancement of Colored People—held a "speak-in" at an Austin City Council meeting. With the help of Claude Allen, a white English professor at Huston-Tillotson College, the two men staged a filibuster in an attempt to force the City Council to consider a ban against racial discrimination and to form a Human Relations Committee. The speak-in began shortly after 10:00 a.m., when Overton took the floor under the guise of protesting the first item on the council agenda, authorization of a refund contract for water and sewer mains in University Hills. Overton then began to read from the book *Black Like Me*, by John Howard Griffin. Shifting his weight from one foot to the other, Overton paused only to compare situations in the book to conditions in Austin. Mayor Lester Palmer twice tried to interrupt Overton by saying that the council's schedule called for consideration of other matters, but Overton kept reading, telling Palmer he "needed just a few more minutes." At 2:00 p.m., the two sides agreed to take a ninety-minute break. Overton then read for another half hour before turning the floor over to Allen. Allen then began an extemporaneous speech about the immorality of racism and the need for whites to give African American their civil rights. The council paused for dinner at 6:00 p.m. but agreed to let Allen have the floor again at 7:30. He resumed his speech, which lasted until 12:30 in the morning, to a standing-room only crowd.[1]

While Overton and Allen spoke, UT students packed the City Council room, while another two hundred students demonstrated outside, joined by nationally known folksinger Joan Baez. Some students questioned Baez's motives for attending the demonstration, believing that neither she nor those listening to her were truly committed to changing life for African Americans in Austin. "They want to come and sing songs," former UT student Jeff Shero said, "but not to protest. Tell them not to just sing songs, but to demonstrate." Asked UT senior Don Hill, "While other people have been protesting, where have you been?" "This is not hootenanny," Hill continued. "There is a park down the block. Why don't you take them there to sing?" he asked Baez. Baez then wondered whether she should sing at all, expressing discomfort at the idea that her fans probably were indeed more interested in seeing her perform than in partaking in the demonstration. "I often feel angry because people clap and then go home to their segregated houses," Baez told a reporter. After asking those in attendance to stay and join the protest afterward, Baez led the crowd in the singing of several freedom songs. She then left to catch a train, and with her departed most of the crowd.[2] Although many of the students had attended simply to see Baez perform, many more of them—like their counterparts in other parts of the South—continued their efforts to open up all segments of the country to all people.

Quiet Progress

By the mid-1960s, racial segregation in public colleges was slowly disappearing. According to a *Dallas News* survey, of the country's fifty tax-supported state universities, all but two or three admitted African American students. In addition, historically black colleges continued to increase in their enrollment despite integration at these white colleges. At the University of Texas, black enrollment remained stagnant between about 125 and 200 even though other predominantly white colleges and universities experienced increases in African American enrollment, in part because of the continued mistreatment of African Americans on the Austin campus. For example, Rosetta Williams, a senior sociology major, endured racist remarks from Professor Robert Hopper on the first day of the 1969 spring semester: Hopper told his class, "I want feedback from the students because I don't want you sitting around like a bunch of niggers nodding your heads not saying anything." Although enraged, Williams chose to say nothing to Hopper but instead spoke with the department chair, Lear Ashmore, who said she sympathized with Williams and would speak with Hopper to "try to determine what his intentions were in making such a statement." Unsatisfied with Ashmore's response, Williams went to the university ombudsman and recounted Hopper's statement. Although the ombudsman told her that "such complaint is endemic to this university," he advised her to drop the class because Hopper had tenure and could say whatever he wanted. Two days after the incident, Hopper called Williams and apologized, and he also apologized in class. Williams, however, worried that the university's passive response would simply "encourage the prevalence of bigotry and racial prejudice to an extent that will seriously cause the deterioration of those interracial relations which have gradually grown here."[3]

African American students also felt isolated among the sea of white students at the university. In the 1970–71 school year, UT enrolled fewer than three hundred African American students and less than a thousand Mexican American students, although African Americans comprised 13 percent of the state population and Mexican Americans 17 percent. Not surprisingly, black UT students such as Brenda Walker constantly complained about feeling lonely on campus. Ernest White, a black freshman studying accounting, said he often felt "out of place, like when you walk up to someone, and he acts like you're not there." According to sophomore Don Boney, however, the white students were "not hostile, they ignore, they tolerate you." Other black students, like Beverly Washington and Joyce Herbert, lived and interacted with white students but had black best friends.[4]

Because of these feelings of loneliness and isolation, black UT students longed for a place on campus to call their own. In 1969 African American students proposed that the Texas Union Board of Directors create an Afro-American Studies Room. The purpose of the room, according to the students' proposal, was to promote "better cultural interchanges on the Texas campus." Moreover, "such a room shall concentrate on providing continuous art works, paintings, reading material, and atmosphere to emphasize the part that Afro-Americans, especially Texas graduates, have contributed to the American history." Despite its name, the room would be open to all students because there could be "no interchange of culture where there is no communication." The Texas Union's board responded positively, and the Afro-American Studies Room opened in 1970 on the union's second floor. Designed around an Afrocentric theme, the room had a small library, a study area, a lounge, a display area, and a place for speakers. It was, according to Almetris Duren, "a place . . . where blacks could meet one another and feel comfortable."[5]

Other aspects of the campus slowly opened to African American students. In 1965, Anitha Mitchell became the first African American selected for Mortar Board, a national honor society of senior women. Earlier that year, the Cactus Goodfellow, a university organization, had elected Mitchell, making her the first African American to join the group. The same year, the Forty Acres Club, a relaxing place for university faculty and staff, alumni, and their friends that had opened in May 1962, also admitted African Americans, thus ending several years of student and faculty protests about a segregated facility so close to UT's campus and so closely associated with the school.[6]

The Forty Acres Club's ground floor housed a lobby, offices, and a dress shop; the next three floors contained forty-two suites and rooms with hotel accommodations for friends and faculty members; and the top floor contained a health club with steam baths and athletic equipment. The club's original policy had stated that faculty members would be allowed to bring guests, regardless of their color, "from other universities or persons coming to Austin in connection with University affairs." Less than a month after the club opened, however, the management refused to serve a visiting African American Peace Corps officer. This denial of service was cited as one of the reasons that the university lost out on a $257,000 Peace Corps contract. The club also denied use of its facilities to members wishing to schedule professional meetings if African Americans would be in attendance. When asked about the change in policy, D. M. "Buck" McCullough, president of the ownership corporation and spokesperson for the Forty Acres Club, pointed out that the club was privately owned and thus had a right to establish its own policies. Six members of Students for Direct Action subsequently picketed the club, carrying signs that said, "First class universities don't support second-class policies" and "This is a club for 'discriminating' admission based on color." The group also handed club members a letter that said that although the club was private, it was linked to the university because a professor had scheduled a graduate seminar there and because the administration entertained official visitors there. Third-year law student Boren Chertkov vowed to keep up the demonstrations "until the university participation" in the club ended. Some faculty groups protested the club's policy by scheduling social events elsewhere. Several professors worried that the university would have to turn down numerous conferences and meetings if the facility remained a segregated place.[7]

In September 1962, the club abolished its faculty-staff advisory board "to prevent further embarrassment to the University and to the Forty Acres Club, and in an effort to show once and for all—that the University has no official connection with this club." That fall, the Committee of Nine, a group that had originated from a resolution adopted at a September meeting of the American Association of University Professors, decided to pressure the Forty Acres Club to reinstate its "originally agreed-upon policy on guests and memberships" and to admit African American guests. A three-person committee composed of Dr. Joseph Jones, professor of English; Dr. Reece McGee, associate professor of sociology; and Dr. Arthur M. Cory, associate professor of English proposed that the Ex-Students' Association consider building a joint Faculty Club–Alumni Home that would be open to all affiliated with the University of Texas regardless of race. The committee also sent a letter to Frank Erwin, the attorney for the Forty Acres Club, requesting a meeting with club directors. In October, the two groups met informally but agreed to keep the proceedings private. Despite the fact that the committee called for another meeting with the club's directors, that meeting was never held.[8]

Because the club insisted on continuing its segregation policy, the *Daily Texan* urged all faculty members who disagreed with the club's policy to withdraw their memberships until the club became "willing to reinstate its policy allowing members to bring all guests to the club." Professor J. Frank Dobie, who resigned from the Forty Acres Club, said, "I've only been once, and I wouldn't think it's good enough to invite a Negro to, myself. It's in poor taste. There are very loud noises." McCullough refused to comment on the resignations the club had received, telling the press, "I don't know how many resignations have been received, and I won't know for several weeks." The number of resignations apparently had some effect on the club's policy, but a visit by President Lyndon Johnson set a new policy in motion. On January 6, 1964, Andrew T. Hatcher, an African American member of LBJ's press staff, was among the guests at a cocktail party that the Texas Press Club hosted at the Forty Acres Club and was served drinks. The fact that Hatcher was served clearly had more to do with the club directors not wanting to embarrass themselves in front of President Johnson than with any change in the club's policy with regard to segregation, a state of affairs confirmed a few days thereafter when Clifton Winstead, chair of the club's Board of Directors, issued a statement saying that no such change had occurred. Three days later, however, the six-man Board of Directors voted unanimously to change its policy to allow "as guests those persons who are official guests of The University of Texas." When asked if this new policy included Negroes, Winstead replied, "Oh, yes." African Americans could be certified as "official guests" if a university official called or brought them to the club.[9]

The new policy still did not permit African Americans to become members of the club. Noting some of the progress made in the advancement of civil rights for African Americans, Professor Alfred Schild believed that the board of the Forty Acres Club had simply "walked an inch" when the rest of the country had "walked a mile." He urged other members of the faculty not to rejoin the Forty Acres Club if they had resigned from it, to resign if they were currently members, and not to bring guests there. "The action proposed," Schild wrote, "is primarily a matter of decency and morals. I cannot keep my self-respect if I do not respect the rights and the self-respect of my fellows."[10] The Forty Acres Club would not open its doors to African American members until the early 1970s.

After many years of stalling, the Longhorn Band also finally accepted African American members in 1964. One of UT's most visible student organizations since it played during all home and most away football games, the band was funded by a wealthy donor who was also rumored to be "a big racist" who had said that he would do all he could to keep the band segregated. Discussion about whether to integrate the band had first occurred almost ten years earlier, in the fall of 1956, when the regents first admitted African American undergraduates. Seven African American freshmen had asked director Vincent DiNino about trying out for the band. In a letter to Dean of Student Life Arno Nowotny, DiNino reported that band members had reacted quite positively to the idea of integrating the band as long as the African Americans "met the required standards of playing and were of top quality character." DiNino concurred. Nowotny agreed to allow DiNino to use his "excellent judgment" when selecting members for the Longhorn Band.[11] Nevertheless, the band remained segregated.

Because of the band's high visibility, many students and prointegration groups wanted to see it desegregated. In the fall of 1963 the Campus Interracial Committee asked Ed Guinn to try out for the band. Guinn, a sophomore from Fort Worth, had thought about joining the band when he first enrolled at the University of Texas. However, after learning that the band was segregated, Guinn and his father asked E. W. Doty, the dean of fine arts, how the band could be segregated when the regents had ordered other parts of the school integrated. Doty replied that because the band was not part of the music department, there was nothing he, the school, or the regents could do. Moreover, because the band was funded by a wealthy private donor, Doty thought that neither Guinn nor any other African American would be marching with the Longhorn Band any time soon. Consequently, Guinn lost interest.[12]

In February 1964, Guinn was surprised to read an article in the *Daily Texan* reporting that he had been accepted as a member of the Longhorn Band in the fall of 1963 and that he had "decided because of his heavy course schedule to wait" until the spring semester. Moreover, said the article, Guinn had played with the band at a UT–Southern Methodist University football game. None of this was true. The article renewed Guinn's interest in the band, and he auditioned for DiNino shortly thereafter. The audition was embarrassing: "I was asked to play rote notes," Guinn remembered, "the kind of stuff you'd expect to give a high school student, not a college student." DiNino then announced to the *Daily Texan* that Guinn had joined the band, although the director had not discussed the matter with Guinn. DiNino then issued Guinn a uniform, which was too small. Guinn made only one appearance with the band, a spring 1964 rally for the basketball team. The first tune the band played was "Dixie," probably, Guinn believed, to alienate him: "It was quite clear that my appearance in the band was an affront to their way of life," Guinn said.[13] Still, the Longhorn Band had finally been integrated, and other African Americans have followed in Guinn's footsteps with more success.

One of the last academic barriers to fall at the University of Texas was the hiring of African American faculty. In April 1964, one month before they ordered the integration of dorms, the regents approved the hiring of Dr. Ervin S. Perry as a professor of civil engineering. Perry thus became the first African American to teach at a white southern university. Perry, a native of Coldspring, Texas, had graduated from Prairie View A & M with a bachelor of science degree in civil engineering in 1956. During the summer of 1959, Perry entered graduate school in civil engineering at the University of Texas while working as an assistant professor of civil engineering at Prairie View. He received a master of science degree in 1961 and a Ph.D. in 1964. Although conscious of the civil rights movement on campus, Perry did not participate in any social protests, although he did take an active role in the lives of his African American students. He served as the sponsor for the Negro Association for Progress and adviser to the Afro-American Culture Committee.[14]

Students and faculty alike were excited by Perry's appointment. John McKetta, dean of the Engineering School, said he spent the first week after Perry's hiring became public answering questions. "Ervin Perry is an outstanding person as well as an outstanding student," McKetta told the press. "He is a tremendous research worker. We consider him the best available Ph.D. engineering candidate who is graduating this year—anywhere in the world." Students, according to McKetta, responded "with glee" upon hearing of Perry's appointment. He had been a teaching assistant in the department and was quite popular. Perry considered his new appointment "just a job," and improving race relations was not his objective "in any way." When Perry died of cancer in 1970, at the age of thirty-four, the

Texas House adopted a resolution by Representative Paul Silber of San Antonio recognizing Perry's achievements in becoming the first African American full-time faculty member at the University of Texas. The university further honored him in 1977 by naming its new $21 million social science and humanities library after him and Carlos Castañeda, a former Mexican American professor of Spanish and Latin American history at UT. At the time, the Perry-Castañeda Library was the third-largest academic library building in the United States (behind Harvard and Yale).[15]

The Crisis Is Conscious

The rise of Malcolm X in the early 1960s signaled the beginning of an ideological split in the civil rights movement. Frustrated by the slow pace of change and having witnessed violence and murder at the hands of white southerners, younger African Americans were beginning to rally around the beliefs of Stokely Carmichael, black power, and the Black Panther Party—that is, self-defense tactics, self-determination, political and economic power, and racial pride. UT's black students increasingly came to view the university as "a racist White-man's Country Club." In an October 26, 1966, *Daily Texan* article, some twenty black students gave their definition of black power. Jackie Kimbrough, a junior psychology major, described it as a movement toward "a racial consciousness, which is almost nil at this point." Gus Lyons, a junior physics major, said that "black power doesn't mean black supremacy, but it lets the black man know he doesn't have to be white to be somebody." Norman Bonner, a junior government major, said of black power, "Its purpose is to instill 'somebodiness' into the Negro community, and it is succeeding in bolstering sagging morale." Said Ed Dorn, a senior government major, "Black power has an emotive power for the underprivileged, frustrated Negro—much like 'Hook 'em Horns' has for other groups." A junior sociology major said, "What the whole thing should mean is black participation in power."[16] To this end, UT's African American students began to form organizations aimed at winning support and empowerment from the white power structure.

One such organization was United Niggers Integrating Texas (UNIT). Despite its militant-sounding name and the fact that its members proposed reclaiming the power of the epithet *nigger*, UNIT helped African American freshmen and transfer students make the transition to the university. Another group, the Student Organization of Afro-American Unity, sought to foster the personal growth and development "of each and every Black student, and to help him/her become everything he is capable of becoming—personally, socially, as well as academically—by means of cooperation, education, sound communication and recreation." The Blacks was an all-encompassing organization whose sphere of activities included academic, economic, and social aspects of black student life and its relationship to the University of Texas. In conjunction with the ideals of the black power movement, The Blacks sought to "develop the potential of Black people by promoting Black identity" through working to obtain "the necessary modifications and changes within the University as well as the Austin community."[17]

In the late 1960s, students began the effort to create an ethnic studies department at the University of Texas. Black students wanted the university to offer courses in the study of African American life and culture. In the fall of 1968, George Washington Jr., one of the first African American graduates of the UT School of Law, taught the university's first course in African American history as part of the American studies program. "The Negro in American Culture" had thirty-five enrolled students, only five of them African American. When asked if he were discouraged by the relatively few African Americans taking the class, Washington replied, "No, I am not disappointed. . . . I think it's a representative number of those enrolled in the University."[18]

In the fall of 1968, assistant professors of history Dr. Lewis L. Gould and Dr. James Curtis arranged for ten scholars of African American history and culture to take part in "an ambitious public lecture series" under the title "The Negro in American History." According to history department chair William H. Goetzmann, the wide range of subjects to be discussed in the lectures "will help focus attention on the research and study possibilities inherent in the field of Negro history." Author Ralph Ellison (whose lecture was "The Negro and the American Literary Tradition") and Thomas Cripps (whose lecture was "The Hollywood Negro and the Myth of the Southern Box Office") captivated audiences with their talks. At the conclusion of the very popular and well-attended lecture series, Curtis and Gould organized select papers from the lecture into a book, *The Black Experience in America: Selected Essays*.[19]

In early 1969, the history department hired its first African American faculty member, Henry A. Bullock, formerly chair of Texas Southern University's Department of History and Sociology. Shortly after Bullock's hiring, on February 27, 1969, a group consisting of members of the Afro-Americans for Black Liberation (AABL) and Mexican American Youth Organization (MAYO) sent a list of demands to University of Texas President Norman Hackerman. The two organizations were frustrated with what they perceived as the slow pace of change at UT as well as a lack of racial and ethnic diversity on campus. Specifically, AABL believed that the university had "continually excluded black students from full participation in campus affairs, exposed them to racist attitudes and situations . . . and [had] completely ignored their needs." AABL's demands included (1) a black studies department with fifty professors, all black; (2) free admission for a minimum of two thousand minority students; (3) rent-free housing for all minority students; (4) Third World instructors in all departments; (5) the immediate dismissal of Board of Regents member Frank Erwin and the appointment of Third World members to half of the board's seats; (6) the conversion of the LBJ Library into the Malcolm X Studies Building; (7) the removal of racist faculty and staff, as determined by a vote of an audience at least half of whose members came from the Third World; (8) the recognition of holidays in honor of Malcolm X and Dr. Martin Luther King Jr. along with the abolition of San Jacinto Day, the celebration of Texas's independence from Mexico; (9) the removal from decision-making procedures of all UT social and other organizations deemed racist; (10) the establishment of an ethnic studies center funded by the university but located in and controlled by the East Austin community; and (11) the immediate rehiring of Larry Caroline, an assistant professor of philosophy whose contract had not been renewed. In general, the members of AABL and MAYO believed that an ethnic studies department would foster black and brown pride as well as provide a space for African American and Mexican American intellectual thought. White students and administrators who saw these demands, however, viewed them as "vague," "racist," "unrealistic," and "ridiculous." Nonetheless, Hackerman responded to some of the groups' concerns, calling for the creation of the Faculty Ad Hoc Committee on Ethnic Studies, which he charged with making recommendations "specifically concerned with ethnic studies and with the needs of minority students." In May 1969, the committee submitted its report and recommendations to the Faculty Council. Among other things, the committee recommended that "adequate treatment of the Afro-American and Mexican-American experience be made a part of existing courses where it is relevant." It also recommended that the university "establish and fund a research institute . . . to oversee and encourage the conduct of research into the Afro-American experience and its cultural and historical antecedents" and that the university step up its recruitment of Mexican American and African American students.[20]

In June 1969, the Board of Regents approved the opening of the Ethnic Studies Center and the hiring of Bullock as its first director. The center would focus on all people of color, not just African Americans. Although most Mexican

American and African American students wanted separate departments for the two disciplines, the Ethnic Studies Center jointly housed the Mexican American Studies Center and the Afro-American Studies Center. After MAYO demanded a separate Chicano studies program, black students held rallies and protests in support of a separate black studies program and submitted their own proposals to university administrators. In the 1971–72 academic year, the Ethnic Studies Center was divided into the Black Studies Center, headed by acting director Geneva Gay, and the Mexican American Studies Center, headed by Dr. Americo Paredes.[21]

In the fall of 1973, the Black Studies Center became the African and Afro-American Studies and Research Center under the Division of General and Comparative Studies. "In the development of foreign area specialization," said Dr. James R. Roach, dean of the Division of General and Comparative Studies, "American higher education has come last and fairly recently to the African continent." As Dr. John Warfield, the center's new director, worked to make studying African and African American history a "legitimate academic pursuit," university administrators came to recognize the necessity of understanding the emerging importance of Africans and African Americans in the "global village where we all have to live." Consequently, those at the university studying to be teachers were now required to take two courses in African American or Mexican American studies. Moreover, students could also major in ethnic studies; by the early 1980s, they could get a bachelor of arts degree in African American studies or Mexican American studies.[22]

When Sheila Walker took over as director of the center (now named the Center for African American Studies) in 1991, its function and purpose changed. Many African American graduate and undergraduate students criticized Walker for her lack of leadership, for a lack of cooperation between CAAS and other departments on campus, and for offering inadequate undergraduate courses. Students also criticized Walker for not attending scheduled exams and dissertation defenses, for misappropriating CAAS funds, for taking extended vacations during the academic year, for handing over control of CAAS to the department's secretary, and for arbitrarily awarding fellowship monies. In December 2000, a group of black graduate students wrote to Walker, whose tenure was up for review, to ask her to resign. They also sent a copy of the letter to appropriate university administrators in hopes of persuading them not to give Walker another five-year contract. Black undergraduate students led by Katherine Kaliski also wrote to university administrators to call for Walker's ouster, citing as their chief complaint the fact that there were not enough upper-division African American studies courses (some semesters there were none) for someone to earn a degree in African American studies. Walker resigned from the directorship in December 2000, shortly after the letters were delivered. In March 2001, Edmund (Ted) Gordon, a professor of anthropology, became CAAS's director, with Joni Jones, a professor of performance studies, as associate director.[23] Gordon has worked tirelessly to bring CAAS back to prominence both on campus and throughout the United States.

Minority Recruitment and Retention

One of the most difficult tasks facing university administrators in the late 1960s and early 1970s was the recruitment and retention of students of color. Compounding this difficulty was a perceived lack of communication between administrators and minority students. In an attempt to open up a dialogue between the two groups, Trudie Preciphs, an African American administrator in the Office of the Dean of Students, recommended that her office "set the pattern for others to follow by striving to seek the most effective ways of dealing with racial issues and problems." Preciphs suggested that staffers in the dean's office participate in a "black awareness" program to be held during three consecutive coffee conferences. Such a program, Preciphs argued, would provide professional development for UT staff members as well as increase awareness "on the part of the staff regarding the 'Black Experience' and its concomitant problems (problems that can and do affect the Black students on this campus)." "Material pertaining to the 'Black Experience,'" Preciphs wrote to Dean of Students James P. Duncan, "will be presented in a rational and factual manner in order to promote bi-racial understanding and cooperation, to allow staff to probe and come to terms with their own feelings in an atmosphere conducive to change and accepting of differences."[24]

Preciphs arranged for four speakers to talk about the "black experience" in America—Mrs. J. E. Craft of Dallas, who had been influential in integrating the Texas State Fair and who had brought the first African American student to North Texas State University; Dr. James Turner, director of the Africana Studies Program and Research Center at Cornell University; John Erickson, founder of Ministry among Neighbors, a program designed to improve black/white relationships in the Austin church community; and Jess Preciphs, a graduate student in social work who worked with Erickson's program. The speakers were a resounding success. Twenty-three of the twenty-four people who returned questionnaires evaluating the program rated its effectiveness as "very good" or "good." "This was more than just becoming aware of Blackness," wrote one program participant, "it was a becoming aware of logic and simplicity." Wrote another participant, "This was a fantastic experience. Not only have I been 'awakened'—informed—but it has given me a look at the people (staff) with whom I work." Many participants agreed that the program represented an important first step in addressing many of the issues that kept black and Latino students from attending the University of Texas at Austin.

The university also endorsed certain recruiting programs as a way to increase the number of black and brown students. One successful program was the Program for Educational Opportunity (PEO). First implemented in the 1968–69 school year, PEO assisted "educationally, culturally, and financially disadvantaged students who appeared capable of succeeding in college on the basis of recommendations and interviews, but not necessarily on the basis of conventional entrance exams." Students admitted to the university under PEO were provided with personal counselors, tutors, tuition, room and board, and books. Many people believed that a program such as PEO was necessary given that so many African American and Mexican American students attended inadequate and underfunded schools, thus making standardized tests such as the American College Test and Scholastic Aptitude Test unfair criteria for judging potential success in college. "The students recognize their deficiencies and understand the competition they are up against," said PEO coordinator Elizabeth Wellborn in 1969. "Our goal . . . is to bring the students in and give them a chance to operate in the world." In its first year, twelve African Americans and thirteen Mexican Americans attended the university under PEO. Twenty-two of these students did well enough to be eligible to return to the university, although only sixteen enrolled in the fall of 1969. Because of the program's overwhelming success, on May 26, 1969, the Faculty Council voted unanimously to expand PEO to include three hundred students. Nonetheless, on August 1, 1969, the Board of Regents voted to eliminate PEO, stating that "no funds appropriated by the Legislature, including local institutional funds, shall be expended for the direct recruitment of students who otherwise would not have had an opportunity for higher education."[25]

Many PEO supporters believed that the regents had canceled the program not because of lack of money but because of racism. In these supporters' eyes, the regents did not want to see a significant increase in the number of African American and Mexican American students on campus. "The Regents' decision was a strong reaction against the Faculty Council recommendation for the expansion of PEO," wrote one of the program's proponents. "Twenty-five additional blacks and chicanos wouldn't be too visible, but 300 is a different matter entirely." African American and Mexican American students, along with their white sympathizers, mobilized to protest the regents' decision. Ben Rodriguez, a UT student, requested that the Texas State Legislature call the regents to appear to explain the decision, and Senator Joe Bernal of San Antonio did so. Speaking at the Capitol before legislators, minority representatives, and university students, Board of Regents Chair Frank C. Erwin Jr. stated that the "program was an out-and-out effort to recruit ethnic minority students who clearly could not meet entrance standards required of other students," Erwin said. "We are turning down thousands of students each year who cannot meet our entrance requirements, and it does not seem to me and to the other members of the Board that we can continue to turn down thousands of applicants of Irish, Scotch, Yugoslav, Japanese, Chinese, Italian, French, and other descents on the ground that they cannot meet our admission standards and at the same time deliberately admit Afro-Americans and Mexican-Americans who fail to meet the same standards." Erwin did, however, agree to keep commitments to the twenty-two students entering the university in the fall of 1969 under PEO. [26]

Erwin's words did little to calm supporters of PEO, who believed that Erwin was saying that PEO represented "discrimination in reverse" and that the university's duty was to educate only those who qualified for admission, not to serve as a social worker. Said a *Daily Texan* editorial, "The Regents killed a project that was moving in the right direction—toward taking on a social responsibility by improving the fate of disadvantaged students who otherwise would not have had an opportunity for a higher education." Protests against the regents' decision continued into the fall semester. Some supporters of PEO placed signs on campus, while others wrote to the *Daily Texan* on the program's behalf. White UT student Ron Hubbard said that PEO would "touch all facets of University life" and continued, "I believe the program, if allowed to grow to the amounts recommended by the Faculty Council, would fill a void in the University of Texas student body."[27] Student Association Vice President Ernie Haywood, an African American, urged students to attend a panel discussion in the Geology Building to become more informed about the pros and cons of PEO, and the next day the association sponsored a pro-PEO rally on the West Mall. [28]

Erwin did voice support for two programs, the Provisional Admission Program and Project Info. The provisional program, which the regents voted to expand at the same time that they canceled PEO, allowed Texas students who did not meet regular admission requirements to enroll at the university in a spring or summer session after graduation from high school. If the student earned at least a 2.0 grade point average in twelve hours of specified courses, he or she could become a regular student. Critics contended that the program was geared toward helping middle-class rather than disadvantaged students. Students accepted into the provisional program often received little or no financial aid from the university, which considered them "high-risk" applicants. Most students from disadvantaged backgrounds—a disproportionate number of them African American or Mexican American—lacked the resources to pay for college immediately after matriculating from high school, and because of the intensity of the summer classes, university administrators discouraged provisional students from working.[29]

Many minority high school students were, however, able to take advantage of Project Info. Founded by students in 1968, Project Info was originally sponsored by UT's Ex-Students' Association. Delegations of volunteer students, faculty, and community representatives visited high schools in disadvantaged areas throughout Texas to inform academically qualified students about admission requirements, financial aid, and campus life. The visitors also provided "insight into the experiences that might hinder some students in their consideration of the University of Texas at Austin as a college choice." One of the program's goals was to increase the number of minority students so that the campus population would become more representative of the state's ethnic composition. At its September 12, 1969, meeting, members of the Board of Regents voted to make Project Info an official program of the University of Texas at Austin, administered by the Office of the Dean of Students. "The Board of Regents . . . supports the objectives of this program to encourage high school students to plan to attend institutions of higher education," the minutes of the regents' meeting read.[30] Administrators at the University of Texas were taking another step to address the school's racial history and to make African American and Mexican American students feel more welcome on the campus.

If I were to describe the [University of Texas] environment, I would not suggest that it is racist. But it is extremely ignorant and naïve. This is even more dangerous because both of these are fodder for racism and racists. People have no clue about what I'm going through. . . . When I am asked to recruit or give an interview and people ask about UT, I feel as if I am asked to say that racism or problems don't live here. But they do in many different forms. And I won't stop saying that they don't until UT is a place for *all* students. —Marlen Whitley, an African American graduate of the University of Texas School of Law, 2001

Epilogue

On September 29, 1992, two white Texans, Cheryl J. Hopwood of Universal City and Stephanie C. Haynes of Austin, filed a lawsuit in U.S. District Court against the University of Texas School of Law, charging that they were being denied the constitutional guarantee of equal protection under the law after the UT Law School rejected their applications while admitting what Hopwood and Haynes argued were less qualified African Americans. Both women claimed that they met the law school's admission requirements and "would have been admitted to the UT law school this fall were it not for preferential admission policies that give special treatment to blacks and Hispanics."[1]

On August 19, 1994, Judge Sam Sparks issued his ruling in the *Hopwood* case: "The court holds that the aspect of the law school's affirmative action program giving minority applicants a 'plus' is lawful. . . . Although under current law the goal of diversity is sufficient by itself to satisfy the compelling governmental interest element of strict scrutiny, the objective of overcoming past effects of discrimination is an equally important goal of the law school's affirmative action program." Sparks also found that "a statistical analysis of the 1992 admissions data supports the defendants' assertion of the non–race based weakness in the plaintiffs' applications." "Therefore," Sparks wrote, "the court finds the defendants have not met the burden of producing credible evidence that legitimate, nondiscriminatory grounds exist for the law school's denial of admission to each of the four plaintiffs and that, in all likelihood, the plaintiffs would not have been offered admission even under a constitutionally permissible process." Sparks found that the plaintiffs had not proven that they had incurred any actual damages other than the cost of applying to law school, so he ordered that the plaintiffs be allowed to reapply to law school without incurring further administrative costs. The court also awarded each plaintiff "nominal damages of one dollar."

The plaintiffs appealed. On March 18, 1996, a clerk of the appellate court in New Orleans read the eighty-one-page opinion of the U.S. Court of Appeals for the Fifth Circuit in *Hopwood, et al., v. State of Texas, et al.* By a vote of two to one, the court overturned Sparks's ruling: "We agree with the plaintiffs that any consideration of race or ethnicity by the law school for the purpose of achieving a diverse student body is not a compelling interest under the Fourteenth Amendment." The opinion concluded, "In sum, the use of race to achieve a diverse student body, whether as a proxy for permissible characteristics, simply cannot be a state interest compelling enough to meet the steep standard of strict scrutiny. These latter factors may, in fact, turn out to be substantially correlated with race, but the key is that race itself not be taken into account. Thus, that portion of the district court's opinion upholding the diversity rationale is reversibly flawed." In August 1996, Texas Attorney General Dan Morales advised Texas colleges and universities to operate on a race-neutral basis. He interpreted the *Hopwood* ruling as applying to all student programs, efforts at recruitment and retention of minority students, and tutoring specifically directed toward minority students. The following February, Morales finalized this advice in an official opinion. He also advised University of Texas officials to dismantle a three-hundred-thousand-dollar-a-year minority hiring program that had helped to bring a record number of African American and Hispanic professors to UT's campus between 1988 and 1997.[2] Formerly segregated and forced to integrate by a 1950 U.S. Supreme Court decision, the University of Texas was now, forty-seven years later, forbidden from considering race in its admissions decisions.

The *Hopwood* case was not the first national attack on affirmative action. In fact, affirmative action has come under attack since its inception in the late 1960s. The first major challenge to affirmative action occurred in *Regents of the University of California v. Bakke* (1978), in which the U.S. Supreme Court forbade the use of racial quotas but allowed race to comprise one factor in admission decisions. Challenges to the concept of racial diversity and racial integration in higher education and other settings are becoming more and more common as Americans debate whether the use of racial criteria is ever moral or constitutional in our "color-blind" society. For example, the repeal of affirmative action in higher education in California, Florida, and Michigan as well as at the University of Maryland, where the courts ruled against race-specific scholarships, seems to suggest that Americans no longer view race as a significant handicap. Contemporary race theorists and even the U.S. Supreme Court now debate the desirability of any form of race consciousness.[3] In a peculiar way, intensive efforts to ensure racial parity and racial equality have again become unpopular. Whites claiming reverse discrimination have, for the most part, argued successfully that such efforts have gone too far.

To legally address the dearth of black and Hispanic undergraduate students at the University of Texas and Texas A & M University, then-Governor George Bush signed into law what has become known as the Top 10 Percent Plan. Under this plan, all Texas students who graduate in the top 10 percent of their high school class would receive automatic admission to any public college or university in the state. Supporters of this new law argued that this plan would increase the number of minority students on the campuses of the state's two major universities. Opponents of the plan, however, had much to criticize. While the plan in theory represented a good-faith effort to remedy the decline in the number of African American and Mexican American students without using affirmative action, the plan would only work in practice if high schools remained segregated and therefore might "actually inhibit integration in elementary and secondary schools." "We're playing little games to allow us to ignore the appalling racial gap in achievement in elementary schools, and this just continues to get these schools off the hook," said Abigail Thernstrom, a Republican member of the U.S. Commission on Civil Rights and a senior fellow at the Manhattan Institute. "These plans compound a moral problem that Americans should be up in arms about."[4] Other observers worried that an influx of students from weaker schools would lower the quality of education offered at Texas's select universities at the same time that students from stronger suburban schools could not even gain admission to those institutions. Moreover, the plan failed to address the lack of African American and Mexican American students in graduate and professional schools.

The most compelling issue that the Top 10 Percent Plan does not address, however, is African American and Hispanic American students' lingering feelings of mistrust. Many observers believe that the University of Texas at Austin and

Texas A & M have not adequately addressed the negative racial climate that still exists on both campuses. African American student Onaje Barnes said that when it came time to select a college, his family and friends warned him not to go to UT "because, quite frankly, the environment of UT is known for racism among black people. Hopwood, and other recent incidents in the past, have put African Americans in a certain mindset about UT. A lot of older people told me not to come here, but I felt that I could deal with any issues that arise."[5] To make African American and Hispanic American students feel more welcome, the University of Texas Ex-Students' Association created the Longhorn Opportunity Scholarship, which awards four thousand dollars to incoming minority students. The University of Texas president regularly visits predominantly minority high schools throughout the state to encourage students to consider attending UT. Despite all of these efforts, the number of minority students remains below the level reached prior to *Hopwood*. Until and unless the University of Texas at Austin honestly deals with its past, it will continue to be seen as a campus that does not welcome African American and Mexican American students.

Proponents of affirmative action and other race-conscious programs received a welcome victory in 2003, when the U.S. Supreme Court ruled five to four that with the "stain of generations of racial oppression . . . still visible in our society," the University of Michigan Law School's "narrowly tailored use of race in admissions decisions to further a compelling interest in obtaining the educational benefits that flow from a diverse student body is not prohibited by the Equal Protection Clause." Writing for the majority in *Grutter v. Bollinger*, Justice Sandra Day O'Connor acknowledged the nation's history of racism and the importance of looking at race as one factor in the admission process. "By virtue of our Nation's struggle with racial equality," she wrote, minority students "are both likely to have experiences of particular importance to the Law School's mission, and less likely to be admitted in meaningful numbers on criteria that ignore those experiences."[6]

As those affiliated with UT continued to think about ways to make the state's flagship campus more appealing to African American and Hispanic American students and to distance itself from its racist past, UT Law Professor Lino Graglia threw the school back into the national spotlight. In his September 1997 remarks to Students for Equal Opportunity, a group formed to oppose affirmative action, Graglia said that "Blacks and Mexican-Americans are not academically competitive with whites" because members of these groups grow up in cultures that "seem not to encourage achievement. Failure is not looked upon with disgrace." His words set off a firestorm. Students, alumni, and some faculty called for

Graglia's dismissal, Jesse Jackson came to Austin and led a rally of five thousand students in front of the Main Building, and the University of Texas again found itself reminded of its long and peculiar racial past while attempting to defend the progress it had made.

These contemporary difficulties associated with racial equality have, of course, a broader historical context. This book has shown how administrators at the University of Texas always remained conscious of race even as they were desegregating. These administrators were so aware of race, in fact, that they noticed it at every turn as a way of ensuring that integration would occur but would not represent full integration. Whether a black woman played the romantic lead opposite a white man in a university-produced play, whether blacks lived in the same dormitories as whites, and whether blacks played on the same sports teams as whites, UT officials always retained an unwillingness to let integration go "too far." This volume has also shown how UT administrators remained more sensitive to the needs and the concerns of both latent and blatant white supremacists than to the needs and concerns of African American students. Heman Sweatt could go to the law school, but administrators and professors seemed to care very little about whether he could (or would) succeed there. Barbara Smith was obviously the best singer for *Dido and Aeneas*, but her blackness alone was enough to disqualify her from the opera. Excellent black athletes could attend UT as students but not as student-athletes. Blackness clearly functioned almost as a limit to the full expressions of humanity that African Americans could offer and served as a profound and sobering reminder of the persistence of white supremacy. Similarly, the Drag's restaurants, barbershops, and other businesses cared more about how their white patrons would feel about having the establishments serve black customers than about the excluded black customers. African American students felt and perhaps still feel the discomfort of being included by law yet uninvited. Men and women such as Ed Guinn and Barbara Smith endured public and private insults daily, sometimes with great reserve and grace, sometimes with anger.

In *Brown v. Board of Education*, the U.S. Supreme Court ruled segregation unconstitutional because it harmed black children irreparably, psychologically, and spiritually. In this volume, several African Americans suggest—in their own words and in the reiterations of their experiences at UT—that limited integration can be no less harmful, that in fact it emotionally and psychologically damaged those who attended the university. These early black students said that although UT claimed to welcome them, they were treated as unwelcome, undeserving, and unwanted. African American John Chase said that he experienced some hostility from white students and received hate mail with racial slurs.[7] Some white students greeted Heman Sweatt by burning a cross on the lawn of the School of Law. In retrospect, the fact that desegregation at UT occurred relatively peacefully despite all these insults is rather amazing. Whites—including members of the Board of Regents, state politicians, UT administrators, and some faculty—went to great lengths to maintain white privilege even as the rest of the nation, including other parts of the South, were looking for ways to remedy the injustices inflicted on the region's blacks.

UT's experiences with limited integration remain instructive. In recent years, as debates swirl around the desirability of race consciousness and race-based programs, we wonder whether even limited integration will survive. Cheryl Hopwood's insistence on color-blindness and a race-neutral admission policy and Lino Graglia's comments about the academic talents of African Americans and Mexican Americans likely will result in fewer minority students at the law school. This development may suggest that even limited integration is too much for institutions such as the University of Texas. In addition, the Fifth Circuit Court of Appeals' rejection of UT's racial history as somehow germane to its admissions policies encourages the institution to forget a past that (remembered or not) continues to inform its present in powerful ways, including a continued legacy of African American and Hispanic American distrust. The result could be the further diminution of the presence of African Americans at UT, a development that the most white supremacist university regent might welcome. By showing the continued persistence of white racism at UT, this book has explored the ways in which white supremacy may be so deeply imbedded in American culture that it never disappears but simply changes form. In light of *Hopwood* and of other challenges to affirmative action policies, it seems plausible that African American students continue to feel less than welcome at UT more than fifty-six years after *Sweatt*. This work has shown the need for deep thinking about UT's odd past, not just by progressive faculty and students but by all members of UT's community. We must remain ever vigilant in the face of the changing nature of racial discrimination.

Notes

Abbreviations

AA	*Austin American*
AAS	*Austin American-Statesman*
CAH	Center for American History, University of Texas at Austin
Chancellor's Office Records	University of Texas Chancellor's Office Records, Center for American History, University of Texas at Austin
Dean of Students Records	University of Texas Dean of Students Records, Center for American History, University of Texas at Austin
DMN	*Dallas Morning News*
DT	*Daily Texan*
HI	*Houston Informer*
President's Office Records	University of Texas President's Office Records, Center for American History, University of Texas at Austin
TLL	Tarlton Law Library, University of Texas at Austin

Preface

1. Bell, *Silent Covenants*, 3.

2. Bell, *Faces*, x; Goldberg, *Anatomy of Racism*; Dudziak, "Desegregation as Cold War Imperative"; Omi and Winant, *Racial Formation*.

3. See Foley, *White Scourge*; Montejano, *Anglos and Mexicans*.

4. See D'Souza, *End of Racism*; Thernstrom and Thernstrom, *America*; Sowell, *Affirmative Action Reconsidered*. In *Gratz v. Bollinger* (2003), the U.S. Supreme Court struck down the University of Michigan's affirmative action policy with regard to undergraduate admissions. In *Grutter v. Bollinger* (2003), the Court ruled five to four that the University of Michigan Law School's "narrowly tailored use of race in admissions decisions" was constitutional.

5. Susan Curtis, *First Black Actors*, x–xi; Sharon Jayson, "Minority Numbers up at UT," *AAS*, September 17, 2000, B1. Peggy Holland, who graduated from the University of Texas in 1962, said that it took her more than twenty years to forgive the school and the students for what she endured during her five years of attendance. She would not return to the campus until 1983, when the university for the first time invited back all black alumni as a way to heal the wounds of the past (conversation with author, November 3, 1998).

6. Clarissa Garcia, letter to author, November 17, 1997. In 1932, Garcia's husband, Osbaldo, became the first Mexican American to graduate from the law school.

Introduction

1. Barr, *Black Texans*, 2–18.

2. Winegarten, *Black Texas Women*, 85–88, 90.

3. Du Bois and Dill, *College-Bred Negro American*, 7; Du Bois, "Higher Education"; Du Bois, *Autobiography*, 212. For a good discussion of this debate, see Kevin Gaines, *Uplifting the Race*.

4. Du Bois, "Talented Tenth"; Du Bois, "Training of Negroes," 410–11. See also Woodson, *Mis-Education*.

5. Sayles, *Constitution*, 329.

6. Such schools included Paul Quinn College (1872) in Austin, Wiley College (1873) in Marshall, Bishop College (1881) in Marshall, Tillotson College (1877) in Austin, and Guadalupe College (1884) in Seguin. Most of the institutions of higher learning for African Americans were located in East Texas. For an excellent discussion of historically black private colleges in Texas, see Heintze, *Private Black Colleges*.

7. Sayles and Sayles, *Early Laws*, 74; Vincent P. Franklin and Anderson, *New Perspectives*, 62.

8. Frantz, *Forty-Acre Follies*, 1–9; Fontaine and Burd, *Jacob Fontaine*, 64. Other

excellent monographs on the history of the University of Texas are Berry, *UT Austin*; Berry, *UT History 101*; Eckhardt, *On This Hallowed Ground*; Garner, *Texas, Our Texas*.

9. Fontaine and Burd, *Jacob Fontaine*, 64, 65; Frantz, *Forty-Acre Follies*, 11.

10. Frantz, *Forty-Acre Follies*, 3.

11. Until the 1940s, all of the senior members of the history department were southerners. As one critic observed, "As long as Texans handled the American history field, the institutions of the South were considered safe at the University of Texas" (Frantz, *Forty-Acre Follies*, 3).

12. Dugger, *Our Invaded Universities*, 14–18; for more information on the standoff between Governor Ferguson and the University of Texas, see 11–18, 23, 28.

13. Ibid., 23, 26–28.

14. Green, *Establishment*, 70–72.

15. Dugger, *Our Invaded Universities*, 45.

16. Ibid., 41; Green, *Establishment*, 86.

17. Barr, *Black Texans*, 42.

18. In 1958, an East Texas jury acquitted a white police chief of murder because he claimed that the black man he killed had had a knife, even though other officers testified that the man had no weapon and had raised his hands to surrender. Two years later, four Texas whites cut KKK into the chest of Felton Turner, an African American man (Barr, *Black Texans*, 183, 190).

19. See Frankenberg, *White Women, Race Matters*; Wells-Barnett, *Red Record*, 29; Barr, *Black Texans*, 45; Hyman and Sheatsley, "Attitudes," 3. Both Frankenberg and Wells-Barnett argue that many of the black men charged with the crime of raping white women were innocent of these charges.

20. James Farmer, conversation with author, February 7, 1997; Tushnet, *Making Civil Rights Law*, 129.

21. See, for example, Clark, *Schoolhouse Door*; Barrett, *Integration at Ole Miss*; Cohodas, *Band Played Dixie*; Bullock, *History of Negro Education*. At the time Bullock published this book, he was a professor of history at Texas Southern University; two years later, he would become the first African American history professor at the University of Texas.

22. Pratt, *We Shall Not Be Moved*; A. G. McNeese Jr. to Thornton Hardie, November 6, 1962, box 217, folder "Segregation," Chancellor's Office Records; Barksdale, "Power Structure," 52.

23. Dugger, *Our Invaded Universities*, 41, 43, 45–47, 72; Green, *Establishment*, 70–72, 84, 86. The regents at first attempted to abolish tenure but did not succeed.

24. In general, most of the white people who lived in East Texas came originally from Alabama, Mississippi, Louisiana, and Tennessee. Consequently, their background, attitudes, and viewpoints with respect to African Americans were southern. Conversely, many of those from the central and western parts of the state had originated in Kansas,

Colorado, Nebraska, New Mexico, Oklahoma, and other nonsouthern regions. This fact, combined with the relatively few African Americans in those parts of the state, meant that a more liberal attitude toward desegregation existed.

25. Sara Hebel, "'Percent Plans' Don't Add Up," *Chronicle of Higher Education*, March 21, 2003, A23.

26. Cohodas, *Band Played Dixie*.

27. Duren with Iscoe, *Overcoming*; Religious Workers' Association of Texas, "A Study of Desegregation and Integration at the University of Texas," 1963, box 128, folder "Integration," President's Office Records; Gould and Sneed, "Without Pride or Apology."

Chapter One. African Americans at the School of Law

1. Baade, "Law at Texas," 161.

2. Simkins, "Why the Ku Klux Klan," 735.

3. *Sweatt v. Painter*, 635. Article 7 of the 1875 Texas Constitution stated that "separate schools shall be provided for the white and colored children, and impartial provision shall be made for both." The article was repealed in 1969 (Tushnet, *Making Civil Rights Law*, 147).

4. Baade, "Law at Texas," 183; Frantz, *Forty-Acre Follies*, 200.

5. Frantz, *Forty-Acre Follies*, 200, 204; Tushnet, *Making Civil Rights Law*, 116–36; *Dallas Express*, October 20, 1938, 14; Marion Curry, conversation with author, November 19, 1998. Curry later returned to the University of Texas after its integration and earned a master of arts degree in education.

6. Charles Bolivar, conversation with author, April 12, 1999. After four decades in California, Bolivar moved back to Texas in 1994. Of the nine children in his family, he is the only one who has returned to Texas. "The others refuse to move back here," he said, "because they remember what Mama and Daddy said about the state."

7. Gillette, "NAACP in Texas," 49; Gillette, "Blacks Challenge the White University," 322.

8. Frantz, *Forty-Acre Follies*, 203; T. S. Painter to Rev. Davis, March 14, 1946, box 20B.a, folder "Negroes in Colleges, 1939–54," President's Office Records. Rainey's support for segregated educational facilities can be seen in his backing of Senate Bill 140, which appropriated $3.35 million to set up a university in Houston and a Negro A & M on the site of Prairie View University. Of these funds, $2 million was to be spent for land and buildings. The bill also called for an emergency appropriation of $350,000 to make available professional courses at Prairie View (Homer P. Rainey to Texas Legislature, October 1942, box 45, folder "Heman Sweatt," President's Office Records).

9. Tushnet, *Making Civil Rights Law*, 137–49; William T. Rives, "State Aids Negro,"

DMN, May 20, 1946, 2. U.S. government figures showed that in 1946, Texas had 7,701 white lawyers and only 23 black lawyers (U.S. Bureau of the Census, *Statistical Abstract of the United States, 1946* [Washington, D.C.: U.S. Government Printing Office, 1946], 17–30).

10. For additional information on Marshall and his work in the NAACP, see Tushnet, *Making Civil Rights Law*, 137–49.

11. Gillette, "Heman Marion Sweatt," 159, 165.

12. "African American Sues for Admission," *DT*, December 18, 1946, 1.

13. Gillette, "Heman Marion Sweatt," 164.

14. Ibid., 162, 164; "Heman Marion Sweatt," *DT*, December 18, 1946, 1; Heman Marion Sweatt, "Why I Want to Attend the University of Texas," *Texas Ranger*, September 18, 1947, 40.

15. Gillette, "NAACP in Texas," 59, 159.

16. Alexander B. Andrews to Charles T. McCormick, July 10, 1941, Law School Vertical File, Charles T. McCormick Papers, TLL; Michael Connolly, "Senate Group Urges Negro College Okay," *DT*, February 12, 1947, 2.

17. Gillette, "NAACP in Texas," 59, 60–62.

18. Gillette, "Heman Marion Sweatt," 167; T. S. Painter to Grover Sellers, March 16, 1946, box 45, folder "Heman Sweatt," President's Office Records.

19. Brief for petitioner, *Sweatt v. Painter*, 2; Duren with Iscoe, *Overcoming*, 1; "Sweatt Appeals Case," *Dallas Express*, December 21, 1946, 1; "Sweatt Case on Appeal," *DT*, March 28, 1947, 1.

20. "Sweatt versus the State of Texas," 52; Charles McCormick to Joe Greenhill, September 16, 1947, box 13, folder 10, "Newspaper Clippings, 1947," Texas State University for Negroes School of Law Papers, TLL; "Announcement of Courses for the Spring Semester," 1947, box 45, folder "Texas State University for Negroes, 1946–52," Chancellor's Office Records.

21. Helen Hargrave to Charles T. McCormick, September 26, 1946, box 20 B.a., folder "Negroes in Colleges 1939–45," President's Office Records; Charles McCormick to Joe Greenhill, September 16, 1947, box 13, folder 10, "Newspaper Clippings, 1947," Texas State University for Negroes School of Law Papers.

22. Margaret Mayer, "Possible Damage to Sweatt Case Advanced as One Reason for 'Empty' Negro Law School," *Austin American Capitol*, March 18, 1947, 1.

23. Charles McCormick to Earnest Jones, January 8, 1947, box 1115, folder 6, McCormick Papers; Clint Pace, "UT Negro Law School Enrolls First Student in State History," *Austin American Capitol*, September 22, 1947, 1; Christina Smith, "Former Students, Profs, and Lawyers Remember: Doomed to Repeat It?" *Austin Chronicle*, February 6, 1998, 26; James F. Vachule, " 'Segregation Changes Needed'—Chicago Prof," *DT*, May 15, 1947, 4. According to historian Michael Gillette, Doyle "incurred the disfavor" of the NAACP for registering at the black law school. Doyle later became

TSUN's first graduate and was later cited as the "fine product of segregated schools." After Doyle passed the Texas bar, however, he began filing civil rights lawsuits against the state. Lott transferred to the University of Texas Law School after the Supreme Court's ruling in *Sweatt v. Painter* and became the school's first black law graduate (Gillette, "NAACP in Texas," 60–62).

24. "Testimony in *Sweatt v. Painter*," May 1947, Law School Vertical File, Mc-Cormick Papers; James F. Vachule, "Negro School Equal to UT, Says Law Dean," *DT*, May 14, 1947, 1; "Sweatt's Lawyer Calls Negro School 'Inferior,' " *DT*, May 13, 1947, 1.

25. Dudley Woodward to T. S. Painter, May 12, 1948, box 2Q122, folder "Sweatt," Dudley Woodward Papers, CAH.

26. "Students Vote Sweatt Supports," *DT*, November 19, 1946, 1; "Resolution from Lutheran Students' Association," April 19, 1946, box VF 20/B.a., folder "Sweatt Case 1946," President's Office Records; "NAACP Chapter Organized at UT," *DMN*, July 6, 1948, 6; A. L. Burford to Dudley Woodward, October 3, 1947, box 2Q122, folder "Sweatt," Woodward Papers; Gillette, "NAACP in Texas," 80; Duren with Iscoe, *Overcoming*, 3. Two of the black students at the march had been designated to file a lawsuit against the university to compel the school to admit them to its medical and dental schools. White administrators worried that the formation of an NAACP chapter on UT's campus would cause many of the state's most promising white students to enroll elsewhere to avoid association with the "rabble-rousers" supporting integration at the state's flagship university (Burford to Woodward, October 3, 1947).

27. Bode, *Portrait of Pancho*, 78; Gwendolyn Tubb to T. S. Painter, November 3, 1949, box VF20/F.a, folder "Sweatt Case 1946," President's Office Records; Heman Sweatt to J. Frank Dobie, September 18, 1946, box 118, folder, "Heman Sweatt," Dobie Collection. In general, the novel was about a "college trained Negro" who thinks a government job will protect him from the "racial abuses common in private industrial employment." Sweatt had three tentative titles for this novel: (1) *No Hiding Place*; (2) *If You're Black, Get Back*; and (3) *Some Postmen Have to Ring More Than Once*. I found no indication that the novel was ever completed. Dobie's collection did not contain a draft of Sweatt's proposed novel.

28. Letter to the editor, *Texas Ranger*, October 1947, 4–9; Mrs. J. R. Rice to T. S. Painter, March 2, 1946, George W. Wiley to T. S. Painter, telegram, March 2, 1946, box VF20/B.a., folder "Sweatt Case 1946," President's Office Records.

29. Claude Villarreal, "Student Opinion Poll Shows 55.92 Per Cent for Unsegregated Admissions," *DT*, April 19, 1949, 3; "Texans Stand Pat on Negroes in UT," *DT*, March 21, 1950, 1.

30. Duren with Iscoe, *Overcoming*, 4; Frantz, *Forty-Acre Follies*, 205. George Mc-Laurin was an African American Ph.D. student in education at the University of Okla-homa. Although he was permitted to use the same classroom, library, and cafeteria as white students, the school assigned him a seat in the classroom in a row specified for

black students and a special table in the library and the cafeteria. The Supreme Court ruled that "the conditions under which appellant is required to receive his education deprive him of his personal and present right to the equal protection of the laws; and the Fourteenth Amendment precludes such differences in treatment by the State based upon race."

31. "Integration Statement," *DT*, November 5, 1961, 1; E. H. Powell, e-mail to author, November 3, 1997; W. Page Keeton, interview by Bill Brands, August 4, 1986, Oral History Collection, TLL; Oscar H. Mauzy, interview by Sheree Scarborough, May 17, 1996, Oral History Collection, TLL.

32. E. H. Powell, e-mail to author, November 3, 1997; Mauzy interview.

33. Weberman and Jackson, "*Sweatt* Paints Dim Past," 35, 40; Ernest Goldstein, conversation with author, November 12, 1997. Two students had registered for graduate courses in government, one in sociology, one in library science, one in zoology (genetics), one for a master's in architecture, five in law, and six in education ("First Black U.T. Students Arrive," *Texas Alcalde* 11 [October 1950]: 17).

34. Christina Smith, "Former Students, Profs, and Lawyers Remember," *Austin Chronicle*, February 6, 1998, 27.

35. Corwin W. Johnson, interview by Sheree Scarborough, September 10, 1997, Oral History Collection, TLL; Mauzy interview.

36. Ray Thompson, "Sweatt Remembers UT," *DMN*, May 20, 1979, 17. There is conflicting evidence as to whether Sweatt flunked out of the law school or was kicked out. At the time Sweatt was a law student, professors did not blindly grade students' exams and papers. Keeton said that Sweatt was "impossible," "couldn't write a simple sentence," and "just had a terrible background." These charges are difficult to believe considering that Sweatt had graduated with honors from Wiley College, had received a master's degree from the University of Michigan, and had done some coursework at Columbia University. In a later interview, Keeton said that Sweatt's problems probably "stemmed from the fact that his prelegal background was inadequate. . . . This really goes back to the fact that he had a segregated education" (Keeton interview). Clarence Coleman, Sweatt's direct supervisor at Atlanta University, recalled Sweatt as "one of the best students" Coleman had ever had and as "serious, thorough, innovative, [and] professionally intense" (Tushnet, *Making Civil Rights Law*, 149).

37. "Handwritten Notes of Professor Ruud, Taken at a Committee Meeting," October 31, 1960, Millard H. Ruud Papers (unprocessed), TLL; Keeton interview; W. Page Keeton to T. S. Painter, March 21, 1951, box 9, folder "Negroes," Chancellor's Office Records.

38. "Integration Statement," *DT*, November 5, 1961, 1; Willie Morris, "Integration at U.T.," *Texas Observer*, October 21, 1960, 2; "Handwritten Notes of Professor Ruud, Taken at a Committee Meeting," October 31, 1960, Ruud Papers.

39. W. Page Keeton to Charles Alan Wright, Millard H. Ruud, Ernest Goldstein,

and Roland Loiseaux, box Vf8, folder "Students and Law Classes: Minority Students (general)," W. Page Keeton Papers, TLL.

40. "Handwritten Notes of Professor Ruud, Taken at a Committee Meeting," October 31, 1960, Ruud Papers.

41. Ibid.; Millard H. Ruud to W. Page Keeton, December 14, 1960, Ruud Papers.

42. "Handwritten Notes of Professor Ruud, Taken at a Committee Meeting," October 31, 1960, Ruud Papers; Kilpatrick, *Southern Case for School Segregation*, 93.

43. "Handwritten Notes of Professor Ruud, Taken at a Committee Meeting," October 31, 1960, Ruud Papers.

44. Kilpatrick, *Southern Case for School Segregation*, 93; "Handwritten Notes of Professor Ruud, Taken at a Committee Meeting," October 31, 1960, Ruud Papers; Carter Wesley, "UT Law Coed, Like Drama Student, Slapped by Bias," *HI*, May 11, 1957, 11. One famous Portia is current Texas Republican Senator Kay Bailey Hutchison, who was elected in 1966. In 1970 the law school's student body voted to delete all mention of the Portia contest from the Student Bar Association Election Code. According to Carol Oppenheimer, a member of the Women's Law Caucus, this referendum clearly demonstrated that the Miss Portia Contest "had outlived its usefulness and was to be buried with other passé relics of yesterday and male chauvinism." Students elected the last Portia in 1971 (*Texas Law Forum*, November 22, 1971, 7).

45. Millard H. Ruud to W. Page Keeton, December 14, 1960, Ruud Papers.

46. Ibid.; "Handwritten Notes of Professor Ruud, Taken at a Committee Meeting," October 31, 1960, Ruud Papers.

47. U.S. Kerner Commission, *Report of the National Advisory Commission on Civil Disorders* (Washington, D.C.: U.S. Government Printing Office, 1968).

48. "The University of New Mexico School of Law Announces a Special Scholarship Program in Law for American Indians," 1971, box K13, folder "CLEO Reports," Keeton Papers; Carl, "Shortage of Negro Lawyers"; Caolo, "Negro Student."

49. Keeton interview.

50. Marc Franklin to Frank Walker, March 31, 1967, Millard H. Ruud to W. Page Keeton, July 29, 1968, February 8, 1970, Ruud Papers.

51. Lyke Thompson, "Conflict Marks Frank Erwin's Career," *DT*, August 14, 1970, 2; Millard H. Ruud to William Huie, November 12, 1972, Ruud Papers; Duren with Iscoe, *Overcoming*, 201; Sheree Scarborough, telephone conversation with author, February 4, 1998; Bertha Means, telephone conversation with author, September 20, 2000. When the governor appointed Erwin as chair, the faculty voted 242 to 197 to express its disapproval and ask for his resignation. Only 609 out of more than 7,000 students voted to support Erwin. Erwin found disfavor when he personally ordered a bulldozer to raze trees on Waller Creek to make way for a Memorial Stadium expansion. In protest, students marched on the administration building and barricaded the entrances with limbs of the dead trees. UT President Norman Hackerman resigned shortly after Erwin's bull-

dozing. Within three months, four other university administrators resigned: Chancellor Harry Ransom, Vice President for Academic Affairs Gardner Lindzey, Executive Vice Chancellor for Academic Affairs John J. McKetta, and Vice Chancellor for Academic Programs William Livingston (Lyke Thompson, "Conflict Marks Frank Erwin's Career," *DT*, August 14, 1970, 2).

52. Millard H. Ruud to William Huie, February 8, 1972, Ruud Papers; Lyke Thompson, "Law Student Program Booted by Regents," *DT*, August 16, 1973, 1.

Chapter Two. Desegregation of Educational Facilities

1. *Brown v. Board of Education* combined pending desegregation cases in Virginia, Delaware, South Carolina, and Washington, D.C.

2. For a discussion of integration at North Texas University, see Marcello, "Reluctance versus Reality."

3. Religious Workers' Association of Texas, "A Study of Desegregation and Integration at the University of Texas," 1963, p. V-3, box 128, folder "Integration," President's Office Records.

4. H. Y. McCown to Logan Wilson, May 26, 1954, box 9, folder "Negroes," Chancellor's Office Records.

5. Williamson, *Crucible of Race*, 306–9; Williamson, *New People*, 10–12; Wells-Barnett, *On Lynchings*; Cohen, *At Freedom's Edge*, 215. Williamson argues that almost three-quarters of the lynchings did not involve charges of rape or attempted rape (*Crucible of Race*, 309).

6. Geduld, *Focus on D. W. Griffith*, 98–99.

7. Logan Wilson to H. Y. McCown, November 12, 1954, box 125, folder "Desegregation," Chancellor's Office Records; McCaslin, "Steadfast in His Intent," 25–26. Not to be outdone on the segregation issue, Republican gubernatorial candidate Reuben Senterfitt asked the Texas State Department of Public Safety to launch an all-out immediate investigation of the NAACP. Senterfitt said he was concerned that the NAACP had strong ties to the Communist Party: "The people of Texas, Negro as well as white, are entitled to know if the objectives of the NAACP and the Communist Party are accidentally the same or as the result of careful design" (Jones, "Status," 337).

8. H. Y. McCown to John Willis Hargis, September 7, 1954, box 34, folder "Desegregation," Chancellor's Office Records; J. C. Goulden, "Segregation Decision Due," *DT*, July 8, 1955, 1. Pennington speculates that the university revoked Ford's admission because he announced that he planned to try out for the UT football team (see chapter 5). John W. Walker, who had been admitted for petroleum engineering, filed suit in the San Antonio district court. His suit was dropped (Pennington, *Breaking the Ice*, 116).

9. Willie Morris, "Regents to Discuss Court Decision Soon," *DT*, June 7, 1955, 1.

10. Kenneth Knopp, "Desegregation Faculty Subject," *DT*, November 11, 1954, 1; Carol Querolo, "Integration Subject of Panel Discussion," *DT*, March 18, 1955, 1.

11. "Regents Open U. of T. to Negroes in Fall of 1956," *Fort Worth Star-Telegram*, July 8, 1955, 1; F. Lanier Cox to Mrs. H. E. Brown, February 27, 1956, box 34, folder "Desegregation," Chancellor's Office Records. The University of Oklahoma had integrated before the University of Texas, but Oklahoma could be considered a border state. The UT regents also announced that all qualified students would be admitted to the graduate school "regardless of whether the desired programs of study" were "offered at the state-supported Negro institutions" ("Regents Open U. of T. to Negroes in Fall of 1956," *Fort Worth Star-Telegram*, July 8, 1955, 1). In October 1955, the U.S. Supreme Court voided section 7, article VII, of the Texas Constitution and Article 2900 of the Texas statutes, both of which provided for separate schools for black and white children (Tushnet, *Making Civil Rights Law*, 139). Increased college enrollment resulted in part from the post–World War II GI Bill (see Olson, *G.I. Bill*).

12. H. Y. McCown to Logan Wilson, May 21, 1955, box 102, folder "Desegregation," President's Office Records. The plan worked. The university registrar admitted 45.6 percent of white students who took the exam during the 1956 academic year but only 19.6 percent of blacks who took the test.

13. "Regents Vote to End Segregation at TWC," *El Paso Herald Post*, July 8, 1955, 1; "A Historic Decision," *DT*, July 12, 1955, 2; Richard M. Morehead, "Austin Studying Integration; No Problem Foreseen at UT," *DMN*, July 13, 1955, 1; Jeann Thompson to Tom Sealy, April 3, 1956, Mary E. Post to Board of Regents, July 26, 1955, box 34, folder "Desegregation," Chancellor's Office Records.

14. Jones, "Status," 337; "Segregation Views: Intense, Varied," *DT*, June 7, 1955, 2; Lloyd S. Riddle to Board of Regents, July 16, 1955; M. Barn to Logan Wilson, n.d., box 34, folder "Desegregation," Chancellor's Office Records; Barbara Ray, " '47 Segregation Talks Fierier Than Today's," *DT*, December 5, 1954, 3; Helen Schafer, "Boycotts as Bullwhips Clutched in KKK Hands," *DT*, December 5, 1954, 3.

15. Don Fairchild, "UT Student Integration Study Told," *AAS*, July 9, 1956, 1; Vincent R. DiNino to Arno Nowotny, September 12, 1956, box 34, folder "Desegregation," Chancellor's Office Records. The majority of black Texans lived in East and Central Texas, where Jim Crow laws remained in force. Galveston, Texas, had been the scene of a terrible race riot following the return of black soldiers from World War I, and that part of the state was still reeling from the effects of that riot and subsequent racial tensions. Residents of West Texas, which was home to large ranches, independent farmers, and few African Americans, seemed to have a more liberal view on race than people in other areas of the state (Kenneth Knopp, "Desegregation Faculty Subject," *DT*, November 11, 1954, 1).

16. James Prentice, telephone conversation with author, February 17, 2001; Barbara Ray, " '47 Segregation Talks Fierier Than Today's," *DT*, December 5, 1954, 3. For a

discussion of the civil rights movement before 1950, see Egerton, *Speak Now against the Day*.

17. Shirley Strum, " 'Crazy College Kids' Take Calm Viewpoint," *DT*, December 5, 1954, 3; James Prentice, telephone conversation with author, February 17, 2001.

18. H. Y. McCown to Logan Wilson and C. P. Boner, September 19, 1961, box 53, folder "Desegregation," Chancellor's Office Records.

19. "90 Negroes Due to Enter UT This Fall," *DMN*, July 30, 1956, 1; "Right for Now," *DT*, October 4, 1956, 1; Clark, *Schoolhouse Door*, xvii; Barrett, *Integration at Ole Miss*, 83–123.

20. Barbara Ray, " '47 Segregation Talks Fierier Than Today's," *DT*, December 5, 1954, 3; Willie Jordan, telephone conversation with author, January 17, 1997.

21. McCaslin, "Steadfast in His Intent," 25–26; Susan Smith, "Building a Legacy, One First at a Time," *AAS*, October 9, 1999, A11; Leon and Peggy Holland, conversation with author, November 3, 1998; Pennington, *Breaking the Ice*, 116; Mary Ann Roser, "No Grudge for New Alumni Chief," *AAS*, September 4, 1999, B5. John Chase became the first African American licensed as an architect in the State of Texas, appointed to the U.S. Commission of Fine Arts, and named a University of Texas Distinguished Alumnus. In July 1998, Chase also became the first African American president of the university's Ex-Students' Association.

22. "Final Report of the Human Relations Commission," June 28, 1957, H. Y. McCown to Logan Wilson, May 21, 1957, box 102, folder "Desegregation," Chancellor's Office Records. While studying at the University of Illinois, Ford had been a member of the school's swimming, wrestling, and football teams.

23. Leon Holland, conversation with author, November 3, 1998; McCaslin, "Steadfast in His Intent," 36; Carl Howard, "Desegregated, Not Integrated at University, Says Student," *DT*, November 7, 1957, 3.

24. H. Y. McCown to Logan Wilson, May 21, 1957, box 102, folder "Desegregation," Chancellor's Office Records.

25. Religious Workers' Association of Texas, "A Study of Desegregation and Integration at the University of Texas," 1963, p. II-9, box 128, folder "Integration," President's Office Records; H. Y. McCown to Logan Wilson and C. P. Boner, May 21, 1957, box 102, folder "Desegregation," Chancellor's Office Records. In the summer of 1959, the Student Association passed a bill calling for integrated bathrooms in the Student Health Center, and the following fall the "white" and "colored" signs came down. Fears about blacks appearing on stage did not extend to well-known performers such as Duke Ellington and Harry Belafonte, both of whom performed on campus to capacity crowds.

26. Executive dean and director of the Medical Branch to Harry Ransom, July 20, 1961, box 85, folder "Desegregation," Chancellor's Office Records. The regents integrated the Medical Branch not because they thought it was the right thing to do but because the NAACP had begun to gather litigants for another lawsuit to force the

legislature to integrate the Medical Branch or build a "separate but equal" medical college for African Americans. Knowing that the state could not afford to maintain two medical schools, the regents admitted African Americans to the Medical Branch (Carter Wesley, "First Negro to Enter U.T. Medical," *HI*, May 16, 1949, 1).

27. Executive dean and director of the Medical Branch to Harry Ransom, July 20, 1961, box 85, folder "Desegregation," Chancellor's Office Records.

28. Wales H. Madden to Thornton Hardie, October 6, 1961, box 85, folder "Desegregation," Chancellor's Office Records.

29. Harry Ransom to Board of Regents, November 3, 1961, box 217, folder "Segregation," Chancellor's Office Records.

30. Wales H. Madden to Thornton Hardie, October 6, 1961, box 85, folder "Desegregation," Chancellor's Office Records.

31. Gwen Jordan, "Jordan Asks Opponents to Give Negroes Chance," *DT*, October 27, 1961, 4.

32. "A Request to the Board of Regents of the University of Texas from the Human Relations Commission of the Students' Association of the University of Texas," April 26, 1961, Leo Hughes to Joseph Smiley, May 22, 1961, box VF 32B/b, folder "Desegregation/Integration," President's Office Records; Joseph Smiley to Leo Hughes, May 25, 1961, box 85, folder "Desegregation," Chancellor's Office Records.

33. "UT Adds Negro to Faculty," *Negro Labor News*, June 16, 1962, 1. A. G. McNeese Jr. to W. W. Heath, June 20, 1962, box 85, folder "Desegregation," Chancellor's Office Records.

34. Wales H. Madden to Thornton Hardie, October 6, 1961, box 85, folder "Desegregation," Chancellor's Office Records.

35. Ernest Goldstein to Harry Ransom, October 22, 1961, Wales Madden to Thornton Hardie, November 2, 1961, Harry Ransom to the Committee on Minority Groups, September 20, 1960, box 85, folder "Desegregation," Chancellor's Office Records.

36. William Boyd, "Let's Shoulder Our Responsibility," *DT*, November 7, 1961, 2; Religious Workers' Association of Texas, "A Study of Desegregation and Integration at the University of Texas," 1963, p. V-2, box 128, folder "Integration," President's Office Records.

37. "Platform Endorsed by Student Party," *DT*, February 7, 1961, 1; Beth McClimon, "Integration, Tuition Emerge as Issues," *DT*, March 15, 1961, 3.

38. "Statement from the Board of Regents of the University of Texas to the Administration for the Secretary of the General Faculty, the Students' Association, and Representatives of Other Groups Which Had Submitted Petitions and Resolutions Concerning Integration Policies at the Main University in Austin," July 22, 1961, box 85, folder "Desegregation," Chancellor's Office Records; Religious Workers' Association of Texas, "A Study of Desegregation and Integration at the University of Texas," 1963, p. II-5, box 128, folder "Integration," President's Office Records; "Press Release by

Chancellor Ransom for A.M. Papers, Including the *DT*," November 10, 1961, box 162, folder "Desegregation," Chancellor's Office Records.

39. Gwen Jordan, "Jordan Asks Opponents to Give Negroes Chance," *DT*, October 27, 1961, 4; Thornton Hardie to Harry H. Ransom, Joseph R. Smiley, and Board of Regents, September 18, 1961, box 85, folder "Desegregation," Chancellor's Office Records.

40. "Aid Drive to Begin for 400 Negroes," *DT*, February 2, 1962, 3.

41. "Freeze Out," *DT*, September 19, 1962, 3; Charmayne Marsh, "PE Department Not to Use Rink," *DT*, September 20, 1962, 1.

42. Anonymous to Logan Wilson, March 24, 1960, box 69, folder "Desegregation," Chancellor's Office Records; Carl Howard, "Desegregated, Not Integrated at University, Says Student," *DT*, November 7, 1957, 3; "Statement from the Board of Regents of the University of Texas to the Administration for the Secretary of the General Faculty, the Students' Association, and Representatives of Other Groups Which Had Submitted Petitions and Resolutions Concerning Integration Policies at the Main University in Austin," July 22, 1961, box 85, folder "Desegregation," Chancellor's Office Records.

Chapter Three. Desegregation on and off Campus

1. Ed Guinn, conversation with author, September 26, 2000.

2. Carl Huntley, conversation with author, January 17, 1999. Huntley remembered going to a UT-Iowa football game and rooting for Iowa because the school had African American football players. Jolene Hall also told me that she attended home football games "just to root for the black players on the other team" (telephone conversation with author, February 13, 2001).

3. H. Y. McCown to Logan Wilson and C. P. Boner, May 21, 1957, box 102, folder "Desegregation," Chancellor's Office Records.

4. Woodward, *Strange Career*, 117; Carl Huntley, conversation with author, January 17, 1999; H. Y. McCown to Logan Wilson and C. P. Boner, May 21, 1957, box 102, folder "Desegregation," Chancellor's Office Records; Harry Ransom to H. Y. McCown, September 15, 1956, box 53, folder "Desegregation," Chancellor's Office Records.

5. Seale, "Barbara Smith Conrad," 26; Nancy McMeans, "Barbara Smith Came to UT for Education," *DT*, May 9, 1957, 3.

6. "Eyes of Texas," 44; "Statement to the Faculty," May 14, 1957, box 102, folder "Desegregation," Chancellor's Office Records; Massa, "Conrad's Sad Song," 11; E. L. Wall, "Reprisals, Threats Bar Negro Singer," *Houston Chronicle*, May 7, 1957, 7; "Statement of the Committee of Counsel on Academic Freedom and Responsibility," May 23, 1957, box 102, folder "Desegregation," Chancellor's Office Records. College of Fine Arts officials said that that the delay in telling Smith was "deliberate" because they wanted her to get the "full benefit (in connection with a credit course she was taking in music)" of

training during rehearsals (Mark Smith, "Negro Girl Withdrawn from UT Opera Cast," *DT*, May 8, 1957, 1).

7. Mark Smith, "Negro Girl Withdrawn from UT Opera Cast," *DT*, May 8, 1957, 1; "Negro Ousted from Role as Lead in U of T Opera," *DMN*, May 8, 1957, 1; "Blames 'Starry-Eyed Liberals' in Uproar over Change in U.T. Cast," *Amarillo Daily News*, May 8, 1957, 3; "Eyes of Texas," 44.

8. "Statement to the Faculty," May 14, 1957, box 102, folder "Desegregation," Chancellor's Office Records; Nancy McMeans, "Wilson Labels Coed's Removal as UT Decision," *DT*, May 12, 1957, 1.

9. "U. of T. Faculty Split in Opinion on Negro Issue," *Fort Worth Star-Telegram*, June 19, 1957, 1; Gould and Sneed, "Without Pride or Apology," 81; "Statement to the Faculty," May 14, 1957, box 102, folder "Desegregation," Chancellor's Office Records; Raymond Orr to Logan Wilson, May 11, 1957, Mrs. Ferris Galbreath to Logan Wilson, May 11, 1957, box 30/B.b, folder "Opera Casting Incident," President's Office Records; Barbara Ray, " '47 Segregation Talks Fierier Than Today's," *DT*, December 5, 1954, 3.

10. Charles Smith to editor, *DT*, May 10, 1957, 3; "Representatives Swung in Effigy Early Thursday," *DT*, May 10, 1957, 1; "Students Start Opera Petition," *DT*, May 12, 1957, 1; "Eyes of Texas," 44; Mark S. Smith, "Young Demos, Republicans Urge Discrimination Probe," *DT*, May 9, 1957, 1.

11. Marion Butts, "U of T President Acted out of Sequence," *Dallas Express*, May 25, 1957, 6; Jim Mathis, "8 Solons Apologize to UT Negro Student," *Houston Post*, May 10, 1957, 2; T. H. McKee to C. P. Boner, May 9, 1957, Allan Metz to Logan Wilson, May 12, 1957, box 30/B.b, folder "Opera Casting Incident," President's Office Records; "Eyes of Texas," 44.

12. "Negro Ousted from Role as Lead in U of T Opera," *DMN*, May 8, 1957, 1; "Silber Fires Questions at Meeting," *DT*, June 7, 1957, 1; Gould and Sneed, "Without Pride or Apology," 82–83; "U.T. Professors Split on Negro Coed Action," *Houston Chronicle*, June 19, 1957, 4; "U. of T. Faculty Split in Opinion on Negro Issue," *Forth-Worth Star Telegram*, June 19, 1957, 4.

13. "Statement of the Committee of Counsel on Academic Freedom and Responsibility," May 23, 1957, box 102, folder "Desegregation," Chancellor's Office Records.

14. *DMN*, May 12, 1957, 12; "To Act on Hope," *DT*, May 10, 1957, 2; Carter Wesley, "UT Law Coed, Like Drama Student, Slapped by Bias," *HI*, May 18, 1957, 11; "Encourage the Barbara Smiths," *HI*, May 18, 1957, 17; Anita Brewer, "Negro Silent about Ouster," May 8, 1957, *AA*, May 8, 1957, 3.

15. Anita Brewer, "Negro Silent about Ouster," *AA*, May 8, 1957, 3; Frank N. Manitzas, "Coed Says Ouster Best for Integration," *AA*, May 9, 1957, 1; "Barbara Smith Says Education, Not Publicity, Is Her UT Aim," *HI*, May 18, 1957, 11; Nancy McMeans, "Barbara Smith Came to UT for Education," *DT*, May 9, 1957, 1.

16. "Smith Refuses Belafonte Aid; to Stay Here," *DT*, May 12, 1957, 1.

17. Ibid.; Bradford Daniel, "Polite Applause Greets Bad Opera," *DT*, May 12, 1957, 7; "Eyes of Texas," 44; James Prentice, telephone conversation with author, February 17, 2001.

18. Massa, "Conrad's Sad Song," 11; "Negro Girl Sings Recital on Campus," *AA*, November 15, 1958, B1; "Girl Singer Wins Praise of Teacher," *AA*, January 1, 1959, B1; "Barbara Smith to Study Voice," *DT*, February 3, 1959, 3; Inez Jeffery, "UT Alumna Finds Success in Singing Career," *AAS*, May 21, 1979, B1–3; "Girl Wins Praise of Teacher," *Austin Statesman*, January 28, 1959, B1.

19. Massa, "Conrad's Sad Song," 11; Candace Beaver, "Conrad Returns to UT with Honors," *DT*, June 15, 1987, 8; "Of Weeds . . . and Flowers," 1–2; Brett Polen, "Voice of Reason," *DT*, December 7, 1990, 4.

20. H. Y. McCown to Logan Wilson, May 21, 1957, box 102, folder "Desegregation," Chancellor's Office Records.

21. Jo Eickmann, "Petition to Request Change in 'Minstrels,'" *DT*, November 10, 1960, 1.

22. "Hecklers Object to 'Jim' Pickets," *DT*, November 11, 1960, 3; "Statement from Texas Cowboys," *DT*, November 11, 1960, 3; David Magrill to editor, *DT*, November 12, 1960, 3.

23. Lott, *Love and Theft*, 3; "Minstrel Complaint Endorsed by YD's," *DT*, November 11, 1960, 1; "Texas Cowboys Give Statement," *DT*, November 11, 1960, 3; Duren with Iscoe, *Overcoming*, 14.

24. Foner, *Reconstruction*; Genovese, *Roll, Jordan, Roll*; Litwack, *Been in the Storm*; Stampp, *Peculiar Institution*; "UT Slave Trade Hits Bull Market in Wild Bidding," *DT*, November 4, 1960, 1.

25. "Martin Luther King to Lecture Tonight," *DT*, March 9, 1962, 1; Jeanne Reinert, "Capacity Crowd Hears King Slam Segregationists," *DT*, March 11, 1962, 1, 8.

26. "Dr. King Speaks to Capacity Crowd at UT," *Capital City Argus*, March 16, 1962, 1; Thornton Hardie to Harry Ransom, Joseph Smiley, Board of Regents, Leon Jaworski, and Franklin Denius, October 26, 1962, box 162, folder "Desegregation," Chancellor's Office Records.

27. "Demonstrators Protest Birmingham Violence," *DT*, May 15, 1963, 1; "Austin Protesters Mourn Negro Girls," *DT*, September 18, 1963, 1; "Students Asked to Back Negroes," *DT*, May 14, 1963, 1.

28. Dave McNeely, "Cope Captures Vote: Meredith Gets OK," *DT*, September 28, 1962, 1; "UT's Telegram to Mississippi Divides Students," *DT*, October 2, 1962, 3.

29. "Students Note Period of Silence," *DT*, October 3, 1962, 1; T. S. Bailey to editor, *DT*, October 2, 1962, 3.

30. "Anxious Moments in Search of Reason," *DT*, October 21, 1962, 2.

31. Handbill passed out by Booker T. Bonner, box 4A242, folder "C" file, 1971–77, Almetris Duren Papers, CAH. Bonner was not a newcomer to the integration struggles at

UT. In 1961, he held a three-day hunger strike and sit-in in front of the Texas Theater on the Drag as a protest against racial segregation. At that time, he was a thirty-three-year-old senior with a wife and six children and studying to be a teacher. He held the protests, he said, to counteract claims that African American students were happy with segregation. "I'm here to show that they are not," Bonner said. "I may not like this movie, or I may not like the way a certain barber cuts my hair, but I would certainly like the right of choice. . . . The reason for my not eating is to show the seriousness of this matter. It is not just a stunt" (Carolyn Coker, "Bonner to Go Hungry," *DT*, March 7, 1961, 3).

32. Handbill passed out by Booker T. Bonner, box 4A242, folder "C" file, 1971–77, Duren Papers; Crawford and Keever, *John B. Connally*, 224–25.

33. Charmayne Marsh, "Sports, Band, Others Suspended from Blanket Tax; UT Quits NSA," *DT*, March 29, 1963, 1; Ed Guinn, conversation with author, September 26, 2000.

34. "Should We Kick?" *DT*, April 5, 1963, 3; Charmayne Marsh, "Athletics Council Gets B-Tax Money," *DT*, April 5, 1963, 1; Bob DuPont Jr., "Assembly Bewitched, Bothered, Bewildered by Segregation Issue," *DT*, April 10, 1963, 1.

35. Donald Hill, "Negro Student Views Problem as Emotional," *DT*, May 16, 1958, 3.

36. "Statement of the Human Relations Committee," June 28, 1957, box 2/E32 (CDL), folder "Negro Housing," Dean of Students Records; "Report on Negro Housing and Eating Facilities," September 29, 1957, box 2/E32 (CDL), folder "Integration," Dean of Students Records.

37. Religious Workers' Association of Texas, "A Study of Desegregation and Integration at the University of Texas," 1963, p. IV-3, box 128, folder "Integration," President's Office Records.

38. "UT's Protesting Pickets," *DT*, March 13, 1960, 3; Religious Workers' Association of Texas, "A Study of Desegregation and Integration at the University of Texas," 1963, p. IV-4, box 128, folder "Integration," President's Office Records.

39. Bob Moore, "150 Students Renew Lunch Room Threats," *DT*, April 26, 1960, 1; Bettye Swales, "Local Café Integration Demanded in 7 Days," *DT*, April 21, 1960, 1; Julia Salter and Bob Moore, "Students Promise Sit-Ins; Ask LBJ to Support Move," *DT*, April 27, 1960, 1.

40. "TV Help Asked for Integration," *DT*, April 28, 1960, 1; Bob Moore, "Counters Refuse Service in 'Sit-In Strike' by 150," *DT*, May 1, 1960, 1.

41. "Pickets Lauded by Austin Group," *DT*, April 28, 1960, 1; "Garwood Urges 'Hands Off' until Settlement Reached," *DT*, April 29, 1960, 1.

42. Bob Moore and Julia Salter, "Bi-Racial Student Group," *DT*, April 28, 1960, 1; "Garwood Urges 'Hands Off' Until Settlement Reached," *DT*, April 29, 1960, 1; "Pickets Lauded by Austin Group," *DT*, April 28, 1960, 1; Bob Moore, "Counters Refuse Service in 'Sit-In Strike' by 150," *DT*, May 1, 1960, 1.

43. Robbie Downing, "SA Endorses Cause of Racial Protesters," *DT*, May 5, 1960,

1; "The Firing Line," *DT*, May 5, 1960, 3; "Pro-Integration Group Organized," *DT*, November 30, 1960, 3.

44. Larry Thompson, "Two Different Views Heard on Integration," *DT*, November 30, 1960, 3; David Slider, "600 Sign Request to Integrate Cafes," *DT*, December 7, 1960, 1.

45. Larry Thompson, "Integration Group Escapes 'Y' Bombing," *DT*, November 30, 1960, 1; Bert Campbell, "Bomb Try Brings Arrest of Students," *DT*, December 1, 1960, 1; Kuhlman, "Direct Action," 554. One of the students, Bill McKnight, was later charged with murdering a twenty-one-year-old University of Texas coed, Kelley Parker, in Bandera County ("Student Arrested for Murder," *DT*, March 21, 1962).

46. Kuhlman, "Direct Action," 554.

47. Jo Eickmann, "Integration Ideology Approved by Leaders," *DT*, April 26, 1960, 4; "Negro Haircuts on SA Agenda," *DT*, May 12, 1960, 3; "SA Refused to Vote on Barbershop Issue," *DT*, May 13, 1960, 3; Karen Kirkland, "Grievance Committee to Study Barber Shops," *DT*, November 11, 1960, 3; Jim Bryant, "Merchants Worry about Customers," *DT*, December 9, 1960, 5. Barbers also refused to cut the hair of dark-skinned Mexican American students.

48. Charles Miles, conversation with author, January 22, 1998; Peggy and Leon Holland, conversation with author, November 3, 1998; Jim Bryant, "Merchants Worry about Customers," *DT*, December 9, 1960, 5; Ed Horn, "Ticket Buyers on Drag Again," *DT*, December 7, 1960, 1.

49. Ed Horn, "Ticket Buyers on Drag Again," *DT*, December 7, 1960, 1.

50. Jim Bryant, "Merchants Worry about Customers," *DT*, December 9, 1960, 5; Ed Horn, "Ticket Buyers on Drag Again," *DT*, December 7, 1960, 1; "The Firing Line," *DT*, December 20, 1960, 3; Leon Holland, conversation with author, November 3, 1998; Kuhlman, "Direct Action," 556.

51. "FACT Letter Hits Stand-Ins," *DT*, December 20, 1960, 1; James Farmer, conversation with author, February 7, 1997; Carl Huntley, conversation with author, January 17, 1999; Jim Bryant, "Merchants Worry about Customers," *DT*, December 9, 1960, 5; Bob Savage, "Bill Controls Race Sit-Ins," *DT*, April 25, 1961, 1.

52. Jim Hyatt, "Theater Protests Resume," *DT*, January 13, 1961, 1; David Slider, "Signs Carried," *DT*, January 8, 1961, 1; Leon Holland, conversation with author, November 3, 1998; Don Myers, "2 Youths Arrested in Picket Assault," *DT*, January 11, 1961, 1; "Austin Man Jailed in Picketer Assault," *DT*, January 21, 1961, 3. A judge fined the first youth, who was twenty-one, five dollars plus forty-two dollars in court costs and ordered him to serve two weeks in jail. The second youth was only sixteen, and his sentence was remanded to juvenile court.

53. Chandler Davidson, "Beware the Jabberwock," *DT*, February 8, 1961, 3.

54. Goldfield, *Black, White, and Southern*, 5. For an in-depth discussion of Elkins's slave personalities, see Elkins, *Slavery*.

55. Ed Guinn, conversation with author, September 26, 2000; Chandler Davidson, "Beware the Jabberwock," *DT*, February 8, 1961, 3; Byron A. Bassell Jr., "Compromise for Drag Theaters," *DT*, September 29, 1961, 1.

56. "Group to Picket for Integration," *DT*, March 3, 1963, 1; "Picketers Approach Paramount, State," *DT*, March 10, 1963, 1; "Integrationists Continue Action," *DT*, March 17, 1963, 1.

57. "CORE Members Asked 'to Go Fish,' " *DT*, March 17, 1963; Jim Davis, "Picketers Carry Signs at Restaurant," *DT*, May 12, 1963, 1.

58. Bruce Maxwell, "Parade to Protest Racial Discrimination," *DT*, April 4, 1963, 1; John Moore to editor, *DT*, April 25, 1963, 3.

59. Ed Guinn, conversation with author, September 26, 2000; "Barbershop to Serve Negroes," *DT*, January 20, 1963, 1; Bruce Maxwell, "Austin Hotels to Desegregate," *DT*, February 8, 1963, 1; Volma Overton, conversation with author, November 8, 1994.

60. Delta Upsilon Fraternity, *Our Record*, 8.

61. Paula Giddings and Lawrence Otis Graham, *Our Kind of People: Inside America's Black Upper Class* (New York: HarperCollins, 1999).

62. Religious Workers' Association of Texas, "A Study of Desegregation and Integration at the University of Texas," 1963, p. III-7, box 128, folder "Integration," President's Office Records.

63. Ibid., II-5, III-8; Pat Rusch, "One Big 'Cannot'—A Negro Student's Life," *DT*, December 6, 1960, 4.

64. Pat Rusch, "One Big 'Cannot'—A Negro Student's Life," *DT*, December 6, 1960, 4; Religious Workers' Association of Texas, "A Study of Desegregation and Integration at the University of Texas," 1963, box 128, folder "Integration," President's Office Records. For the formation of whiteness in the United States, see Allen, *Invention of the White Race*; Omi and Winant, *Racial Formation*; Roediger, *Wages of Whiteness*. This phenomenon did not, of course, extend to brown-skinned Mexican immigrants, who were "welcomed" (tolerated?) only when they came to do jobs that whites did not want to do. For Mexicans and Mexican Americans in Texas, see Montejano, *Anglos and Mexicans*; for black, Anglo, and Mexican workers in Texas, see Foley, *White Scourge*.

65. Jack Holland to H. Y. McCown, June 26, 1958, box 53, folder "Desegregation (9/1/56–8/31/58)," Chancellor's Office Records; Religious Workers' Association of Texas, "A Study of Desegregation and Integration at the University of Texas," 1963, p. III-7, box 128, folder "Integration," President's Office Records; "Negro Sorority, Fraternity Establish Groups on Campus," *DT*, January 15, 1960, 5.

66. Giddings, *In Search of Sisterhood*, 137; Margaret Peck to H. Y. McCown, August 5, 1958, Dorothy Gebauer to Arno Nowotny, June 23, 1958, box 53, folder "Desegregation (9/1/56–8/31/58)," Chancellor's Office Records.

67. "Negro Sorority, Fraternity Establish Groups on Campus," *DT*, January 15, 1960, 5; Margaret Peck to Arno Nowotny and H. Y. McCown, February 3, 1959, Margaret

Peck to Arno Nowotny, February 22, 1960, box CDL2/E31, folder "Negro Students," Dean of Students Records.

68. Pat Rusch, "One Big 'Cannot'—A Negro Student's Life," *DT*, December 6, 1960, 4.

69. Carl Huntley, conversation with author, January 17, 1999.

70. Jolene Hall, telephone conversation with author, February 13, 2001; Carl Huntley, conversation with author, January 17, 1999; "Greek Integration: 'Duty,' 'Unnatural,'" *DT*, November 21, 1963, 3.

71. Kaye Northcott, "UT Could Lose Aid If Greeks Don't Mix," *DT*, June 25, 1965, 1.

72. "Black Student Directory, 1974–1975," box 4A256, folder "Minority Student Services," Duren Papers.

Chapter Four. Dormitory Integration

1. Hank Ezell, "Lynda Leaves Dorms as CIC Demonstrates," *DT*, December 8, 1963, 1.

2. Carolyn Coker, "Racial Suit Postponed," *DT*, February 17, 1963, 1; "Defendants' Brief in Support of Motion to Dismiss, *Sanders v. Ransom*, Civil Action No. 1231," in box 4Ze234, folder "Race Relations and Dormitory Lawsuit, University of Texas, 1961–69," Richard Morehead Papers, CAH.

3. Carolyn Coker, "Social Policies Come to Light," *DT*, June 14, 1963, 1.

4. James P. Hart to Logan Wilson, April 1, 1953, F. C. McConnell to Logan Wilson, April 22, 1953, box 9, folder "Negroes," Chancellor's Office Records; H. Y. McCown to C. P. Boner, September 12, 1955, G. W. Landrum to Logan Wilson and C. P. Boner, September 19, 1956, box 2/E32 (CDL), folder "Negro Housing," Dean of Students Records. Davis decided to go to college out of state.

5. H. Y. McCown to C. P. Boner, September 12, 1955, G. W. Landrum to Logan Wilson and C. P. Boner, September 19, 1956, "Final Report of the Desegregation Commission of The University of Texas," June 1, 1955, box 2/E32 (CDL), folder "Negro Housing," Dean of Students Records.

6. "Minutes from the Board of Regents Meeting," July 8, 1955, box 34, folder "Desegregation," Chancellor's Office Records; "University Regents Vote to Desegregate," *Texas Observer*, July 13, 1955, 4; "UT News Release," March 8, 1956, box 34, folder "Desegregation," Chancellor's Office Records.

7. "Progress as Rapidly as Opinion Will Allow," *DT*, May 16, 1958, 3; "Negro Housing Shows Crickets and Discontent," *DT*, October 13, 1959, 5. Representatives of the university would later claim that integration of the dorms had actually begun in 1953 because the first dormitory for African American men housed "one foreign white, one Chinese, and one Hispanic" (Arno Nowotny to Margaret Peck, November 8, 1961, box 64, folder "Negro Students," President's Office Records).

8. Arno Nowotny to C. P. Boner, September 7, 1956, box 2/E32 (CDL), folder "Negro Housing," Dean of Students Records; Richard Vansteenkiste, "Negro Men Limited in Housing to San Jacinto, Brackenridge," *DT*, December 8, 1960, 3; "Bids Up, Huts Down for Cliff Courts," *DT*, September 18, 1960, 3; Leon Holland, conversation with author, November 3, 1998.

9. Arno Nowotny to C. P. Boner, September 7, 1956, G. W. Landrum to C. P. Boner, June 1, 1955, box 2/E32 (CDL), folder "Negro Housing," Dean of Students Records.

10. Arno Nowotny to C. P. Boner, September 7, 1956; G. W. Landrum to C. P. Boner, September 11, 1956, F. C. McConnell to G. W. Landrum, June 1, 1955, box 2/E32 (CDL), folder "Negro Housing," Dean of Students Records.

11. J. B. Dannenbaum to Logan Wilson, December 16, 1954, J. B. Dannenbaum to Leroy Jeffers, December 29, 1954, Arno Nowotny to J. B. Dannenbaum, December 20, 1954, box 34, folder "Desegregation," Chancellor's Office Records; Arno Nowotny to Logan Wilson, December 8, 1954, box 2/E32 (CDL), folder "Negro Housing," Dean of Students Records.

12. Arno Nowotny to Logan Wilson, December 8, 1954, H. Y. McCown to C. P. Boner, September 12, 1955, "Eliza Dee Hall flyer," box 2/E32 (CDL), folder "Negro Housing," Dean of Students Records; C. P. Boner to Almetris Duren, August 15, 1956, box 4125A, folder " 'D,' 1941–71," Duren Papers.

13. Handwritten note by Harry Ransom, November 18, 1959, box 2/E32 (CDL), folder "Negro Housing," Dean of Students Records.

14. Ibid.; F. C. McConnell to G. W. Landrum, June 1, 1955, box 2/E32 (CDL), folder "Negro Housing," Dean of Students Records.

15. "Report of the Special Committee on Student Housing, 1956," box 4A242, folder "D," Duren Papers; Harry Ransom to Logan Wilson, April 22, 1958, Harry Ransom to Dorothy Gebauer, G. W. Landrum, H. Y. McCown, and F. C. McConnell, March 21, 1958, G. W. Landrum to Logan Wilson, February 19, 1958, box 2/E32 (CDL), folder "Negro Housing," Dean of Students Records.

16. "Report of the Special Committee on Student Housing," December 4, 1959, box 4A242, folder "Housing Troubles, 1958–78," Duren Papers; Robbie Thomas to editor, *DT*, September 26, 1956, 3.

17. Logan Wilson to Nancy McMeans, October 10, 1956, "Residence Hall Bulletin," n.d., box 2/E32 (CDL), folder "Negro Housing," Dean of Students Records.

18. Logan Wilson to Nancy McMeans, October 10, 1956, "Residence Hall Bulletin," n.d., H. Y. McCown to Logan Wilson and Harry Ransom, May 9, 1958, box 2/E32 (CDL), folder "Negro Housing," Dean of Students Records; June Brewer, conversation with author, November 10, 1998.

19. "Almetris Co-op Open to 32 Negro Women," *DT*, December 8, 1960, 3; "Almetris Co-op," *AAS*, March 31, 1975, B1; "Minimum Sanitation Standards for Student Residences at the University of Texas," quoted in "A Report of the Grievance Com-

mittee of the Students Association," October 22, 1959, box 3U370, folder "Minority Concerns," Harry Ransom Papers, CAH; Center for American History, University of Texas at Austin, *Blacks at the University of Texas* (videotape, 1983), Duren Papers; Peggy Holland, conversation with author, November 3, 1998.

20. Ku Klux Klan to the Duren House, n.d., box 4A242, folder " 'C' file, 1971–77," Duren Papers; Center for American History, *Blacks at the University of Texas*.

21. Handwritten note by Harry Ransom, November 1, 1959, box 2/E32 (CDL), folder "Negro Housing," Dean of Students Records.

22. Donald Hill, "Negro Student Views Problem as Emotional," *DT*, May 16, 1958, 3.

23. "Integration Report: Housing, Eating, Recreation," *DT*, May 16, 1958, 3.

24. Ibid.; Donald Hill, "Negro Student Views Problem as Emotional," *DT*, May 16, 1958, 3.

25. "Desegregation Is Not Enough," *DT*, May 16, 1958, 3.

26. "Committee Airs Negro Students' Dorm Problems," *DT*, October 16, 1959, 1.

27. Jerry Conn, "Negro Housing Shows Crickets and Discontent," *DT*, October 13, 1959, 3.

28. Ibid.

29. "Shocking Dreariness," *DT*, October 20, 1959, 3; "Housing for Negro Women," box 41A25, folder " 'D' file, 1959–75," Duren Papers.

30. "Well-Done Housing Study," *DT*, October 29, 1959, 2; Harry Ransom to Frank Cooksey, November 20, 1959, box 2/E32 (CDL), folder "Negro Housing," Dean of Students Records.

31. Roger Shattuck to Harry Ransom, November 4, 1959, Harry Ransom to Committee on Minority Groups, December 20, 1960, box 3U370, folder "Minority Concerns," Ransom Papers.

32. Ed Guinn, conversation with author, September 26, 2000; "Whitis Dorm— Improved Negro Housing," *DT*, December 8, 1960, 2.

33. "Landrum Tells Facts of UT Negro Housing," *DT*, December 8, 1960, 3; Frank Cooksey to Logan Wilson, October 15, 1959, box 2/E32 (CDL), folder "Negro Housing," Dean of Students Records; Jim Hyatt, "Minority Groups Study Alive, Smiley Tells Faculty Council," *DT*, September 19, 1961, 1; Ed Dorn, conversation with author, December 16, 1997.

34. "Negroes Ousted from Kinsolving Cafeteria Line," *DT*, April 29, 1960, 1.

35. "Integration at U.T.," *Texas Observer*, October 21, 1960, 3–8; Religious Workers' Association of Texas, "A Study of Desegregation and Integration at the University of Texas," 1963, p. II-5, box 128, folder "Integration," President's Office Records; "Negroes Ousted from Kinsolving Cafeteria Line," *DT*, April 29, 1960, 1; Linda Maxwell to editor, *DT*, May 3, 1960, 3; Carlos Dominguez to editor, *DT*, May 5, 1960, 3.

36. See " 'The Group' Calls Protest Truce, *DT*, March 17, 1960, 1; "Race Protestors Call Talks with Wilson 'Unsatisfactory,'" *DT*, March 16, 1960, 1; "The Protest Movement," *DT*, March 16, 1960, 1; Cabinet of the Wesley Foundation to editor, *DT*, March 30, 1960, 3; "Religious Group Supports Moves for Integration," *DT*, April 5, 1960, 3; David McDonald to editor, *DT*, May 5, 1960, 3.

37. "Integration Dispute at UT," *Texas Observer*, October 17, 1961, 1; John T. Malone to Thornton Hardie, November 1, 1961, box 85, folder "Desegregation," Chancellor's Office Records; Glenn E. Barnett to Joseph Smiley, n.d., box VF 32/B.b, folder "Desegregation: Dormitory Incidents," President's Office Records; Religious Workers' Association of Texas, "A Study of Desegregation and Integration at the University of Texas," 1963, p. II-7, box 128, folder "Integration," President's Office Records.

38. Sam Houston Clinton to Thornton Hardie, November 8, 1961, box 4Ze234, folder "Race Relations and Dormitory Lawsuit," Morehead Papers; Pat Rusch, "Dorm Coeds Hear UT Housing Segregation Restrictions," *DT*, September 27, 1961, 1; "Integration at U.T.," *Texas Observer*, October 21, 1960, 3.

39. Center for American History, *Blacks at the University of Texas*; "Three Negro Girls Visit Kinsolving Lobby Area," *DT*, October 13, 1961, 1; Jolene Hall, telephone conversation with author, February 13, 2001; Jim Hyatt, "Dorm Segregation Violators to Face Disciplinary Action," *DT*, October 19, 1961, 1.

40. Pat Rusch, "Negroes Stage Sit-in at Kinsolving Dorm," *DT*, October 20, 1961, 1; "Integration Dispute at UT," *Texas Observer*, October 17, 1961, 4.

41. "Integration Dispute at UT," *Texas Observer*, October 17, 1961, 4; Glenn E. Barnett to Joseph Smiley, n.d., box VF 32/B.b, folder "Desegregation: Dormitory Incidents," President's Office Records.

42. Glenn E. Barnett to Joseph Smiley, n.d., box VF 32/B.b, folder "Desegregation: Dormitory Incidents," President's Office Records; *General Information Catalog of the Main University*, 1961–62, p. 97, box 4A242, folder "D," Duren Papers.

43. Joseph Smiley to students, October 21, 1961, box VF 32 B/b, folder "Desegregation: Dormitory Incidents, October 1961," President's Office Records; "Integration Dispute at UT," *Texas Observer*, October 17, 1961, 4.

44. " 'Read-Ins' Continue," *DT*, November 8, 1961, 1; David Lopez, "100 Demonstrate before Dormitories," *DT*, November 1, 1961, 1; Jeanne Reinert, "Olian Tells Dormitory Ruling at Student Gathering in 'Y,' " *DT*, November 1, 1961, 1.

45. Goldstein, "How LBJ Took the Bull," 14; Ernest Goldstein to William Huie, October 30, 1961, Ernest Goldstein Vertical File, Law School Archives, TLL.

46. Jim Hyatt, "Regents Decide to Go to Court," *DT*, November 12, 1961, 1; "Statement by the Board of Regents," box 85, folder "Desegregation," Chancellor's Office Records; Leon Holland, conversation with author, November 3, 1998.

47. "Law Professors Warned on Suit," *DMN*, November 12, 1961, A1; Richard M. Morehead, "UT Selects Counsel in Dormitory Suit," *DMN*, December 7, 1961, 1; Dave Crossley, "Law Petition Hits Regents," *DT*, December 5, 1961, 1; Martha Tipps, "UT Regent Chairman Clears Board's Stand to Law School Dean," *DT*, December 13, 1961, 1.

48. Ernest Goldstein, conversation with author, November 4, 1997; Goldstein, "How LBJ Took the Bull," 14; Ernest Goldstein to William Huie, October 30, 1961, Goldstein Vertical File, Law School Archives, TLL.

49. Douglass J. Wilde to A. G. McNeese Jr., May 17, 1962, box 85, folder "Desegregation," Chancellor's Office Records; Anne Apel and Larry Lee, "Integration Stand 'Catalyst' in Loss," *DT*, June 29, 1962, 1.

50. Carolyn Coker, "Integration Suit Lawyers Agree to Month Delay," *DT*, June 11, 1963, 1; "UT States Grounds for Dismissal in Dormitory Integration Suit," *DT*, June 28, 1963, 1.

51. *Sanders, et al., v. Ransom, et al.*, Plaintiffs' Request for Admissions of Fact, January 1, 1963; Jean Kamins Knaiger to Harry Ransom, November 11, 1963, box 102, folder "Desegregation," Chancellor's Office Records.

52. Carolyn Coker, "Social Policies Come to Light," *DT*, June 14, 1963, 1; W. W. Heath to Board of Regents, May 12, 1964, box 102, folder, "Desegregation," Chancellor's Office Records.

53. Jack Holland to Norman Hackerman, September 18, 1964, box 4A260, folder "Housing 1958–75," Duren Papers; "Off-Campus Housing Report to Come Later," *DT*, December 12, 1964, 3.

54. Margaret Peck to staff, May 28, 1965, Almetris Duren's notes to self, June 2, 1965, Norman Hackerman to deans, chairs, and other administrators, June 1, 1964, box 4A242, folder "UT Dormitories Integrated, Official Statement, 1964," Duren Papers; Anita Brewer, "Last Racial Wall at UT Falls: Dorms Integrated," *AAS*, May 17, 1964, A1; "Heath Sums up Texas," *DT*, January 8, 1965, 1; "Regents Complete UT Desegregation," *DT*, May 18, 1964, 1.

55. F. C. McConnell to James H. Colvin, May 19, 1964, box VF 32B/b, folder "Desegregation," President's Office Records; Jane Greer to F. C. McConnell, June 24, 1965, box 34, folder "Desegregation," Chancellor's Office Records; Louise Chilton Bryan to Board of Regents, May 21, 1964, Addie Barlow Frazier to W. W. Heath, February 9, 1964, box 102, folder "Desegregation," Chancellor's Office Records.

56. Jack Holland to Norman Hackerman, June 4, 1965, box 4A260, folder "Housing 1958–75," Duren Papers; Charmayne Marsh, "Loss of Whitis Puts Negroes Back in Bind," *DT*, March 10, 1965, 1; Lucy Horton, "Crisis Still Looms in Negro Housing," *DT*, November 13, 1966, 1.

57. Lucy Horton, "Crisis Still Looms in Negro Housing," *DT*, November 13, 1966, 1; "UT Dorms Integrated after Long Struggle," *DT*, May 5, 1972, 5.

Chapter Five. Black Integration of the Athletic Program

1. Jack Keever, "Black Alumnus Airs Views on UT Racism," *DT*, November 21, 1972, 7; Bert Adams, "History in the Making," *Capital City Argus*, April 2, 1962, 1; Bill Little, "Texas Southern Dominates Relays," *DT*, April 8, 1962, 7.

2. "Interim Report of the Committee on Minority Groups," February 1961, "A Request to the Board of Regents of the University of Texas from the Human Relations Commission of the Students' Association of the University of Texas," December 6, 1958, box 85, folder "Desegregation," Chancellor's Office Records; Harry Ransom to H. Y. McCown, September 15, 1956, Logan Wilson to H. Y. McCown, "Confidential Memo Concerning the Participation of Negro Students in Intercollegiate Athletics," October 13, 1956, box 53, folder "Desegregation (9/1/56–8/31/58)," Chancellor's Office Records.

3. Fitzpatrick, *And the Walls Came Tumbling Down*, 46–47, 118.

4. James P. Hart to Board of Regents, May 20, 1953, box VF 20/B.a., folder "Sweatt Case 1946," President's Office Records; Bobby Carter to Logan Wilson, April 20, 1953, box 9, folder "Negroes," Chancellor's Office Records; "Meeting of the Board of Regents, May 29, 1953," box 9, folder "Negroes," Chancellor's Office Records.

5. Fitzpatrick, *And the Walls Came Tumbling Down*, 45; Olsen, "The Black Athlete: A Shameful Story," 17.

6. Betty Anne Thedford to Logan Wilson, October 16, 1956, box 53, folder "Desegregation (9/1/56–8/31/58)," Chancellor's Office Records; "Record of Understanding with President Clement French, of Washington State College, Concerning the Football Game Scheduled at the University of Texas between That Institution and This One on October 2, 1954, in Austin," box 34, folder "Desegregation," Chancellor's Office Records.

7. Betty Anne Thedford to Logan Wilson, October 16, 1956, box 53, folder "Desegregation (9/1/56–8/31/58)," Chancellor's Office Records; "Record of Understanding with President Clement French, of Washington State College, Concerning the Football Game Scheduled at the University of Texas between That Institution and This One on October 2, 1954, in Austin," box 34, folder "Desegregation," Chancellor's Office Records; Pennington, *Breaking the Ice*, 116.

8. Leroy Jeffers to Tom Sealy, August 25, 1954, H. Y. McCown to Marion G. Ford Jr., July 23, August 16, 1954, J. L. Shanklin to H. Y. McCown, August 25, 1954, box VF 20/B.a., folder "Negroes in Colleges 1939–," President's Office Records; Pennington, *Breaking the Ice*, 116; "Ford Abandons UT Bid to Enter Wiley College," *AA*, September 10, 1954, B1.

9. Sterling Holloway to Logan Wilson, September 13, 1958, box 85, folder "Desegregation," Chancellor's Office Records; Carter, "Negro in College Athletics," 208; *Howard University Hilltop*, April 29, 1924, 2, box 4A242, folder "D," Duren Papers.

10. Logan Wilson to C. P. Boner and H. Y. McCown, December 9, 1955, box 85, folder "Negroes," President's Office Records. For an excellent discussion of the evolution of the black "superathlete" and white perceptions of him, see Hoberman, *Darwin's Athletes*. Among other things, Hoberman argues that some whites began to change their perceptions about the talents of black athletes following Jesse Owens's success in the 1936 Olympics, but not until Jackie Robinson integrated Major League Baseball in 1947 did the barrier preventing whites and blacks from competing together begin to fall.

11. H. Y. McCown to Logan Wilson and C. P. Boner, September 19, 1956, box 53, folder "Desegregation," Chancellor's Office Records.

12. Lanier Cox to C. P. Boner, July 2, 1956, box CDL2/E32, folder "Integration, 1961–62," Dean of Students Records; Pat Rusch, "One Big 'Cannot'—A Negro Student's Life," *DT*, December 6, 1960, 5.

13. "Baylor Due Protest on Negro's Case," *Fort Worth Star-Telegram*, November 8, 1958, A3; W. R. White to Logan Wilson, November 14, 1958, Logan Wilson to W. R. White, November 15, 1958, H. Y. McCown to W. J. Hall, November 17, 1958, box 69, folder "Desegregation," Chancellor's Office Records.

14. Pennington, *Breaking the Ice*, 116; Pat Rusch, "One Big 'Cannot'—A Negro Student's Life," *DT*, December 6, 1960, 5; Ed Olle to H. Y. McCown, October 21, 1959, box 9, folder "Negroes," Chancellor's Office Records. In 1958, Ford graduated from UT with a degree in chemical engineering. He then went on to receive a master's and later a doctorate in dental science. In 1963, Ford was chosen as a Fulbright Scholar, and he did postgraduate work at the University of Bonn in West Germany. He returned to Houston and opened a dental practice.

15. Clinton A. Givans to Dana X. Bible, October 3, 1956, Dana X. Bible to Clinton A. Givans, October 5, 1956, H. Y. McCown to C. P. Boner, October 11, 1956, box CDL2/E32, folder "Integration, 1961–62," Dean of Students Records.

16. H. Y. McCown to C. P. Boner, October 11, 1956, box CDL2/E32, folder "Integration, 1961–62," Dean of Students Records.

17. Dana X. Bible to C. P. Boner, September 11, 1956, G. W. Landrum to Harry Ransom, October 18, 1957, box 53, folder "Desegregation," Chancellor's Office Records.

18. Sterling Holloway to Logan Wilson, September 13, 1958, Sterling Holloway to M. T. Harrington, August 31, 1960, box 85, folder "Desegregation," Chancellor's Office Records; Henderson, "Negro Athlete," 78.

19. H. Y. McCown to Logan Wilson, November 10, 1959, box CDL2/E32, folder "Integration, 1961–62," Dean of Students Records.

20. Sterling Holloway to M. T. Harrington, August 31, 1960, box 85, folder "Deseg-

regation," Chancellor's Office Records; Sterling Holloway to John S. Redditt, June 28, 1960, box 102, folder "Desegregation," Chancellor's Office Records; "To Do a Little Better," 54.

21. Sterling Holloway to M. T. Harrington, August 31, 1960, box 85, folder "Desegregation," Chancellor's Office Records.

22. M. T. Harrington to Sterling Holloway, September 7, 1960, J. Wayne Reitz to Harry Ransom, October 31, 1961, O. C. Aderhold to Harry Ransom, November 1, 1961, Troy H. Middleton to Harry Ransom, October 27, 1961, A. D. Holt to Harry Ransom, November 14, 1961, George L. Cross to Harry Ransom, October 28, 1961, box 85, folder "Desegregation," Chancellor's Office Records; Pennington, *Breaking the Ice*, 136.

23. "Coffey Prefers Texas," *AAS*, March 5, 1960, C1; "Guess They Know What They're Doing," *DT*, March 7, 1961, 7. Coffey decided to attend the University of Washington, where he had much success on the football team.

24. "Committee Studies Athletic Integration," *DT*, April 11, 1961, 1; Executive Board of Campus Interracial Committee to Board of Regents, John Connally, and attorney for UT in dorm suit, November 4, 1961, box 4124A, folder "Integration of Housing, 1959–81," Duren Papers; Debbie Howell, "Sports Integration OK'd by Assembly," *DT*, May 12, 1961, 1.

25. "Introductory Statement and Resolution on Racial Desegregation from the General Faculty," May 9, 1961, box 85, folder "Desegregation," Chancellor's Office Records; Executive Board, Campus Interracial Committee, to Board of Regents, September 27, 1963, box 102, folder "Desegregation," Chancellor's Office Records; "Athletic Integration Readied for Vote," *DT*, October 12, 1961, 1; Jim Hyatt, "Athletic Integration Referendum Goes before Student Body Today," *DT*, October 25, 1961, 1.

26. Mody C. Boatright to John Burdine, December 18, 1961, box 85, folder "Desegregation," Chancellor's Office Records.

27. Ibid.; Thornton Hardie to Wales H. Madden Jr., October 9, 1961, "Interim Report of the Committee on Minority Groups," February 1961, "Statement from the Athletic Council," November 17, 1961, box 85, folder "Desegregation," Chancellor's Office Records; "End of Race Ban Asked in Sports," *DT*, January 1, 1962, 1.

28. Sterling Holloway to John Redditt, February 4, 1962, box 85, folder "Desegregation," Chancellor's Office Records; Wales Madden Jr., telephone conversation with author, November 8, 2000.

29. Bertha Means, telephone conversation with author, September 20, 2000.

30. "Royal Sees Meeting on UT Integration," *DMN*, November 12, 1963, 12; "Royal Says Negro Athletes 'Welcome,' " *DMN*, November 19, 1963, 10.

31. "SWC Action for Negroes Draws Near," *DMN*, November 19, 1963, 10; "TCU

Integrates Most Facilities," *DT*, January 28, 1964, 3; "Baylor Athletics Open to Negroes," *DT*, November 24, 1964, 6; "Houston Follows Texas' Lead, Integrates Athletic Program," *DT*, November 20, 1963, 6.

32. Seaborn Jones to Harry Ransom, January 2, 1964, E. J. Schutze to W. W. Heath, November 14, 1963, box 102, folder "Desegregation," Chancellor's Office Records; Ira Carroll to Joseph Smiley, January 4, 1964, box VF 32B/b, folder "Desegregation/Integration," President's Office Records; "A Sensible Move," *DT*, November 21, 1963, 2.

33. Bill Little, "Royal Says All Sports Now Open to Negroes," *DT*, November 10, 1963, 1; A. Rogers Mielly to Harry Ransom, November 19, 1963, Harry Ransom to A. Rogers Mielly, December 16, 1963, box 102, folder "Desegregation," Chancellor's Office Records.

34. "Two Negro Sprinters in Track Workouts," *DT*, December 4, 1963, 1; Pennington, *Breaking the Ice*, 134.

35. Pennington, *Breaking the Ice*, 120, 84–85, 92. LeVias was not the first African American to play in an SWC football game. John Westbrook broke the color barrier on September 10, 1966, one week before LeVias appeared in a game. Westbrook, who played for Baylor University, said he was miserable and lonely at Baylor and twice thought about committing suicide. He died at age thirty-five of a massive heart attack ("First Black SWC Player Dead at 35," *DMN*, December 19, 1983, 16).

36. W. W. Heath to Thornton Hardie, November 5, 1962, box 162, folder "Desegregation," Chancellor's Office Records; Karen Elliot and Larry Upshaw, "All-White Sports Decried by NAP," *DT*, May 12, 1967, 1; Bill Little, telephone conversation with author, November 9, 2000.

37. Lucy Horton, "Negro Group Doubts Coach," *DT*, May 14, 1967, 1; Karen Elliot and Larry Upshaw, "All-White Sports Decried by NAP," *DT*, May 12, 1967, 1; Sharon West, "Royal Discredits NAP Complaints," *DT*, May 14, 1967, 1.

38. "Longhorns Recruit First Negro Player," *DT*, February 15, 1968, 1; Bill Little, telephone conversation with author, November 9, 2000; Pennington, *Breaking the Ice*, 126. Although Curry became the first African American to wear a football varsity uniform, he never made the traveling squad and was not listed on the 1968 roster. He quit the team and left the school before the 1969 spring semester.

39. Pennington, *Breaking the Ice*, 126; Jack Keever, "Black Alumnus Airs Views on UT Racism," *DT*, November 21, 1972, 7; Charles Pace, telephone conversation with author, November 10, 2000; Bill Little, telephone conversation with author, November 9, 2000.

40. Banks, *Darrell Royal Story*, 155, 161; Reid, "Coach Royal Regrets," 250; "Six Black Football Players Charge Racism," *Capital City Argus*, November 24–December

1, 1972, 1–2; Jack Keever, "Royal Fights Racist Image," *DT*, November 16, 1972, 8. Top black athletes who left Texas to play college football included Bubba Smith, Gregg Pruitt, Tody Smith, and Joe Washington; they played for such college football giants as Michigan State, UCLA, Oklahoma, Purdue, and Notre Dame (Pennington, *Breaking the Ice*, 130).

41. Banks, *Darrell Royal Story*, 154.

42. Toback, "Longhorns and Longhairs," 70.

43. Bryan Martin, "Black Problems," *DT*, March 12, 1970, 3.

44. Roosevelt Leaks, conversation with author, July 25, 1998; Jack Keever, "UT Must 'Pay Price' for Years of Racism," *DT*, November 14, 1972, 7.

45. Jack Keever, "UT Must 'Pay Price' for Years of Racism," *DT*, November 14, 1972, 7; " 'Money' a Big Factor in Recruiting Blacks," *DT*, November 15, 1972, 7; "Royal Fights Racist Image," *DT*, November 16, 1972, 8; "UT Racist Image Puzzles Royal," *DT*, November 17, 1972, 10.

46. Miguel McKay, conversation with author, February 27, 2001; Donnie Little, conversation with author, November 14, 2000; Brian Jones, conversation with author, November 7, 2000. Founded in 1957, the Longhorn Men's Hall of Honor represents "one of the most cherished athletic traditions at the University of Texas at Austin." Inductees comprise "a distinguished circle of individuals who have made a distinct and lasting contribution to The University," according to the Hall of Honor plaque in Belmont Hall. Few athletes of color have been so honored. As of 2005, only fifteen African Americans and two Mexican Americans had been inducted into the Hall of Honor. Reeves was honored in November 2000. Although forgotten after his death, Reeves was quite popular and well respected during his tenure with the UT football team. After Reeves suffered a stroke while working the Texas A & M football game, students collected money to pay for his medical bills, although he died shortly thereafter. The *Houston Post* called Reeves "the University's most enduring character connected with football" (Hall of Honor plaque, November 2000, Belmont Hall, University of Texas at Austin).

Chapter Six. Desegregation from 1964 to the Present

1. Volma Overton, conversation with author, November 8, 1994.

2. "Baez Appears, Aiding Protest," *DT*, April 3, 1964, 1.

3. "Personal Report by Richard M. Morehead, Austin Bureau of the News," November 22, 1965, box 3F279, folder "Classified Files: College Enrollment Including Negroes, 1965–67," Morehead Papers; Rosetta Williams to Peter Flawn, January 20, 1969, box 4A256, folder "Miscellaneous, 1960–77," Duren Papers.

4. Elizabeth Wellborn to James Duncan, June 9, 1971, box CDL2/E36, folder "Minority Affairs Information," Dean of Students Records; Debbie Hay and Henry Wells,

"Social Life Called Deficient," *DT*, April 14, 1971, 3; "Boney: Untiring, Energetic," *DT*, April 23, 1973, 3; Joyce Herbert, conversation with author, July 25, 1998.

5. "Proposal for Afro-American Studies Room," October 1969, box 4A270, folder "Afro-American Studies Room," Duren Papers. The regents had rejected a previous proposal submitted by students because the Afro-American Studies Room would have been open only to African American students. The Texas Union had a separate Mexican American Culture Room. Like the Afro-American Studies Room (later renamed the Afro-American Culture Room), the Mexican American Culture Room served as a place where Mexican American students could meet and feel comfortable. The room was also used for receptions, committee meetings, and other cultural events. Because of the special nature of the rooms, neither could be used as the offices of any university or nonuniversity organization or group ("Proposal for Afro-American Studies Room," October 1969, box 4A270, folder "Afro-American Studies Room," Duren Papers).

6. Joan McAfee, "Anitha Mitchell . . . Outstanding at UT," *DT*, July 17, 1956, 5; "Forty Acres Club to Be Segregated," *DT*, February 8, 1961, 1; "Forty Acres Club: Too Exclusive," *DT*, February 10, 1961, 1.

7. Anne Apel and Larry Lee, "Integration Stand 'Catalyst' in Loss," *DT*, June 29, 1962, 1; "Silent Scholars to Speak Out," *DT*, March 1, 1963, 1; "UT Students Picket Club for Bigotry," *DMN*, July 31, 1962, A1.

8. Joseph Jones to editor, *DT*, February 27, 1964, 3; "Committee of 9 Releases Letter on Faculty Club," *DT*, October 28, 1962, 1; "Full Text of the Report Issued by the Special Committee on Faculty Club Facilities," *DT*, October 28, 1962, 3.

9. "Silent Scholars to Speak Out," *DT*, March 1, 1963, 1; J. Frank Dobie to editor, *DT*, October 5, 1962, 3; Mary Oles, "Club Stays Comment about Faculty's Stand," *DMN*, March 6, 1963, 11; Charmayne Marsh, "40 Acres Club Serves Negro Newspaperman," January 7, 1964, 1; "Half a Loaf," *DT*, January 8, 1964, 2.

10. Alfred Schild to Harry Ransom, Frank Erwin, and Board of Regents, February 11, 1964, box 64, folder "Desegregation," Chancellor's Office Records.

11. Ed Guinn, conversation with author, September 26, 2000; Vincent R. DiNino to Arno Nowotny, September 12, 1956, box 85, folder "Desegregation," Chancellor's Office Records.

12. Ed Guinn, conversation with author, September 26, 2000.

13. "Negro Playing in 'Show Band,'" *DT*, February 5, 1964, 1; Ed Guinn, conversation with author, September 26, 2000.

14. Richard M. Morehead, "UT Names First Negro to Faculty," *DMN*, May 12, 1964, 1; "Paper by Daphne Lambert for Professor Juliet E. Walker," spring 1979, box 41A20, folder "Negroes," Duren Papers.

15. Richard M. Morehead, "UT Names First Negro to Faculty," *DMN*, May 12, 1964, 1; Carolyn Coker, "Perry Eyes Calm Future," *DT*, May 12, 1964, 3; "House Honors Black UT Prof," *San Antonio Express*, February 22, 1971, B1. Carlos Castañeda graduated

from the University of Texas Phi Beta Kappa with a bachelor's degree in history in 1921. After receiving a master's degree, Castañeda left the University of Texas to teach Spanish at the College of William and Mary in Williamsburg, Virginia. He eventually returned to UT and earned a doctorate in history in 1933. Castañeda worked as a librarian at the Latin American Collection until 1946, after which he devoted his time to teaching and numerous scholarly projects ("Speech of President Lorene Rogers at the Ceremony That Dedicated the PCL to Perry and Castañeda," November 19, 1977, "UT News Release," August 24, 1977, box 4A247, folder "Perry-Castañeda Library, 1976–77," Duren Papers).

16. Carmichael and Hamilton, *Black Power*; "Pamphlet from 'The Blacks' and Mexican-American Youth Organization, n.d., box 4A270, folder "The Blacks," Duren Papers; Duren with Iscoe, *Overcoming*, 15; Judy Burton, "Negroes Evaluate Black Power," *DT*, October 26, 1966, 3.

17. "Black Student Directory, 1974–1975," box 4A256, folder "Minority Student Services," Duren Papers.

18. Christina Smith, "Former Students, Profs, and Lawyers Remember: Doomed to Repeat It?" *Austin Chronicle*, February 6, 1998, 26; "New Course Tours American Negro Life," *DT*, October 4, 1968, 3.

19. "Hon. John G. Tower of Texas, in the Senate of the United States, Tuesday, Oct. 1, 1968," box 3J426, folder "Correspondence: Lecture Series, Oct.–Dec. 1968," Lewis L. Gould Papers, CAH.

20. Dr. William Goetzmann, conversation with author, November 30, 2000; "Report to the Faculty Council by the Faculty Ad Hoc Committee on Ethnic Studies," May 26, 1969, box CDL2/E36, folder "Special Programs and Ethnic Affairs," Dean of Students Records; Duren with Iscoe, *Overcoming*, 18.

21. Flyer for "The Blacks," February 17, 1972, box 4A269, folder "The Blacks," Duren Papers; John Warfield, conversation with author, April 14, 1997.

22. "The University of Texas at Austin News and Information Service, Press Release," January 14, 1974, box 4A256, folder "Blacks: Integration," Duren Papers.

23. Vincent Woodard, conversation with author, December 19, 2000; Katherine Kaliski, conversation with author, December 19, 2000; Stephen Ward, conversation with author, March 29, 2001.

24. Trudie Preciphs to James Duncan, December 9, 1971, box CDL2/E36, folder "Special Programs and Ethnic Affairs, Project Info," Dean of Students Records.

25. Ibid.; "Results of Questionnaire on Racial Awareness Program," January 31, 1972, "Report to the Faculty Council by the Faculty Ad Hoc Committee on Ethnic Studies," May 26, 1969, box CDL2/E36, folder "Special Programs and Ethnic Affairs, Project Info," Dean of Students Records; Cynthia Knight, "Regents Lack Understanding of PEO Plans, Claims Panel," *DT*, November 5, 1969, 3; "PEO Facts and Figures," October 30,

1969, box 4A247, folder "Project PEO and CLEO, 1969–73," Duren Papers; Duren with Iscoe, *Overcoming*, 20.

26. Mark Morrison, "Regent Erwin Supports Project Info while Defending Board's PEO Stand," *DT*, August 22, 1969, 1. PEO's total financial expenditure was approximately $38,000, including private and matching federal monies. The university appropriated no direct funds for PEO except for two part-time and one full-time staff members ("PEO Facts and Figures," October 30, 1969, "Support PEO," n.d., box 4A247, folder "Project PEO and CLEO, 1969–73," Duren Papers).

27. Mark Morrison, "Regent Erwin Supports Project Info while Defending Board's PEO Stand," *DT*, August 22, 1969, 1; "Death of PEO," *DT*, August 12, 1969, 1; Ron Hubbard to editor, *DT*, November 3, 1969, 3.

28. Mark Morrison, "Regent Erwin Supports Project Info while Defending Board's PEO Stand," *DT*, August 22, 1969, 1; "Death of PEO," *DT*, August 12, 1969, 1; Ron Hubbard to editor, *DT*, November 3, 1969, 3; Ernie Haywood, "PEO Support Advocated," *DT*, November 3, 1969, 3.

29. Mark Morrison, "Regent Erwin Supports Project Info while Defending Board's PEO Stand," *DT*, August 22, 1969, 1; Rick Keeton, "PEO Supporters Now Hope New Program Given a Chance," *AAS*, November 2, 1969, 1. Elizabeth Wellborn, PEO coordinator, described a student as financially disadvantaged when his or her family's income fell below a certain level, academically deficient when his or her SAT score fell below 800, and culturally deprived when he or she had no vision of education beyond high school (Cynthia Knight, "Regents Lack Understanding of PEO Plans, Claims Panel," *DT*, November 5, 1969, 1). By 2000, university administrators vowed to end the program because too many students were being admitted into and completing the summer program, thus making the freshman class too large (Mark Roser, "Regents to End Provisional," *AAS*, September 5, 2000, B1); however, the program still exists.

30. "Report to the Faculty Council by the Faculty Ad Hoc Committee on Ethnic Studies," May 26, 1969, box CDL2/E36, folder "Special Programs and Ethnic Affairs," Dean of Students Records; Elizabeth Wellborn to counselor at Abernathy High School in Abernathy, Texas, August 3, 1971, "Minutes of Meeting of the Board of Regents, the University of Texas System," September 12, 1969, box CDL2/E36, folder "Project Info," Dean of Students Records.

Epilogue

1. A. Phillips Brooks, "Suit Challenges UT Law School Admissions Policy," *AAS*, September 30, 1992, A1.

2. Mary Ann Roser, "Citing Hopwood Ruling, UT Ends Faculty Minority-Hiring Program," *AAS*, January 7, 1999, A1.

3. See *Podberesky v. Kirwan*; California Proposition 209 (1996); *Adarand v. Pena*, in which the Supreme Court held that the awarding of federal construction contracts must not rely on even "benign" racial classifications or classifications intended to assist underrepresented minorities; *Shaw v. Reno*, in which the Supreme Court held that districting boundaries that cannot be explained on grounds other than racial ones would be presumptively unconstitutional; and *J. A. Croson Company v. J. A. Guy, Inc., et al.*, in which the Supreme Court ruled that set-asides for minority contractors violated the Fourteenth Amendment.

4. Sara Hebel, " 'Percent Plans' Don't Add Up," *Chronicle of Higher Education*, March 21, 2003, A24.

5. Ibid.; Aarti Shah, "Race Issues Influence UT Community," *DT*, February 7, 2002, 1–3.

6. At the same time it decided *Grutter v. Bollinger*, however, the Court struck down the University of Michigan's affirmative action policy with regard to undergraduate admissions in *Gratz v. Bollinger*.

7. Mary Ann Roser, "No Grudge for New Alumni Chief," *AAS*, September 4, 1999, B5. John Chase was the first African American licensed as an architect in the state of Texas, appointed to the U.S. Commission of Fine Arts, and named a University of Texas Distinguished Alumnus. In July 1998 Chase also became the first African American president of the university's Ex-Students' Association.

Selected Bibliography

Archival and Manuscript Sources

Center for American History, University of Texas at Austin.
  Almetris Duren Papers. Lewis L. Gould Papers. Richard Morehead Papers. Harry Ransom Papers. University of Texas Chancellor's Office Records. University of Texas Dean of Students Records. University of Texas President's Office Records. Dudley Woodward Papers.
Harry Ransom Center, University of Texas at Austin.
  J. Frank Dobie Manuscript Collection.
Tarlton Law Library, University of Texas at Austin.
  Ernest Goldstein Vertical File. *Hopwood v. State of Texas.* W. Page Keeton Papers. Charles T. McCormick Papers. NAACP Papers. Millard H. Ruud Papers (unprocessed). *Sweatt v. Painter.* Texas State University for Negroes. Students and Law Classes.

Legal Cases and Judicial Decisions

Adarand v. Pena, 515 U.S. 200 (1995).

Brown v. Board of Education I, 347 U.S. 483 (1954).

Brown v. Board of Education II, 349 U.S. 294 (1955).

Cheryl J. Hopwood, et al., v. State of Texas, et al., No. A-92-CA-563-SS (1994).

Cheryl J. Hopwood, et al., v. State of Texas, et al., No. 94–50569 (1996).

Gaines v. Canada, 305 U.S. 337 (1938).

Gratz v. Bollinger, U.S. 539 (2003).

Grutter v. Bollinger, U.S. 539 (2003).

J. A. Croson Company v. J. A. Guy, Inc., et al., 525 U.S. 871 (1998).

Leroy Sanders, et al., v. Harry H. Ransom, Chancellor, et al., Civil Action No. 1231.

Loans v. State, 50 Tenn. 287 (1871).

McLaurin v. Oklahoma State Regents, 339 U.S. 637 (1950).

Plessy v. Ferguson, 163 U.S. 537 (1896).

Podberesky v. Kirwan, 514 U.S. 1128 (1995).

Shaw v. Reno, 509 U.S. 630 (1993).

Sweatt v. Painter, 339 U.S. 629 (1950).

Periodicals

Amarillo Daily News
Austin American
Austin American Capitol
Austin American-Statesman
Austin Capital City Argus
Austin Chronicle
Austin Daily Texan
Austin Texas Ranger
Boston Patriot Ledger
Dallas Express
Dallas Morning News
Dallas News
El Paso Herald Post
Fort Worth Star-Telegram
Houston Chronicle
Houston Informer
Houston Post
Negro Labor News
New York Times

San Antonio Express
Time
Washington Times

Secondary Sources

Aleinikoff, T. Alexander. "A Case for Race-Consciousness." *Columbia Law Review* 91 (1991): 1060–1125.

Allen, Theodore. *The Invention of the White Race: Racial Oppression and Social Control.* London: Verso, 1994.

Allport, Gordon. *The Nature of Prejudice.* New York: Perseus, 1954.

Anderson, James D. *The Education of Blacks in the South, 1860–1935.* Chapel Hill: University of North Carolina Press, 1988.

Ansley, Frances Lee. "Stirring the Ashes: Race, Class, and the Future of Civil Rights Scholarship." *Cornell Law Review* 74 (1989): 993–1077.

Ayers, Edward. *The Promise of the New South: Life after Reconstruction.* New York: Oxford University Press, 1993.

Baade, Hans W. "Law at Texas: The Roberts-Gould Era (1883–1983)." *Southwestern Historical Quarterly* 86 (October 1982): 161–96.

Balibar, Etienne, and Immanuel Wallerstein. *Race, Nation, Class: Ambiguous Identities.* London: Verso, 1992.

Balkin, Jack M. *What "Brown v. Board of Education" Should Have Said: The Nation's Top Legal Experts Rewrite America's Landmark Civil Rights Decision.* New York: New York University Press, 2002.

Banks, Jimmy. *The Darrell Royal Story.* Austin, Tex.: Eakin, 1998.

Banton, Michael. *Promoting Racial Harmony.* New York: Cambridge University Press, 1985.

Bardaglio, Peter W. "Shameful Matches: Regulation of Interracial Sex and Marriage." In *Sex, Love, Race: Crossing Boundaries in North American History,* edited by Martha Hodes. New York: New York University Press, 1999.

Barksdale, E. C. "The Power Structure and Southern Gubernatorial Conservatism." In *Essays on Recent Southern Politics,* edited by Harold M. Hollingsworth. Arlington: University of Texas Press for the University of Texas at Arlington, 1979.

Barr, Alwyn. *Black Texans: A History of Negroes in Texas, 1528–1971.* Austin, Tex.: Jenkins, 1985.

Barr, Alwyn, and Robert A. Calvert, eds. *Black Leaders: Texans for Their Times.* Austin: Texas State Historical Association, 1981.

Barrera, Mario. *Race and Class in the Southwest: A Theory of Racial Inequality.* Notre Dame, Ind.: University of Notre Dame Press, 1980.

Barrett, Russell H. *Integration at Ole Miss.* Chicago: Quadrangle, 1965.

Barzun, Jacques. *Race: A Study in Modern Superstition.* New York: Harcourt, Brace, 1937.

Bauböck, Rainer, Agnes Heller, and Aristide R. Zolberg, eds. *The Challenge of Diversity: Integration and Pluralism in Societies of Immigration.* London: Ashgate, 1996.

Beals, Melba Pattillo. *White Is a State of Mind: A Memoir.* New York: Berkeley, 2000.

Bell, Derrick. *And We Are Not Saved: The Elusive Quest for Racial Prejudice.* San Francisco: Harper, 1989.

———. *Faces at the Bottom of the Well: The Permanence of Racism.* New York: Basic Books, 1993.

———. *Race, Racism, and American Law.* 4th ed. Gaithersburg, Md.: Aspen Law and Business, 2000.

———. *Silent Covenants: "Brown v. Board of Education" and the Unfulfilled Hopes for Racial Reform.* New York: Oxford University Press, 2004.

Bender, Thomas. *Community and Social Change in America.* New Brunswick, N.J.: Rutgers University Press, 1978.

Bendix, Richard. *Nation-Building and Citizenship: Studies of Our Changing Social Order.* Berkeley: University of California Press, 1976.

Bennett, Michael J. *When Dreams Came True: The GI Bill and the Making of Modern America.* Washington, D.C.: Brassey's, 1996.

Berry, Margaret Catherine. *UT Austin: Tradition and Nostalgia.* San Antonio, Tex.: Marion Koogler McNay Art Museum, 1983.

———. *UT History 101: Highlights in the History of the University of Texas at Austin.* Austin, Tex.: Eakin, 1997.

Bhabha, Homi K. *The Location of Culture.* New York: Routledge, 2004.

Blauner, Robert. *Racial Oppression in America.* New York: HarperCollins, 1972.

Bode, Winston. *Portrait of Pancho: The Life of a Great Texan, J. Frank Dobie.* Austin, Tex.: Pemberton, 1965.

Bohn, Frank. "The Ku Klux Klan Interpreted." *American Journal of Sociology* 50 (1925): 385–407.

Brandt, Nat. *Harlem at War: The Black Experience in World War II.* Syracuse, N.Y.: Syracuse University Press, 1996.

Bullock, Henry Allen. *A History of Negro Education in the South, from 1619 to the Present.* Cambridge: Harvard University Press, 1967.

Bulmer, Martin, and John Solomos, eds. *Researching Race and Racism.* New York: Routledge, 2004.

Burka, Paul. "What's Black and White and Red-Faced All Over?" *Texas Monthly,* December 1997, 141–42, 144, 146.

Caolo, Mike. "The Negro Student: A Law School Dilemma." *Texas Law Forum,* November 1967, 5–6.

Carl, Earl L. "The Shortage of Negro Lawyers: Pluralistic Legal Education and Legal Service for the Poor." *Journal of Legal Education* 21 (February 1967): 21–30.

Carmichael, Stokely, and Charles V. Hamilton. *Black Power: The Politics of Liberation (in America)*. New York: Vintage, 1992.

Carr, Leslie. *"Colorblind" Racism*. Thousand Oaks, Calif.: Sage, 1997.

Carson, Clayborne. *In Struggle: SNCC and the Black Awakening of the 1960s*. Cambridge: Harvard University Press, 1995.

Carson, Clayborne, David J. Garrow, Gerald Gill, Vincent Harding, and Darlene Clark Hine, eds. *The Eyes on the Prize Civil Rights Reader: Documents, Speeches, and First-hand Accounts from the Black Freedom Struggle*. New York: Penguin, 1991.

Carter, Elmer A. "The Negro in College Athletics." *Opportunity* 11 (July 1933): 208–10, 219.

Cashin, Sheryll. *The Failures of Integration: How Race and Class Are Undermining the American Dream*. New York: Public Affairs, 2004.

Cell, John W. *The Highest Stage of White Supremacy: The Origins of Segregation in South Africa and the American South*. London: Cambridge University Press, 1982.

Center for Individual Rights. "Hopwood: A Perfect Mess of an Opinion." Reprinted in *Texas Lawyer*, November 7, 1994, 5.

Chideya, Farai. *The Color of Our Future: Race in the Twenty-first Century*. New York: Harper Perennial, 2000.

Clark, E. Culpepper. *The Schoolhouse Door: Segregation's Last Stand at the University of Alabama*. New York: Oxford University Press, 1993.

Cohen, William. *At Freedom's Edge: Black Mobility and the Southern White Quest for Racial Control, 1861–1915*. Baton Rouge: Louisiana State University Press, 1991.

Cohodas, Nadine. *The Band Played Dixie: Race and the Liberal Conscience at Ole Miss*. New York: Free Press, 1997.

Coleman, Michael C. *American Indian Children at School, 1850–1930*. Jackson: University Press of Mississippi, 1993.

Conley, Dalton. *Honky*. New York: Vintage, 2001.

Cose, Ellis. *A Nation of Strangers: Prejudice, Politics, and the Populating of America*. New York: Morrow, 1992.

Cottrol, Robert J., Raymond T. Diamond, and Leland B. Ware. *"Brown v. Board of Education": Caste, Culture, and the Constitution*. Lawrence: University Press of Kansas, 2003.

Cover, Robert M. *Justice Accused: Antislavery and the Judicial Process*. New Haven: Yale University Press, 1975.

Crawford, Ann Fears, and Jack Keever. *John B. Connally: Portrait in Power*. Austin, Tex.: Jenkins, 1973.

Crawford, Vicki L., Jacqueline Anne Rouse, and Barbara Woods, eds. *Women in the*

Civil Rights Movement: Trailblazers and Torchbearers, 1941–1965. Brooklyn, N.Y.: Carlson, 1990.

Cullen, Jim. *Popular Culture in American History*. Malden, Mass.: Blackwell, 2001.

Curry, Constance, Joan C. Browning, Dorothy Dawson Burlage, Penny Patch, Theresa Del Pozzo, Sue Thrasher, Elaine DeLott Baker, Emmie Schrader Adams, and Casey Hayden. *Deep in Our Hearts: Nine White Women in the Freedom Movement*. Athens: University of Georgia Press, 2002.

Curtis, Gregory. "Affirmative Reaction." *Texas Monthly*, July 1994, 5–92.

Curtis, James C., and Lewis L. Gould, eds. *The Black Experience in America: Selected Essays*. Austin: University of Texas Press, 1970.

Curtis, Michael Kent. *No State Shall Abridge: The Fourteenth Amendment and the Bill of Rights*. Durham, N.C.: Duke University Press, 1986.

Curtis, Susan. *The First Black Actors on the Great White Way*. Columbia: University of Missouri Press, 2001.

Davidson, Osha Gray. *The Best of Enemies: Race and Redemption in the New South*. New York: Scribner, 1996.

Davis, F. James. *Who Is Black? One Nation's Definition*. University Park: Pennsylvania State University Press, 2001.

Davis, Jack E., ed. *The Civil Rights Movement*. Malden, Mass.: Blackwell, 2001.

Delta Upsilon Fraternity. *Our Record: The Manual of Delta Upsilon Fraternity*. New York: Delta Upsilon Fraternity, 1985.

DeMott, Benjamin. *The Trouble with Friendship: Why Americans Can't Think Straight about Race*. New York: Atlantic Monthly Press, 1995.

Dickerson, Debra J. *The End of Blackness: Returning the Souls of Black Folk to Their Rightful Owners*. New York: Pantheon, 2004.

Doane, Ashley W., and Eduardo Bonilla-Silva. *WhiteOut*. New York: Dutton, 2004.

Dollard, John. *Caste and Class in a Southern Town*. Madison: University of Wisconsin Press, 1989.

D'Souza, Dinesh. *The End of Racism: Principles for a Multicultural Society*. New York: Free Press, 1996.

Du Bois, W. E. B. *The Autobiography of W. E. B. Du Bois: A Soliloquy on Viewing My Life from the Last Decade of Its First Century*. New York: International Publishers, 1968.

———. *Black Reconstruction in America, 1860–1880*. New York: Free Press, 1998.

———. "Higher Education." *Crisis* 34 (September 1927): 239.

———. "The Talented Tenth." In *The Negro Problem: A Series of Articles by Representative American Negroes of To-Day*, edited by Booker T. Washington. New York: Ayer, 1903.

———. "The Training of Negroes for Social Power." *Outlook*, October 17, 1903, 409–14.

Du Bois, W. E. B., and Augustus Granville Dill, eds. *The College-Bred Negro American: Report of a Social Study Made by Atlanta University under the Patronage of the Trustees of the John F. Slater Fund*. Atlanta: Atlanta University Press, 1910.

Dudziak, Mary L. "Desegregation as Cold War Imperative." *Stanford Law Review* 41 (November 1988): 61–120.

Dugger, Ronnie. *Our Invaded Universities: Form, Reform, and New Starts*. New York: Norton, 1974.

Duren, Almetris Marsh, with Louise Iscoe. *Overcoming: A History of Black Integration at the University of Texas at Austin*. Austin: University of Texas at Austin, 1979.

Eastland, Terry. *Ending Affirmative Action: The Case for Colorblind Justice*. New York: Basic Books, 1997.

Eckhardt, John. *On This Hallowed Ground*. Austin: s.n., 1980.

Egerton, John. *Speak Now against the Day: The Generation before the Civil Rights Movement in the South*. Chapel Hill: University of North Carolina Press, 1995.

Elkins, Stanley. *Slavery: A Problem in American Institutional and Intellectual Life*. Chicago: University of Chicago Press, 1976.

Elliott, Janet. "*Bakke* of the Legal World? Once Segregated, UT Returns to Court to Defend Race Preferences." *Texas Lawyer*, May 16, 1994, 1–3.

———. "Law-School Challenge: *Bakke* of the Legal World?" *Legal Times*, May 23, 1994, 4–28.

———. "UT Responds to Suit with Policy Changes." *Texas Lawyer*, May 24, 1994, 10.

"The Eyes of Texas." *Time*, May 20, 1957, 44.

Fabre, Geneviève, and Robert O'Meally, eds. *History and Memory in African-American Culture*. New York: Oxford University Press, 1994.

Fairman, Charles. "Does the Fourteenth Amendment Incorporate the Bill of Rights: The Original Understanding." *Stanford Law Review* 2 (1949): 44–120.

Fanon, Frantz. *Black Skin, White Masks*. Translated by Charles Lam Markmann. New York: Grove, 1991.

Farmer, James. *Lay Bare the Heart: An Autobiography of the Civil Rights Movement*. Fort Worth: Texas Christian University Press, 1998.

Fields, Barbara Jeanne. "Ideology and Race in American History." In *Region, Race, and Reconstruction: Essays in Honor of C. Vann Woodward*, edited by J. Morgan Kousser and James M. McPherson. New York: Oxford University Press, 1982.

Fine, Michelle, Lois Weis, Linda Powell Pruitt, and April Burns. *Off White: Readings in Power, Privilege, and Resistance*. New York: Routledge, 2004.

Fitzpatrick, Frank. *And the Walls Came Tumbling Down: The Basketball Game That Changed American Sports*. Lincoln: University of Nebraska Press, 2000.

Foley, Neil. *The White Scourge: Mexicans, Blacks, and Poor Whites in the Texas Cotton Culture*. Berkeley: University of California Press, 1999.

Foner, Eric. *Free Soil, Free Labor, Free Men: The Ideology of the Republican Party before the Civil War*. Oxford: Oxford University Press, 1995.

———. *Reconstruction: America's Unfinished Revolution, 1863–1877*. New York: Harper Perennial Modern Classics, 2002.

Fontaine, Jacob, with Gene Burd. *Jacob Fontaine: From Slavery to the Greatness of the Pulpit, the Press, and Public Service*. San Antonio, Tex.: Marion Koogler McNay Art Museum, 1984.

Frank, D. A. "Colonel W. S. Simkins." *Texas Alcalde*, April 1920, 765–72.

Frankenberg, Ruth. *White Women, Race Matters: The Social Construction of Whiteness*. Minneapolis: University of Minnesota Press, 1993.

Franklin, John Hope, and Alfred A. Moss Jr. *From Slavery to Freedom: A History of African Americans*. New York: Knopf, 2000.

Franklin, Vincent P., and James D. Anderson, eds. *New Perspectives on Black Educational History*. Boston: Hall, 1978.

Frantz, Joe B. *The Forty-Acre Follies*. Austin: Texas Monthly Press, 1983.

Frederickson, George M. *White Supremacy: A Comparative Study in American and South African History*. New York: Oxford University Press, 1982.

Freeman, Denne H. *Hook 'Em Horns: A Story of Texas Football*. Huntsville, Ala.: Strode, 1979.

Gaines, Howell. *My Soul Is Rested: Movement Days in the Deep South Remembered*. New York: Penguin, 1983.

Gaines, Kevin. *Uplifting the Race: Black Leadership, Politics, and Culture in the Twentieth Century*. Chapel Hill: University of North Carolina Press, 1996.

Galston, William A. *Liberal Purposes: Goods, Virtues, and Diversity in the Liberal State*. Cambridge: Cambridge University Press, 1991.

Gans, Herbert. "Symbolic Ethnicity: The Future of Ethnic Groups and Cultures in America." *Ethnic and Racial Studies* 2 (January 1979): 1–20.

Garner, Bryan A., ed. *Texas, Our Texas: Remembrance of the University*. Austin, Tex.: Eakin, 1984.

Geduld, Harry M., ed. *Focus on D. W. Griffith*. Englewood Cliffs, N.J.: Prentice-Hall, 1971.

Genovese, Eugene. *Roll, Jordan, Roll: The World the Slaves Made*. New York: Vintage, 1976.

Giddings, Paula. *In Search of Sisterhood: Delta Sigma Theta and the Challenge of the Black Sorority Movement*. New York: Amistad, 1994.

———. *When and Where I Enter: The Impact of Black Women on Race and Sex in America*. 2nd ed. New York: Amistad, 1996.

Gillette, Michael L. "Blacks Challenge the White University." *Southwestern Historical Quarterly* 86 (July 1995): 321–44.

———. "Heman Marion Sweatt: Civil Rights Plaintiff." In *Black Leaders: Texans for*

Their Times, edited by Alwyn Barr and Robert A. Calvert. Austin: Texas State Historical Association, 1981.

———. "The NAACP in Texas, 1937–1957." Ph.D. diss., University of Texas, 1984.

Gilmore, Glenda Elizabeth. *Gender and Jim Crow: Women and the Politics of White Supremacy in North Carolina, 1896–1920*. Chapel Hill: University of North Carolina Press, 1996.

Gilroy, Paul. *"There Ain't No Black in the Union Jack": The Cultural Politics of Race and Nation*. Chicago: University of Chicago Press, 1991.

Glazer, Nathan. *Affirmative Discrimination: Ethnic Inequality and Public Policy*. Cambridge: Harvard University Press, 1987.

———. *We Are All Multiculturalists Now*. Cambridge: Harvard University Press, 1998.

Goldberg, David Theo, ed. *Anatomy of Racism*. Minneapolis: University of Minnesota Press, 1990.

Goldfield, David R. *Black, White, and Southern: Race Relations and Southern Culture, 1940 to the Present*. Baton Rouge: Louisiana State University Press, 1990.

Goldstein, Ernest. "How LBJ Took the Bull by the Horns." *Amherst* 4 (Winter 1985): 14–24.

Gossett, Thomas F. *Race: The History of an Idea in America*. New York: Oxford University Press, 1997.

Gould, Lewis L., and Melissa R. Sneed. "Without Pride or Apology: The University of Texas at Austin, Racial Integration, and the Barbara Smith Case." *Southwestern Historical Quarterly* 103 (July 1999): 66–87.

Graglia, Lino. *"Hopwood v. Texas*: Racial Preferences in Higher Education Upheld and Endorsed." *Journal of Legal Education* 45 (March 1995): 79–93.

Graham, Hugh Davis. *The Civil Rights Era: Origins and Development of National Policy, 1960–1972*. New York: Oxford University Press, 1990.

Graham, Lawrence Otis. *Member of the Club: Reflections on Life in a Racially Polarized World*. New York: HarperCollins, 1996.

———. *Our Kind of People: Inside America's Black Upper Class*. New York: HarperCollins, 2000.

Grant, Madison. *The Passing of the Great Race; or, The Racial Basis of European History*. New York: Ayer, 1970.

Green, George Norris. *The Establishment in Texas Politics: The Primitive Years, 1938–1957*. Norman: University of Oklahoma Press, 1984.

Greene, Maxine. *The Dialectic of Freedom*. New York: Columbia University Press, 1988.

Greeson, Aaron David. *The Recovery of Race in America*. Minneapolis: University of Minnesota Press, 1995.

Gubar, Susan. *Racechanges: White Skin, Black Face in American Culture*. New York: Oxford University Press, 1997.

Guglielmo, Jennifer, and Salvatore Salerno. *Are Italians White? How Race Is Made in America*. New York: Routledge, 2003.

Gwaltney, John Langston, ed. *Drylongso: A Self-Portrait of Black America*. New York: Vintage, 1981.

Hacker, Andrew. *Two Nations: Black and White, Separate, Hostile, Unequal*. New York: Scribner, 1992.

Hale, Grace Elizabeth. *Making Whiteness: The Culture of Segregation in the South, 1890–1940*. New York: Vintage, 1999.

Handlin, Oscar. *The American People in the Twentieth Century*. Cambridge: Harvard University Press, 1966.

Haney-Lopez, Ian. *White by Law: The Legal Construction of Race*. New York: New York University Press, 1999.

Harris, Cheryl I. "Whiteness as Property." *Harvard Law Review* 106 (1993): 1709–75.

Heintze, Michael R. *Private Black Colleges in Texas, 1865–1954*. College Station: Texas A & M University Press, 1985.

Henderson, Edwin Bancroft. "The Negro Athlete and Race Prejudice." *Opportunity* 14 (March 1936): 77–79.

Higginbotham, A. Leon. *In the Matter of Color: The Colonial Period*. New York: Oxford University Press, 1978.

Hoberman, John. *Darwin's Athletes: How Sport Has Damaged Black America and Preserved the Myth of Race*. Boston: Houghton Mifflin, 1997.

Hodes, Martha Elizabeth, ed. *Sex, Love, Race: Crossing Boundaries in North American History*. New York: New York University Press, 1999.

———. *White Women, Black Men: Illicit Sex in the Nineteenth-Century South*. New Haven: Yale University Press, 1999.

Hollingsworth, Harold M., ed. *Essays on Recent Southern Politics*. Arlington: University of Texas at Arlington, 1970.

hooks, bell. *Black Looks: Race and Representation*. Boston: South End, 1992.

Horsman, Reginald. *Race and Manifest Destiny: The Origins of American Racial Anglo-Saxonism*. Cambridge: Harvard University Press, 1981.

How Race Is Lived in America: Pulling Together, Pulling Apart. New York: Times Books/Holt, 2001.

Hughes, Langston. "Who's Passing for Who?" In *Laughing to Keep from Crying*. New York: Aeonian, 1976.

Hyman, Herbert H., and Paul B. Sheatsley. "Attitudes toward Desegregation." *Scientific American* 195 (December 1956): 35–39.

Ifekwunigwe, Jayne O., ed. *"Mixed Race" Studies: A Reader*. New York: Routledge, 2004.

Ignatiev, Noel. *How the Irish Became White*. New York: Routledge, 1996.

Jaschik, Scott. "Suit against U. of Texas Challenges Law School's Affirmative-Action Effort." *Chronicle of Higher Education*, February 9, 1994, A32–33.

Johnson, Kevin. "Racial Hierarchy, Asian Americans and Latinos as 'Foreigners,' and Social Change: Is Law the Way to Go?" *Oregon Law Review* 76 (August 1997): 348–68.

Jones, William. "The Status of Educational Desegregation in Texas." *Journal of Negro Education* 25 (Summer 1956): 334–44.

Jordan, Winthrop. *White over Black: American Attitudes toward the Negro, 1550–1812*. Chapel Hill: University of North Carolina Press, 1995.

Kallen, Horace. *Culture and Democracy in the United States: Studies in the Group Psychology of the American Peoples*. New York: Boni and Liveright, 1924.

Katznelson, Ira, and Margaret Weir. *Schooling for All: Class, Race, and the Decline of the Democratic Ideal*. New York: Basic Books, 1985.

Kelley, Robin D. G. " 'We Are Not What We Seem': Rethinking Black Working-Class Opposition in the Jim Crow South." *Journal of American History* 80 (June 1993): 75–112.

Kilpatrick, James Jackson. *The Southern Case for School Segregation*. New York: Crowell-Collier, 1962.

King, Desmond. *Separate and Unequal: Black Americans and the U.S. Federal Government*. New York: Oxford University Press, 1995.

King, Martin Luther, Jr. "Letter from a Birmingham Jail." In *Why We Can't Wait*. New York: Harper and Row, 1964.

Kirven, Lamar L. "A Century of Warfare: Black Texans." Ph.D. diss., Indiana University, 1974.

Klarman, Michael J. *From Jim Crow to Civil Rights: The Supreme Court and the Struggle for Racial Equality*. New York: Oxford University Press, 2004.

Kluger, Richard. *Simple Justice: The History of "Brown v. Board of Education" and Black America's Struggle for Equality*. New York: Vintage, 2004.

Knowles, Louis L., and Kenneth Prewitt, eds. *Institutional Racism in America*. Englewood Cliffs, N.J.: Prentice-Hall, 1969.

Kotkin, Joel. *Tribes: How Race, Religion, and Identity Determine Success in the New Global Economy*. New York: Random House, 1993.

Kuhlman, Martin. "Direct Action at the University of Texas during the Civil Rights Movement, 1960–1965." *Southwestern Historical Quarterly* 98 (April 1995): 551–66.

Kull, Andrew. *The Color-Blind Constitution*. Cambridge: Harvard University Press, 1998.

Kymlicka, Will. *Liberalism, Community, and Culture*. New York: Oxford University Press, 1991.

———. *Multicultural Citizenship: A Liberal Theory of Minority Rights*. New York: Oxford University Press, 1995.

Ladino, Robyn Duff. *Desegregating Texas Schools: Eisenhower, Shivers, and the Crisis at Mansfield High.* Austin: University of Texas Press, 1996.

Laue, James H. *Direct Action and Desegregation, 1960–1962: Toward a History of the Rationalization of Protest.* Brooklyn, N.Y.: Carlson, 1989.

Law, Anna O. "Race, Ethnicity, and National Origins in Public Policy—When Should It Matter?" *Georgetown Immigration Law Journal* 10 (1996): 71–76.

Lawrence, Charles R., and Mari J. Matsuda. *We Won't Go Back: Making the Case for Affirmative Action.* Boston: Houghton Mifflin, 1997.

Leatherman, Courtney. "A Public-Interest Law Firm Aims to Defend the Politically Incorrect." *Chronicle of Higher Education,* November 23, 1994, A18–19.

Lemann, Nicholas. *The Promised Land: The Great Migration and How It Changed America.* New York: Vintage, 1992.

Lester, Anthony, and Geoffrey Bindman. *Race and Law.* London: Longman, 1972.

Levine, Ellen. *Freedom's Children: Young Civil Rights Activists Tell Their Own Stories.* New York: Putnam, 2000.

Litwack, Leon F. *Been in the Storm So Long: The Aftermath of Slavery.* New York: Knopf, 1979.

———. *Trouble in Mind: Black Southerners in the Age of Jim Crow.* New York: Knopf, 1998.

Loewen, James W. *The Mississippi Chinese: Between Black and White.* Long Grove, Ill.: Waveland, 1988.

Lott, Eric. *Love and Theft: Blackface Minstrelsy and the American Working Class.* New York: Oxford University Press, 1995.

Malcolmson, Scott L. *One Drop of Blood: The American Misadventure of Race.* New York: Farrar Straus Giroux, 2000.

Mansfield, Harvey C., Jr. *America's Constitutional Soul.* Baltimore: Johns Hopkins University Press, 1993.

Marable, Manning. *Beyond Black and White: Transforming African American Politics.* New York: Verso, 1996.

———. *Race, Reform, and Rebellion: The Second Reconstruction in Black America, 1945–1990.* Jackson: University Press of Mississippi, 1991.

Marcello, Ronald E. "Reluctance versus Reality: The Desegregation of North Texas State College, 1954–1956." *Southwestern Historical Quarterly* 99 (October 1996): 152–85.

Massa, Don. "Conrad's Sad Song Ends on a Happy Note." *Texas Alcalde,* July–August 1984, 10–13.

McCaslin, Richard B. "Steadfast in His Intent: John W. Hargis and the Integration of the University of Texas at Austin." *Southwestern Historical Quarterly* 95 (July 1991): 25–36.

McCloskey, Robert G. *The American Supreme Court*. Chicago: University of Chicago Press, 2004.

McConnell, Michael W. "Originalism and the Desegregation Decisions." *Virginia Law Review* 81 (1995): 947–1140.

McIntosh, Peggy. "White Privilege and Male Privilege: A Personal Account of Coming to See Correspondences through Work in Women's Studies." In *Race, Class, and Gender: An Anthology*, compiled by Margaret L. Andersen and Patricia Hill Collins. Belmont, Calif.: Wadsworth, 1998.

McPherson, James M. *The Struggle for Equality: Abolitionists and the Negro in the Civil War*. Princeton: Princeton University Press, 1964.

Mecklin, John. *The Ku Klux Klan: A Study of the American Mind*. New York: Russell and Russell, 1963.

Miles, Robert, and Malcolm Brown. *Racism*. 2nd ed. New York: Routledge, 2003.

Mills, Nicolaus. *Debating Affirmative Action*. New York: Delta, 1994.

Minow, Martha. *Making All the Difference: Inclusion, Exclusion, and American Law*. Ithaca: Cornell University Press, 1991.

Montejano, David. *Anglos and Mexicans in the Making of Texas, 1836–1986*. Austin: University of Texas Press, 1987.

Moore, Brenda L. *To Serve My Country, to Serve My Race: The Story of the Only African American WACs Stationed Overseas during World War II*. New York: New York University Press, 1998.

Moore, Truman E. *The Slaves We Rent*. New York: Random House, 1965.

Morris, Willie. "Integration at U.T." *Texas Observer*, October 21, 1960, 1–3.

———. *North toward Home*. New York: Vintage, 2000.

Myers, Gustavus. *History of Bigotry in the United States*. Santa Barbara, Calif.: Capricorn, 1943.

Myers, Ken. "UT Admissions Plaintiffs Say Ruling Shortchanges Them." *National Law Journal*, September 5, 1994, A17.

Myrdal, Gunnar. *An American Dilemma: The Negro Problem and Modern Democracy*. New Brunswick, N.J.: Transaction, 1996.

Nalty, Bernard C. *The Right to Fight: African American Marines in World War II*. Washington, D.C.: History and Museum Division, Headquarters, U.S. Marine Corps, 1995.

Nash, Gary B. *Race and Revolution*. Madison, Wis.: Madison House, 1990.

———. *Red, White, and Black: The Peoples of Early America*. Englewood Cliffs, N.J.: Prentice-Hall, 1974.

National Opinion Research Center, Doctorate Data Project. "Summary Report 1999: Doctorate Recipients from United States Universities." http://www.norc.uchicago.edu/studies/sed/sed1999.htm (accessed November 23, 2005).

Nett, Roger. "The Civil Right We Are Not Ready For: The Right of Free Movement of People on the Face of the Earth." *Ethics* 81 (April 1971): 212–27.

Oberst, Paul. "The Strange Career of *Plessy v. Ferguson*." *Arizona Law Review* 389 (1973): 433–41.

"Of Weeds . . . and Flowers." *We* 1 (June 1991): 12.

Ogletree, Charles J. *All Deliberate Speed: Reflections on the First Half-Century of "Brown v. Board of Education."* New York: Norton, 2004.

Okihiro, Gary. *Margins and Mainstreams: Asians in American History and Culture.* Seattle: University of Washington Press, 1994.

Olsen, Jack. "The Black Athlete: The Anguish of a Team Divided." *Sports Illustrated,* July 29, 1968, 20–35.

———. "The Black Athlete: In an Alien World." *Sports Illustrated,* July 15, 1968, 28–41.

———. "The Black Athlete: In the Back of the Bus." *Sports Illustrated,* July 22, 1968, 28–45.

———. "The Black Athlete: Pride and Prejudice." *Sports Illustrated,* July 8, 1968, 18–31.

———. "The Black Athlete: A Shameful Story." *Sports Illustrated,* July 1, 1968, 12–27.

Olson, Keith W. *The G.I. Bill, the Veterans, and the Colleges.* Lexington: University Press of Kentucky, 1974.

Omi, Michael, and Howard Winant. *Racial Formation in the United States: From the 1960s to the 1990s.* New York: Routledge, 1994.

Orfield, Gary, and Susan E. Eaton. *Dismantling Desegregation: The Quiet Reversal of "Brown v. Board of Education."* New York: New Press, 1997.

Page, Clarence. *Showing My Color: Impolite Essays on Race and Identity.* New York: Perennial, 1997.

Park, Robert. *Race and Culture.* Glencoe, Ill.: Free Press, 1950.

Pennington, Richard. *Breaking the Ice: The Racial Integration of Southwest Conference Football.* Jefferson, N.C.: McFarland, 1987.

Peterson, Carla L. *"Doers of the Word": African-American Women Speakers and Writers in the North (1830–1880).* New York: Oxford University Press, 1995.

Peterson, Peter, ed. *Classifying by Race.* Princeton: Princeton University Press, 1995.

Pinsker, Sanford. *Worrying about Race, 1985–1995: Reflections during a Troubled Time.* Troy, N.Y.: Whitston, 1996.

Pole, J. R. *The Pursuit of Equality in American History.* Berkeley: University of California Press, 1978.

Pratt, Robert. *We Shall Not Be Moved: The Desegregation of the University of Georgia.* Athens: University of Georgia Press, 2002.

Reich, Michael. *Racial Inequality.* Princeton: Princeton University Press, 1981.

Reid, Jan. "Coach Royal Regrets." *Texas Monthly*, December 1982, 147–49, 244–46, 248, 250, 252, 254.

Reuben, Richard C. "$1 Damages for Reverse Bias Plaintiffs: 'Mixed Bag' Ruling Strikes Down Law School's Separate Admissions Committees." *ABA Journal* 80 (November 1994): 24–25.

Rice, Lawrence D. *The Negro in Texas, 1874–1900*. Baton Rouge: Louisiana State University Press, 1971.

Robinson, Randall. *The Debt: What America Owes to Blacks*. New York: Dutton, 2000.

Roediger, David. *Towards the Abolition of Whiteness: Essays on Race, Politics, and Working Class History*. London: Verso, 1994.

———. *The Wages of Whiteness: Race and the Making of the American Working Class*. London: Verso, 1991.

Rosen, Jeffrey. "Is Affirmative Action Doomed?" *New Republic*, October 17, 1994, 25–26, 28–29, 34–35.

Rosenberg, Gerald N. *The Hollow Hope: Can Courts Bring about Social Change?* Chicago: University of Chicago Press, 1993.

Rossinow, Doug. *The Politics of Authenticity*. New York: Columbia University Press, 1998.

Rushton, J. Philippe. *Race, Evolution, and Behavior: A Life History Perspective*. New Brunswick, N.J.: Transaction, 1995.

Sandel, Michael. *Democracy's Discontent: America in Search of a Public Philosophy*. Cambridge: Belknap Press of Harvard University Press, 1998.

San Miguel, Guadalupe. *"Let All of Them Take Heed": Mexican Americans and the Campaign for Educational Equality in Texas, 1910–1981*. Austin: University of Texas Press, 1987.

Saxton, Alexander. *The Rise and Fall of the White Republic: Class Politics and Mass Culture in Nineteenth-Century America*. New York: Verso, 1990.

Sayles, John. *Constitution of the State of Texas*. St. Louis: Gilbert, 1888.

Sayles, John, and Henry Sayles. *Early Laws of Texas*. St. Louis: Gilbert, 1888.

Schmidt, Benno. "Principles of Prejudice: The Supreme Court and Race in the Progressive Era: Part 1, The Heyday of Jim Crow." *Columbia Law Review* 82 (1982): 444–72.

———. "Principles of Prejudice: The Supreme Court and Race in the Progressive Era: Part 2, The Peonage Cases." *Columbia Law Review* 82 (1982): 646–94.

———. "Principles of Prejudice: The Supreme Court and Race in the Progressive Era: Part 3, Black Disenfranchisement from the KKK to the Grandfather Clause." *Columbia Law Review* 82 (1982): 835–66.

Schwartz, Bernard. *Super Chief: Earl Warren and His Supreme Court*. New York: New York University Press, 1983.

Seale, Avrel. "Barbara Smith Conrad." *Texas Alcalde*, November–December 1998, 24–29.

————. "Texas Tithe." *Texas Alcalde*, July–August 1998, 14–19.

Shabazz, Amilcar. *Advancing Democracy: African Americans and the Struggle for Access and Equity in Higher Education in Texas*. Chapel Hill: University of North Carolina Press, 2004.

————. "The Opening of the Southern Mind: The Desegregation of Higher Education in Texas, 1865–1965." Ph.D. diss., University of Houston, 1996.

Simkins, W. S. "Why the Ku Klux Klan." *Texas Alcalde*, April 1920, 735–48.

Smallwood, Ernest C., Jr. "Law Schools' Unequal Justice." *Texas Lawyer*, May 16, 1994, 24–25.

Sniderman, Paul M., and Thomas Piazza. *The Scar of Race*. Cambridge: Belknap Press of Harvard University Press, 1993.

Sowell, Thomas. *Affirmative Action Reconsidered: Was It Necessary in Academia?* Washington, D.C.: American Enterprise Institute for Public Research, 1975.

————. *Barbarians inside the Gates and Other Controversial Essays*. Stanford, Calif.: Hoover Institution Press, 1999.

————. *Civil Rights: Rhetoric or Reality?* New York: Morrow, 1984.

Spinner, Jeff. *The Boundaries of Citizenship: Race, Ethnicity, and Nationality in the Liberal State*. Baltimore: Johns Hopkins University Press, 1994.

Stampp, Kenneth M. *The Peculiar Institution: Negro Slavery in the Ante-Bellum South*. London: Eyre and Spottiswoode, 1964.

Steele, Shelby. *The Content of Our Character: A New Vision of Race in America*. New York: Harper Perennial, 1991.

Steinberg, Stephen. *Turning Back: The Retreat from Racial Justice in American Thought and Policy*. Boston: Beacon, 1996.

Stocking, G. *Race, Culture, and Evolution: Essays in the History of Anthropology*. Chicago: University of Chicago Press, 1982.

"Sweatt versus the State of Texas." *Time*, March 24, 1947, 52–53.

Takaki, Ronald T. *A Different Mirror: A History of Multicultural America*. Boston: Little, Brown, 1993.

————. *Iron Cages: Race and Culture in Nineteenth-Century America*. New York: Knopf, 1979.

————. *Strangers from a Different Shore: A History of Asian Americans*. Boston: Back Bay, 1998.

Thernstrom, Abigail M. *Whose Votes Count? Affirmative Action and Minority Voting Rights*. Cambridge: Harvard University Press, 1989.

Thernstrom, Abigail M., and Stephan Thernstrom. *America in Black and White: One Nation, Indivisible*. New York: Simon and Schuster, 1999.

"To Do a Little Better." *Time*, August 29, 1960, 52–57.

Toback, James. "Longhorns and Longhairs: The Setting Is Texas; The Issue Is Football, Blacks, and Hippies." *Harper's*, November 1970, 70–73.

Torruella, Juan. *The Supreme Court and Puerto Rico: The Doctrine of Separate and Unequal.* Río Piedras: University of Puerto Rico Press, 1985.

Trillin, Calvin. *An Education in Georgia: Charlayne Hunter, Hamilton Holmes, and the Integration of the University of Georgia.* Athens: University of Georgia Press, 1991.

Tushnet, Mark V. *Making Civil Rights Law: Thurgood Marshall and the Supreme Court, 1956–1961.* New York: Oxford University Press, 1996.

———, ed. *The Warren Court in Historical and Political Perspective.* Charlottesville: University Press of Virginia, 1993.

U.S. Bureau of Statistics. *Statistical Abstract of the United States, 1947.* Washington, D.C.: U.S. Government Printing Office, 1947.

U.S. Kerner Commission. *Report of the National Advisory Commission on Civil Disorders.* Washington, D.C.: U.S. Government Printing Office, 1968.

van den Berghe, Pierre. *Race and Racism: A Comparative Perspective.* New York: Wiley, 1972.

van Evrie, J. H. *White Supremacy and Negro Subordination; or, Negroes a Subordinate Race.* New York: Evrie, Horton, 1868.

Vera, Hernán, Joe R. Feagin, and Nikitah Imani. *The Agony of Education: Black Students at White Colleges and Universities.* New York: Routledge, 1996.

Walker, Robbie Jean, ed. *The Rhetoric of Struggle: Public Address by African American Women.* New York: Taylor and Francis, 1992.

Walters, Laurel Shaper. "Lawsuit in Texas Turns Racial Justice on Its Head." *Christian Science Monitor*, August 1, 1994, 17.

Walzer, Michael. *Spheres of Justice: A Defense of Pluralism and Equality.* New York: Basic Books, 1983.

Washington, Booker T. *Up from Slavery.* New York: Gramercy, 1993.

Weberman, Bernie, and Steve Jackson. "*Sweatt* Paints Dim Past." *Texas Law Forum*, October 3, 1974, 8.

Wellman, David T. *Portraits of White Racism.* 2nd ed. Cambridge: Cambridge University Press, 1993.

Wells-Barnett, Ida B. *On Lynchings.* Salem, N.H.: Ayer, 1993.

———. *A Red Record: Tabulated Statistics and Alleged Causes of Lynchings in the United States, 1892–1893–1894.* Chicago: Donohue and Henneberry, 1895.

West, Cornel. "The New Cultural Politics of Difference." In *Out There: Marginalization and Contemporary Culture*, edited by Russell Ferguson, Martha Gever, Trinh T. Minh-ha, and Cornel West. Cambridge: MIT Press, 1990.

———. *Race Matters.* New York: Vintage, 1994.

Wicker, Tom. *Report of the National Advisory Commission on Civil Disorders.* New York: Bantam, 1968.

Wilkinson, J. Harvie, III. *From "Brown" to "Bakke": The Supreme Court and School Integration, 1954–1978.* New York: Oxford University Press, 1993.

————. *One Nation Indivisible: How Ethnic Separatism Threatens America*. Reading, Mass.: Addison-Wesley, 1997.

Williams, Patricia. *The Alchemy of Race and Rights*. Cambridge: Harvard University Press, 1992.

Williamson, Joel. *The Crucible of Race: Black-White Relations in the American South since Emancipation*. New York: Oxford University Press, 1984.

————. *New People: Miscegenation and Mulattoes in the United States*. Baton Rouge: Louisiana State University Press, 1995.

Winant, Howard. *Racial Conditions: Politics, Theory, Comparisons*. Minneapolis: University of Minnesota Press, 1994.

Winegarten, Ruthe. *Black Texas Women: 150 Years of Trial and Triumph*. Austin: University of Texas Press, 1995.

Woodson, Carter G. *The Mis-Education of the Negro*. Lawrenceville, N.J.: Africa World, 1990.

Woodward, C. Vann. *Origins of the New South, 1877–1913*. Rev. ed. Baton Rouge: Louisiana State University Press, 1971.

————. *The Strange Career of Jim Crow*. New York: Oxford University Press, 2001.

Wright, Lawrence. "One Drop of Blood." *New Yorker*, July 24, 1994, 25–34.

Yancy, George, ed. *What White Looks Like: African-American Philosophers on the Whiteness Question*. New York: Routledge, 2004.

Young, Iris Marion. *Justice and the Politics of Difference*. Princeton: Princeton University Press, 1990.

Young, Robert. *White Mythologies: Writing History and the West*. New York: Routledge, 2004.

Index